T0340118

TRANSFORMING THE SOCIO ECONOMY WITH DIGITAL INNOVATION

TRANSFORMING THE SOCIO ECONOMY WITH DIGITAL INNOVATION

CHIHIRO WATANABE

Professor Emeritus, Tokyo Institute of Technology,
Meguro, Tokyo, Japan

Research Professor, University of Jyväskylä,
Jyväskylä, Finland

Guest Research Scholar, International
Institute for Systems Analysis (IIASA),
Laxenburg, Austria

YUJI TOU

Associate Professor, Tokyo Institute of Technology,
Meguro, Tokyo, Japan

PEKKA NEITTAANMÄKI

Professor, University of Jyväskylä, Jyväskylä, Finland

ELSEVIER

Elsevier
Radarweg 29, PO Box 211, 1000 AE Amsterdam, Netherlands
The Boulevard, Langford Lane, Kidlington, Oxford OX5 1GB, United Kingdom
50 Hampshire Street, 5th Floor, Cambridge, MA 02139, United States

Notices
Knowledge and best practice in this field are constantly changing. As new research
and experience broaden our understanding, changes in research methods, professional
practices, or medical treatment may become necessary.

Practitioners and researchers must always rely on their own experience and knowledge
in evaluating and using any information, methods, compounds, or experiments
described herein. In using such information or methods they should be mindful of
their own safety and the safety of others, including parties for whom they have a
professional responsibility.

To the fullest extent of the law, neither the Publisher nor the authors, contributors, or
editors, assume any liability for any injury and/or damage to persons or property as a
matter of products liability, negligence or otherwise, or from any use or operation of
any methods, products, instructions, or ideas contained in the material herein.

Library of Congress Cataloging-in-Publication Data
A catalog record for this book is available from the Library of Congress

British Library Cataloguing-in-Publication Data
A catalogue record for this book is available from the British Library

ISBN: 978-0-323-88465-5

For information on all Elsevier publications visit our website at
https://www.elsevier.com/books-and-journals

Publisher: Brian Romer
Editorial Project Manager: Grace Lander
Production Project Manager: Sreejith Viswanathan
Cover Designer: Miles Hitchen

Typeset by TNQ Technologies

Working together
to grow libraries in
developing countries

www.elsevier.com • www.bookaid.org

Contents

8. Conclusion   219

About the authors

Chihiro Watanabe graduated from the University of Tokyo, Japan, and is currently a professor emeritus at the Tokyo Institute of Technology, Japan, a research professor at the University of Jyväskylä, Finland, and a guest research scholar at the International Institute for Applied Systems Analysis (IIASA), Austria (watanabe.c.pqr@gmail.com).

Yuji Tou graduated from, and is currently a specially appointed associate professor at, the Tokyo Institute of Technology, Japan, and is a research officer of the Economic and Social Research Institute of the Cabinet Office, Japan (tou.yuji@gmail.com).

Pekka Neittaanmäki graduated from the University of Jyväskylä, Finland, and is currently a professor in the Faculty of Information Technology, University of Jyväskylä, and a UNESCO Chair on Digital Platforms for Transforming Economies, Finland (pekka.neittaanmaki@jyu.fi).

Preface

As Don Tapscott demonstrated in his 1995 book, *The Digital Economy*, the Internet has dramatically changed how we conduct business and lead our daily lives. The further advancement of digital innovation, including the cloud, mobile services, and artificial intelligence, has accelerated this change significantly and provided new services alongside unprecedented welfare. However, running counter to these gains, productivity in industrialized countries has been faced with an apparent decline, a situation that raises the specter of a possible productivity paradox in the digital economy. Due to this paradox, the limitations of gross domestic product (GDP) statistics in measuring the development of the digital economy have become an important subject.

This mismatch is an old problem rooted in the dynamics of product innovation. Because the mismatch brought about by information and communication technology (ICT) is extremely strong, finding a solution to this issue has become crucial for the digital economy.

With these features of the digital economy as a basis, this book highlights the significance of increasing dependence on what is known as *uncaptured GDP* by postulating that the Internet promotes free culture. The consumption within this culture, in turn, provides utility and happiness to people, but the value of this consumption cannot be captured through GDP data, which solely measure revenue. This added value is defined as uncaptured GDP.

The increasing dependence on uncaptured GDP has also been intensified by a shift in people's preferences from economic functionality to suprafunctionality beyond economic value, which encompasses social, cultural, and emotional values. This shift then induces the further advancement of ICT initiated by the Internet. Therefore, a new coevolution has emerged among the development of the Internet, increasing dependence on uncaptured GDP, and a shift in people's preferences. By analyzing the dynamism of this coevolution, a possible solution to the critical issue of how to measure uncaptured GDP in the digital economy can be obtained.

This book attempts to do so through an intensive empirical analysis of national, industrial, and individual behaviors.

This study includes an empirical analysis of the development trajectory of 500 global ICT firms in the digital economy. The analysis shows that under the circumstances listed above, research and development (R&D)-intensive global ICT firms have been confronting the conflict between the increase in R&D investment (which is indispensable for success in the digital economy) and a decline in productivity.

Further analysis revealed that aiming to avoid this dilemma, these firms have been attempting to activate the latent self-propagating function indigenous to ICT, because this can be activated through network externalities. Once activated, the self-propagating function induces the development of new functionality, leading to suprafunctionality beyond economic value, which corresponds to the shift in people's preferences in the digital economy.

The empirical analysis of six remarkable disruptive business models in the digital economy helps confirm that activation of this self-propagating function can be enabled by harnessing soft innovation resources (SIRs). SIRs are latent innovation resources activated by the digital platform ecosystem and are considered condensates and crystals of the advancement of the Internet.

The identification of SIRs as unique resources enables the development of neo open innovation. This novel concept avoids the dilemma created by increasing R&D and the decline in productivity. Instead, it enables sustainable growth by increasing gross R&D, which encompasses assimilated SIRs. This innovation leads to the operationalization of uncaptured GDP through the effective utilization of SIRs and helps global ICT leaders move in a transformative direction.

This book provides insight into the transformative direction of innovation in the digital economy. This insight can be attributed to the intensive challenge inherent in the synthesis of four-dimensional research, which consists of the following: observations on the forefront of the digital platform ecosystem, a theoretical appraisal, the development of statistical methods and the empirical analysis based on them, and database construction.

Acknowledgments

The research leading to these results is part of a project: "Platform Value Now: Value Capturing in the Fast Emerging Platform Ecosystems," supported by the Strategic Research Council at the Academy of Finland [grant number 293446].

The authors are grateful for the support and collaboration of the co-authors of articles that are referred to in this book. In particular, we would like to thank Dr. Leena Ilmola of IIASA for her advice regarding conceptualization of soft innovation resources, and Dr. Kashif Naveed of the University of Jyväskylä and Dr. Weilin Zhao of the ITOCHU Research Institute for their data construction and analysis contributions to parts of the book.

The authors want to extend our warmest gratitude to both Mr Matti Savonen and Mr Matthew Wuetricht for their invaluable assistance in the administrative and linguistic expertise, respectively. We also wish to thank the publishing team at Elsevier for the support on producing this book.

CHAPTER 1

Introduction

Contents

1.1 Rapid increase in digitalized innovation

The dramatic advancement of the Internet has led to the digital economy, which has changed our daily lives and the way we conduct business (Tapscott, 1994). Further progression of digitized innovation, including the cloud, mobile services, and artificial intelligence, has significantly accelerated this change and provided us with extraordinary services and unprecedented levels of welfare.

Fig. 1.1 illustrates these phenomena by demonstrating the significant correlation between R&D intensity and human resource development in major countries.

Fig. 1.2 illustrates the information and communication technology (ICT)-driven development trajectory of 120 countries in 2016, demonstrating the significant contribution of ICT advancement (as measured by the networked readiness index, or NRI) to economic development (in GDP per capita).

Similarly, Fig. 1.3 illustrates ICT-driven educational development in 120 countries, which demonstrates the significant role of digital innovation in advancing institutional systems (Watanabe et al., 2017). These figures also demonstrate the leading role of Finland and Singapore in ICT-driven institutional development (Watanabe et al., 2015b, 2016a).

Transforming the Socio Economy with Digital Innovation
ISBN 978-0-323-88465-5
https://doi.org/10.1016/B978-0-323-88465-5.00010-6

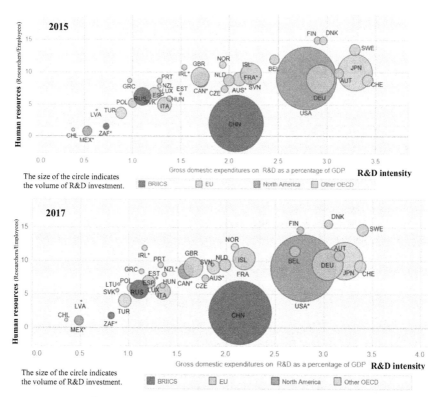

Figure 1.1 Correlation between R&D intensity and human resources in Organisation for Economic Co-operation and Development countries and key partner countries (2015, 2017). *(Source: OECD, 2017, 2019. Main Science and Technology Indicators Databases. OECD, Paris. http://www.oecd.org/sti/inno/researchanddevelopmentstatisticsrds. htm.)*

Fig. 1.4 illustrates the trends in R&D investment of the world's top 20 R&D leaders from 2015 to 2018 and shows the magnitude of R&D investment in the context of global competition in the digital economy. This can be considered a microcosm of the rapid progress of global digital innovation (for details of the data construction, see Table AII-2 in Appendix II).

Fig. 1.5 traces the number of R&D leaders by sector among the world's top 10 R&D-investing companies from 2007 to 2018. This reveals the rapid progress of global digital innovation, as ICT firms have taken the R&D lead in global competition.

Such a trend is supported by Fig. 1.6, which shows the world's biggest companies by market capitalization from 2007 to 2018.

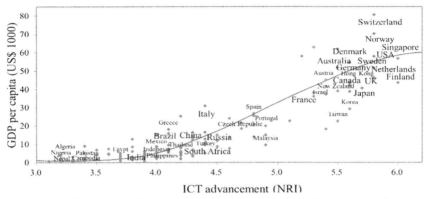

Figure 1.2 *Information and communication technology (ICT)-driven economic development trajectory of 120 countries (2016).* Luxembourg is not included. The networked readiness index (NRI) measures the capacity of countries to leverage ICT for increased competitiveness and well-being (see Appendix II-1). *(Sources: World Economic Forum (WEF), 2016. The Global Information Technology Report 2016. WEF, Geneva; International Monetary Fund (IMF), 2017a. World Economic Outlook Database, IMF, Washington, D.C.)*

1.2 Structural decline in productivity

However, in contrast to such an accomplishment, productivity in industrialized countries has undergone a structural decline (OECD, 2016; US Council on Competitiveness, 2016; IMF, 2017a; The World Bank, 2016), as demonstrated in Fig. 1.7, and raised questions about the apparent productivity paradox of the digital economy.[1] The limitations of GDP statistics in measuring advances in the digital economy have become an important subject (Brynjolfsson and McAfee, 2014; Economist, 2016; IMF, 2017b).

The Organisation for Economic Co-operation and Development (OECD) has posed the question, "Are GDP and productivity measures up to the challenges of the digital economy?" (Ahmad and Schreyer, 2016). The OECD highlights the following seven productivity loopholes derived from the advancement of the digital economy: (1) new forms of intermediation of peer-to-peer services, (2) blurring production boundaries that lead consumers to become producers, (3) consumer durables and investment, (4) free and subsidized consumer products, (5) free assets produced by

---

[1] The causal relationship of digitalization leading to declining productivity is demonstrated in Section **5.3**.

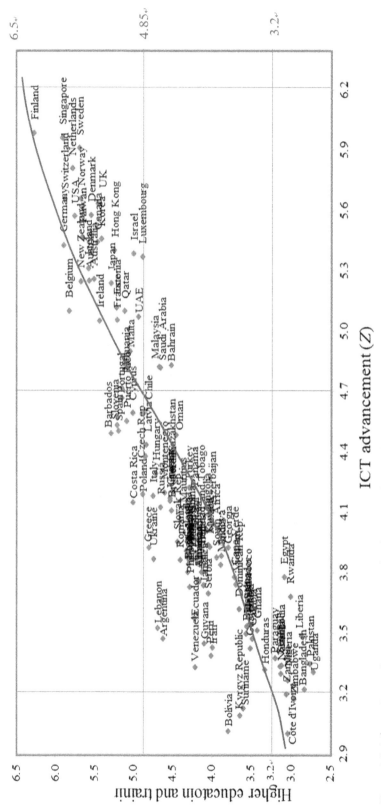

Figure 1.3 Information and communication technology (ICT)-driven educational development in 120 countries (2013). (*Sources: World Economic Forum (WEF), 2013a. The Global Competitiveness Report 2013–2014. WEF, Geneva; World Economic Forum (WEF), 2013b. The Global Information Technology Report 2013. WEF, Geneva.*)

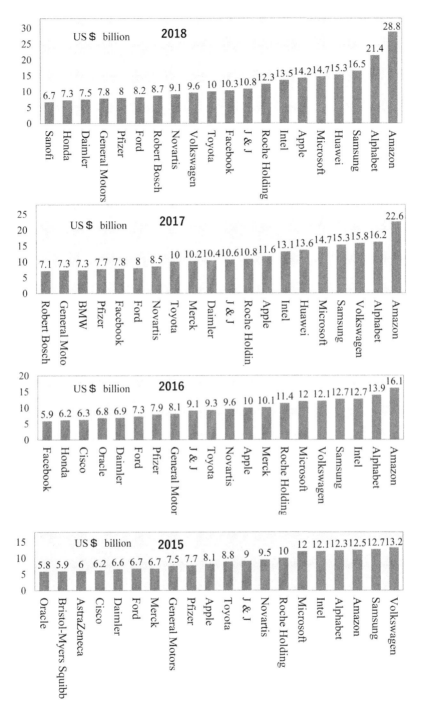

Figure 1.4 Trends in R&D investment for the world's top 20 R&D leaders (2015–18). *(Sources: UNCTAD (2019), Strategy & PwC (2018), US SEC (2020a,b,c,d,e,f,g,h,i), Bosch (2020), Daimler (2019), Ford (2019), Huawei Investment (2020), General Motors (2019), Honda (2019), Novartis (2020), Roche (2020), Samsung Electronics (2019), Sanofi (2020), Toyota (2020), Volkswagen (2020).)*

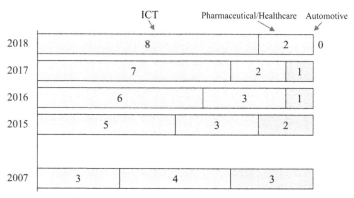

Figure 1.5 Number of R&D leaders by sector among the world's top 10 R&D-spending companies (2007–18). *ICT*, information and communication technology

		1	2	3	4	5	6	7	8	9	10
2018	[7]	Microsoft	Apple	Amazon	Alphabet	Berkshire	Facebook	Tencent	Alibaba	Johnson &J	JPMorgan
2017	[7]	Apple	Alphabet	Microsoft	Amazon	Facebook	Tencent	Berkshire	Alibaba	Johnson &J	JPMorgan
2016	[4]	Apple	Alphabet	Microsoft	Berkshire	Exxon Mobil	Amazon	Johnson &J	JPMorgan	General Elec	Wells Fargo
2015	[4]	Apple	Alphabet	Microsoft	Berkshire	Exxon Mobil	Amazon	General Elec	Johnson &J	Wells Fargo	JPMorgan
2007	[1]	Petrochina	ExxonMobil	General Elec	China Mob	ICBC	Microsoft	Gazprom	Royal Dutch	AT&T	Sinopec

Indicates ICT firms (not including telecommunication firms). [ ] indicates number of ICT firms.

Figure 1.6 Annual ranking of the world's top 10 companies in terms of market capitalization (2007–15). *ICT*, information and communication technology *(Source: The Financial Times (2019), annual issues.)*

households, (6) vague transactions through e-commerce, and (7) mis-measurement of ICT prices.

The above points can be attributed to the advancement of the digital economy initiated by the Internet and to the role of online intermediaries (OECD, 2010; Copenhagen Economics, 2013).

Because GDP is considered the most fundamental yardstick for devising economic policies, a large number of researchers have attempted to understand the issues using GDP as a measurement tool to represent the true picture of the digital economy (e.g., Feldstein, 2017; Syverson, 2017; Groshen et al., 2017; US Council on Competitiveness, 2016; Byrne and Corrado, 2016). However, the fundamental question of how GDP can be used to measure the digital economy remains unanswered (IMF, 2017b).

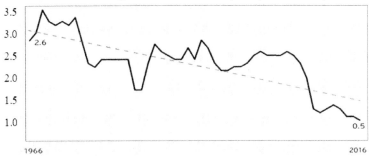

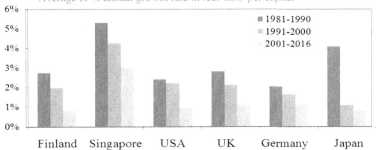

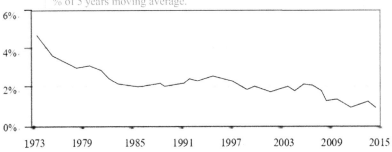

Figure 1.7 The trend in declining productivity in the digital economy. *(Sources: US Council on Competitiveness, 2016. No Recovery: An Analysis of Long-Term U.S. Productivity Decline. US Council on Competitiveness, Washington, D.C; International Monetary Fund (IMF), 2017a. World Economic Outlook Database, IMF, Washington, D.C; The World Bank, 2016. Digital Dividends. The World Bank, Washington, D.C.)*

Without a suitable answer to the foregoing question, decision-making and policy implementation can become biased and misleading. Furthermore, the social well-being enabled by digitization is not considered in identifying a nation's optimal trajectory.

We now confront the economy's third productivity paradox, following the earlier computer-initiated productivity paradox (in the late 1980s and 1990s) and the Internet-initiated productivity paradox (in the early 2010s). The third paradox raises a fundamental question about the myth of GDP.

This mismatch is an old problem rooted in the dynamics of product innovations, and it has affected our statistical understanding of change and growth for decades.

Nobel Laureate in Economics Richard Stone dealt with the challenge of measuring changes in quality in his impactful book *"Quality and Price Indexes in National Accounts"* (Stone, 1956). He suggested that quality differences can be measured if one obtains information based on a set of specifications that explains price differences among different grades of a product in the base period. Since then, intensive efforts to measure the prices of quality changes in new products have been undertaken. The hedonic prices approach introduced by Griliches (1961) has played a central role, while attempts at an appropriate analysis of changes in product quality have continued (Wasshausen and Moulton, 2006).

However, despite these efforts in product quality assessment, national statistical accounts have failed to integrate their sources with these efforts.

1.3 The dilemma of digitalized innovation and productivity decline

As a consequence of the productivity decline, digital leaders have encountered a dilemma when opting for further digital innovation (which is essential for global competition), as investing in such innovation can lead to further declines in productivity.

Fig. 1.8 demonstrates the bipolarization of countries and firms that are less digitalized from those that are highly digitalized. While the former enjoy a virtuous cycle between digitalization and increased productivity, the latter suffer from the conflicting results between the two.

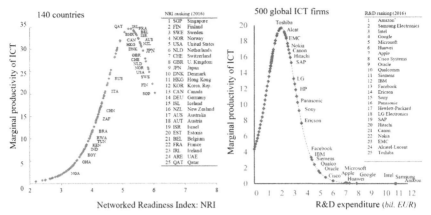

Figure 1.8 Development trajectories of 140 countries and 500 global information and communication technology (ICT) firms (2016). *(Based on Tou, Y., Watanabe, C., Moriya, K., Neittaanmäki, P., 2019a. Harnessing soft innovation resources leads to neo open innovation. Technology in Society 58, 101114; International Monetary Fund (IMF), 2017a. World Economic Outlook Database, IMF, Washington, D.C, World Economic Forum (WEF), 2016. The Global Information Technology Report 2016. WEF, Geneva; European Commission, Joint Research Center, 2017. The EU Industrial R&D Investment Scoreboard 2016. European Commission, Brussels. Ahmad and Schreyer, 2016; Bosch, 2020; Brynjolfsson and McAfee, 2014; Byrne and Corrado, 2016; Copenhagen Economics, 2013; Daimler, 2019; Economist, 2016; European Commission, Joint Research Center, 2017; Feldstein, 2017; Groshen et al., 2017; Honda, 2019; Huawei Investment, 2020; International Monetary Fund (IMF), 2017a, 2017b; McDonagh, 2008; Novartis, 2020; OECD, 2010, 2016, 2017; Roche, 2020; Samsung Electronics, 2019; Sanofi, 2020; Stone, 1956; Strategy & PwC, 2018; Syverson, 2017; Tapscott, 1994; The World Bank, 2016; Tou et al., 2019a, 2019b; Toyota, 2020; UNCTAD, 2019; US Council on Competitiveness, 2016; US Security and Exchange Commission (SEC), 2020a, 2020b, 2020c, 2020d, 2020e, 2020f, 2020g, 2020h, 2020i; Volkswagen, 2020; Watanabe et al., 2015a, 2015b, 2016a, 2016b, 2017, 2018, World Economic Forum (WEF), 2013a, 2013b, 2016.)*

1.4 Two-sided nature of information and communication technology

The structural source of this dilemma can be attributed to the two-sided nature of ICT (Watanabe et al., 2015b). Advances ICT generally contribute to enhancing technology prices through the development of new functionalities. A typical demonstration of this is the iPhone X, which was released in November 2017.[2] However, contrary to the

---

[2] As its functionality has advanced, the price of Apple's smartphone has also increased: iPhone SE (US$ 399), iPhone 6S (US$ 549), iPhone 7 (US$ 649), iPhone 8 (US$ 699), iPhone 8 Plus (US$ 799), and iPhone X (US$ 999).

historical results from traditional ICT, the dramatic advancement of the Internet has resulted in declining ICT prices because digital content is characterized by freebies, easy replication, and mass standardization (Watanabe et al., 2015b).

The continuing drop in ICT prices has resulted in declining marginal productivity for leading ICT firms, because this productivity corresponds to relative prices when firms seek profit maximization in competitive markets.

1.5 Uncaptured GDP

By accounting for the most notable features of the digital economy, this book stresses the significance of the economy's increasing dependence on uncaptured GDP in value creation. It postulates that the Internet promotes a free culture, the consumption of which provides utility and happiness to people. However, these forms of consumer value are not captured in traditional GDP data, which only measure revenue. This added but unaccounted-for value is defined as uncaptured GDP (Watanabe et al., 2015a).

The shift in people's preferences from economic functionality to suprafunctionality that goes beyond economic value to encompass social, cultural, and emotional values (McDonagh, 2008) has induced further advancement of ICT initiated by the Internet, which in turn has intensified the economy's increasing dependence on uncaptured GDP.

1.6 Spin-off coevolution

As a result, a new coevolution in Internet advancement has emerged. Fig. 1.9 (Watanabe et al., 2015a, 2015b, 2016a, 2016b) illustrates this coevolution of the increasing share of uncaptured GDP and the shift in people's preferences. This coevolution can be considered a spin-off from traditional coevolution, which consists of traditional ICT, captured GDP, and economic functionality.

A possible solution to the issue of increasing R&D expenditures coupled with declining productivity in the digital economy can be obtained by analyzing the dynamism of this coevolution (Watanabe et al., 2016a).

With an intensive empirical analysis of national, industrial, and individual behaviors, this book attempts to offer a perspective on this critical issue.

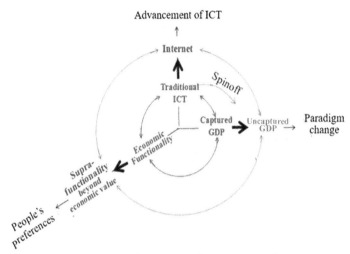

Figure 1.9 *Spin-off dynamism scheme.* Coevolution among the internet, uncaptured GDP, and suprafunctionality.

1.7 Activation of self-propagating function

An empirical analysis of the development trajectory of 500 global ICT firms found that R&D-intensive firms have aimed to avoid the conflict between increased R&D investment and declining productivity. To do so, they have attempted to activate the latent self-propagating function indigenous to ICT (Watanabe et al., 2018). This latent function can be awoken and activated through the network externalities inherent to ICT. The activated self-propagating function then induces new functionality development, leading to a suprafunctionality beyond economic value in the digital economy that corresponds to the shift in people's preferences, as illustrated in Fig. 1.10.

1.8 Soft innovation resources

This study's empirical analysis examines six remarkable disruptive business models that have attempted to harness the potential of the latent innovation resources in the digital economy. This analysis confirms that the self-propagating function can be enabled by harnessing soft innovation resources *(SIRs)*. *SIRs* are latent innovation resources activated by the digital platform ecosystem. *SIRs* are considered the condensates and crystals of the advancement of the Internet because their activation has occurred with the advancement of the Internet (Tou et al., 2019a).

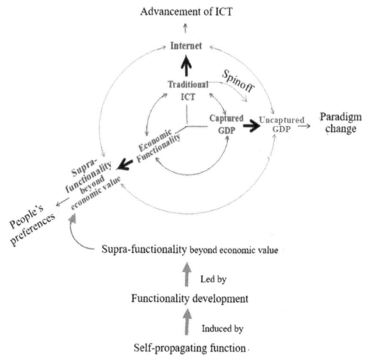

Figure 1.10 Scheme of the transformative strategy to counter declining productivity.

A virtuous cycle emerges—the above dilemma is avoided as people's preferences are satisfied, while further advancement of the Internet is expected through the use of external innovation resources, namely, *SIRs*.

1.9 Neo open innovation

By identifying these unique resources, *SIRs*, within the digital economy. the novel concept of neo open innovation emerges. This concept helps firms avoid the dilemma of declining productivity and enables sustainable growth by expanding gross R&D to include assimilated *SIRs* (Tou et al., 2019a).

As an example, Amazon's neo open innovation is responsible for the company's conspicuous jump in R&D investment to become one of the world's top R&D firms over a short period, as illustrated in Fig. 1.11. At the same time, this increased R&D has driven increases in its sales and market capitalization, as illustrated in Fig. 1.12 while avoiding the dilemma of declining productivity (Tou et al., 2019b). Fig. 1.12 shows the

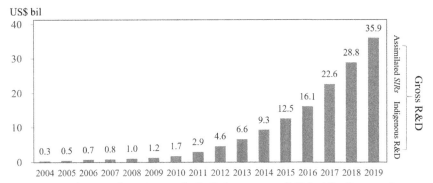

Figure 1.11 The trend in Amazon's R&D investment (2004—19). *(Source: Amazon annual report (annual issues). Tou, Y., Watanabe, C., Moriya, K., Naveed, N., Vurpillat, V., Neittaanmäki, P., 2019b. The transformation of R&D into neo open innovation: a new concept of R&D endeavor triggered by Amazon. Technology in Society 58, 101141.)*

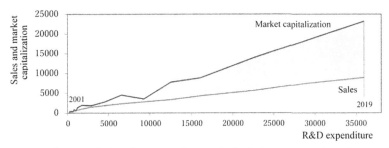

Figure 1.12 The correlation between Amazon's R&D investment, its sales, and its market capitalization a(2001—19; index: 2001 = 100). *(Source: US Security and Exchange Commission (SEC), 2020b. Annual Report Pursuant to Section 13 or 15(d) of the Security Exchange Act of 1934 for the Fiscal Year 2019. Amazon.com, Inc. SEC, Washington, D.C.)*

correlations between Amazon's R&D expenditures, its sales, and its market capitalization. This shows that Amazon has succeeded in driving increased sales and market capitalization through increases in R&D spending, which demonstrates its success in overcoming the dilemma between R&D expansion and productivity declines.

This innovation leads to operationalization of uncaptured GDP through the effective utilization of *SIRs* and paves the way for transformation by global ICT leaders.

This book provides insight into the overall transformative direction of innovation in the digital economy.

This insight can be attributed to the intensive challenge inherent in the book's synthesis of four-dimensional research. This synthesis consists of observations at the forefront of the platform ecosystem, theoretical appraisal, development of statistical methods and empirical analysis, and database construction.

The structure of this book is as follows:

Chapter 2 contrasts the productivity paradox between the Product of Things and Internet of Things societies, thereby highlighting the limitations of GDP for measuring the digital economy. Chapter 3 analyzes the structural sources of this limitation and identifies the key causes of uncaptured GDP in its coevolutionary dynamism. It attempts to measure uncaptured GDP based on its coevolutionary dynamism with Internet advances and shifts in people's preferences. Chapter 4 demonstrates the six remarkable disruptive business models that have emerged from the use of *SIRs* within this dynamism. Chapter 5 postulates the concept of neo open innovation, which utilizes *SIRs* as a solution to the conflict between R&D expansion and subsequent declines in productivity. Chapter 6 examines the disruptive business models of GAFAM (Google, Apple, Facebook, Amazon, and Microsoft), particularly that of Amazon, while demonstrating the significance of neo open innovation through *SIR*-driven transformative R&D. Chapter 7 suggests novel approaches and concepts for the operationalization of uncaptured GDP as an insightful compass. Chapter 8 summarizes significant findings while offering policy suggestions and directions for future research.

Appendix I provides a summary of the basic mathematics for the technoeconomic analysis. Appendix II tabulates the database for the technoeconomic analysis. Appendix III presents figures and tables for the analyses of the six disruptive business models from which new innovations have emerged in response to the use of *SIRs*.

References

Ahmad, N., Schreyer, P., 2016. Measuring GDP in a Digital Economy. OECD Statistics Working Papers, 2016/07. OECD Publishing, Paris.

Bosch, 2020. Annual Report 2019. Robert Bosch AG, Gerlinger. https://assets.bosch.com/media/global/bosch_group/our_figures/pdf/bosch-annual-report-2019.pdf.

Brynjolfsson, E., McAfee, A., 2014. The Second Machine Age: Work, Progress, and Prosperity in a Time of Brilliant Technologies. W.W. Norton & Company, New York.

Byrne, D., Corrado, C., 2016. ICT Prices and ICT Services: What Do They Tell about Productivity and Technology? Economic Program Working Paper Series, EPWP #16-05 The Conference Board, New York.

Copenhagen Economics, 2013. The Impact of Online Intermediaries on the EU Economy. Copenhagen Economics, Copenhagen.

Daimler, 2019. Annual Report 2018. Daimler AG, Stuttgart. https://www.daimler.com/documents/investors/reports/annual-report/daimler/daimler-ir-annual-report-2018.pdf.

Economist, 2016. How to Measure Prosperity. https://www.economist.com/news/leaders/21697834-gdp-bad-gauge-material-well-being-time-fresh-approach-how-measure-prosperity (retrieved 30.04.2016).

European Commission, Joint Research Center, 2017. The EU Industrial R&D Investment Scoreboard 2016. European Commission, Brussels.

Feldstein, M., 2017. Understanding the real growth of GDP, personal income, and productivity. The Journal of Economic Perspectives 31 (2), 145—164.

Ford, 2019. Annual Report 2018. Ford Motor Company, Dearborn. https://s23.q4cdn.com/799033206/files/doc_financials/annual/2018-Annual-Report.pdf.

General Motors, 2019. Annual Report 2018. General Motors Company, Detroit. https://www.sec.gov/Archives/edgar/data/1467858/000146785820000028/gm201910k.htm.

Griliches, Z., 1961. Hedonic price Indexes for automobiles: an econometric analysis of quality change. In: The Price Statistics of Federal Government. NBER, New York, pp. 173—196. NBER Staff Report No. 3, General Series No. 73.

Groshen, E.L., Moyer, B.C., Aizcorbe, A.M., Bradley, R., Friedman, D.M., 2017. How government statistics adjust for potential biases from quality change and new goods in an age of digital technologies: a view from the trenches. The Journal of Economic Perspectives 31 (2), 187—210.

Honda, 2019. Consolidated Financial Results for FY 2018. Honda Motor Co., Ltd., Tokyo. https://global.honda/content/dam/site/global/investors/cq_img/library/financialresult/FY201903_4Q_financial_ result_e.pdf.

Huawei Investment, 2020. 2019 Annual Report. Huawei Investment & Holding Co., Ltd., Shenzen. https://www-file.huawei.com/-/media/corporate/pdf/annual-report/annual_report_2019_en.pdf?la=en.

International Monetary Fund (IMF), 2017a. World Economic Outlook Database. IMF, Washington, D.C.

International Monetary Fund (IMF), 2017b. Measuring the Digital Economy: IMF Statistical Forum. IMF, Washington D.C.

McDonagh, D., 2008. Satisfying needs beyond the functional: the changing needs of the silver market consumer. In: Proceedings of the International Symposium on the Silver Market Phenomenon. Business Opportunities and Responsibilities in the Aging Society, Tokyo.

Novartis, 2020. Annual Report 2019. Novartis AG, Basel. https://www.novartis.com/sites/www.novartis.com/files/novartis-annual-report-2019.pdf.

OECD, 2010. The Economic and Social Role of Internet Intermediaries. OECD, Paris.

OECD, 2016. Tax Challenges in the Digital Economy. OECD, Paris.

OECD, 2017, 2019. Main Science and Technology Indicators Databases. OECD, Paris. http://www.oecd.org/sti/inno/researchanddevelopmentstatisticsrds.htm.

Roche, 2020. Finance Report 2019. Roche Holding AG, Basel. https://www.roche.com/dam/jcr:1e6cfce4-2333-4ed6-b98a-f6b62809221d/en/fb19e.pdf.

Samsung Electronics, 2019. Consolidated Financial Statements. Samsung Electronics Co. Ltd., Seoul. https://images.samsung.com/is/content/samsung/p5/global/ir/docs/2018_con_quarter04_all.pdf.

Sanofi, 2020. Annual Report 2019. Sanofi, Paris. https://www.sanofi.com/-/media/Project/One-Sanofi-Web/Websites/Global/Sanofi-COM/Home/common/docs/investors/2020_03_23_Sanofi-Report-2019-20F.

Stone, R., 1956. Quality and Price Indexes in National Accounts. OEEC, Paris.

Strategy & PwC, 2018. 2018 Global Innovation 1000 Study. Strategy & PwC, New York.

Syverson, C., 2017. Challenges to mismeasurement explanations for the US productivity slowdown. The Journal of Economic Perspectives 31 (2), 165–186.

Tapscott, D., 1994. The Digital Economy: Promise and Peril in the Age of Networked Intelligence. McGraw-Hill, New York.

The Financial Times, 2019. FT Global 500. The Financial Times, New York.

The World Bank, 2016. Digital Dividends. The World Bank, Washington, D.C.

Tou, Y., Watanabe, C., Moriya, K., Neittaanmäki, P., 2019a. Harnessing soft innovation resources leads to neo open innovation. Technology in Society 58, 101114.

Tou, Y., Watanabe, C., Moriya, K., Naveed, N., Vurpillat, V., Neittaanmäki, P., 2019b. The transformation of R&D into neo open innovation: a new concept of R&D endeavor triggered by Amazon. Technology in Society 58, 101141.

Toyota, 2020. Annual Report 2019. Toyota Motor Corporation, Tokyo. https://global. toyota/en/ir/library/annual/.

UNCTAD, 2019. World Investment Report 2019 Based on Statistical Databases of Eikon and Orbis of Ghent University. UNCTAD, Geneva.

US Council on Competitiveness, 2016. No Recovery: An Analysis of Long-Term U.S. Productivity Decline. US Council on Competitiveness, Washington, D.C.

US Security and Exchange Commission (SEC), 2020a. Annual Report Pursuant to Section 13 or 15(d) of the Security Exchange Act of 1934 for the Fiscal Year 2019. Alphabets Inc. SEC, Washington, D.C.

US Security and Exchange Commission (SEC), 2020b. Annual Report Pursuant to Section 13 or 15(d) of the Security Exchange Act of 1934 for the Fiscal Year 2019. Amazon.com, Inc. SEC, Washington, D.C.

US Security and Exchange Commission (SEC), 2020c. Annual Report Pursuant to Section 13 or 15(d) of the Security Exchange Act of 1934 for the Fiscal Year 2019. Apple Inc. SEC, Washington, D.C.

US Security and Exchange Commission (SEC), 2020d. Annual Report Pursuant to Section 13 or 15(d) of the Security Exchange Act of 1934 for the Fiscal Year 2019. Facebook, Inc. SEC, Washington, D.C.

US Security and Exchange Commission (SEC), 2020e. Annual Report Pursuant to Section 13 or 15(d) of the Security Exchange Act of 1934 for the Fiscal Year 2019. Intel Corporation. SEC, Washington, D.C.

US Security and Exchange Commission (SEC), 2020f. Annual Report Pursuant to Section 13 or 15(d) of the Security Exchange Act of 1934 for the Fiscal Year 2019. Johnson & Johnson. SEC, Washington, D.C.

US Security and Exchange Commission (SEC), 2020g. Annual Report Pursuant to Section 13 or 15(d) of the Security Exchange Act of 1934 for the Fiscal Year 2019. Microsoft Corporation. SEC, Washington, D.C.

US Security and Exchange Commission (SEC), 2020h. Annual Report Pursuant to Section 13 or 15(d) of the Security Exchange Act of 1934 for the Fiscal Year 2019. Pfizer Inc. SEC, Washington, D.C.

US Security and Exchange Commission (SEC), 2020i. Annual Report Pursuant to Section 13 or 15(d) of the Security Exchange Act of 1934 for the Fiscal Year 2019. Sanofi. SEC, Washington, D.C.

Volkswagen, 2020. Annual Report 2019. Volkswagen AG, Wolfsburg. https://www. volkswagenag.com/en/InvestorRelations/news-and-publications/Annual_Reports.html.

Wasshausen, D., Moulton, B.R., 2006. The Role of Hedonic Methods in Measuring Real GDP in the United States. BEA Papers 0067. Bureau of Economic Analysis, Washington.

Watanabe, C., Naveed, K., Zhao, W., 2015a. New paradigm of ICT productivity: increasing role of un-captured GDP and growing anger of consumers. Technology in Society 41, 21–44.

Watanabe, C., Naveed, K., Neittaanmäki, P., 2015b. Dependency on un-captured GDP as a source of resilience beyond economic value in countries with advanced ICT infrastructure: similarities and disparities between Finland and Singapore. Technology in Society 42, 104−122.

Watanabe, C., Naveed, K., Neittaanmäki, P., Tou, Y., 2016a. Operationalization of un-captured GDP: the innovation stream under new global mega-trends. Technology in Society 45, 58−77.

Watanabe, C., Naveed, K., Neittaanmäki, P., 2016b. Co-evolution of three mega-trends nurtures un-captured GDP: uber's ride-sharing revolution. Technology in Society 46, 164−185.

Watanabe, C., Naveed, K., Neittaanmäki, P., 2017. Co-evolution between trust in teachers and higher education toward digitally-rich learning environments. Technology in Society 48, 70−96.

Watanabe, C., Naveed, K., Tou, Y., Neittaanmäki, P., 2018. Measuring GDP in the digital economy: increasing dependence on uncaptured GDP. Technological Forecasting and Social Change 137, 226−240.

World Economic Forum (WEF), 2013a. The Global Competitiveness Report 2013−2014. WEF, Geneva.

World Economic Forum (WEF), 2013b. The Global Information Technology Report 2013. WEF, Geneva.

World Economic Forum (WEF), 2016. The Global Information Technology Report 2016. WEF, Geneva.

CHAPTER 2

The productivity paradox and the limitations of GDP in measuring the digital economy

Contents

Transforming the Socio Economy with Digital Innovation
ISBN 978-0-323-88465-5
https://doi.org/10.1016/B978-0-323-88465-5.00005-2

2.1 The increasing significance of the measurement mismatch in the digital economy

2.1.1 The mismatch between the quality of products and statistical sources

The mismatch concerns all our macroeconomic records since their introduction by economist Richard Stone just after World War II.[1] While Stone made a significant contribution to the development and diffusion of the national accounting system, he always stressed a number of concerns (Baranzini and Marangoni, 2015). In his impactful book *Quantity and Price Indexes in National Accounts* (Stone, 1956),[2] Stone dealt with the challenge of measuring changes in quality. He suggested that quality differences can be measured if information can be obtained based on a set of specifications that can explain price differences among different grades of a product in the base period. This was appreciated by "great thoughtfulness, ingenuity, and clarity of exposition and merits the attention of every user of index numbers" (Chipman, 1959).

However, this is a difficult question, and it "might have been more suitably put in a technical supplement" (Moss, 1958); therefore, a "more theoretical and less empirical method of estimating implicit prices seems to be called for" (Chipman, 1959).

In his Nobel Memorial Lectures in 1984, Stone pointed out the difficulty of estimating the prices of new types of goods for national accounting (Stone, 1984).

Market prices do not necessarily reflect longitudinal changes in the quality of products, particularly new products, which results in misleading statistical data. While new products provide better-quality services to their users, they are rarely reflected by a change in their market price. This is an old problem rooted in the dynamics of product innovations, and has affected the statistical understanding of change and growth for decades.

---

[1] Stone produced the national accounts figures covering the years 1938–44 in 1945, which laid a solid foundation for national income accounting in the UK and led to the current System of National Accounts.

[2] This book was published by the OEEC (the current OECD) as a proposal to public officers for the development of an international standard for national accounts (Pesaran and Harcourt, 2000; Baranzini and Marangoni, 2015).

2.1.2 Exacerbation of the mismatch by the digital economy

However, the digital economy has created a more fundamental change than that which took place in the previous decades owing to the following unique features:

(1) The expansion of information and communications technology (ICT) and the digital economy is occurring at a tremendous pace.

(2) Value can be provided free of charge.

(3) ICT prices decrease and productivity declines.

(4) Digital goods are mobile and intangible, thus leading to substantially different business models.

(5) The boundary between consumer and producer is becoming thinner, and consumers are becoming "prosumers."

(6) Barriers to entry are low, causing companies to innovate more seamlessly.

(7) Companies can fully enjoy the network externalities and subsequent self-propagation phenomenon embedded in ICT products and services.[3]

(8) Companies are polarized between those that enjoy network externalities and those that do not.

(9) Digital companies tend toward a gigantic monopoly.

(10) Contrary to a traditional monopoly, this new monopoly can enhance convenience.

Consequently, the digital economy has exacerbated the above mismatch problem (Ahmad and Schreyer, 2016; Watanabe et al., 2018c).

The available statistics inevitably lag behind the reality they are meant to describe. When there is a structural change in the economy, such as digital transformation, the gap between statistics and reality may be so great that the lock-in to the existing statistical framework due to the constellation of interests involved could break (Coyle, 2016).

Although there have been critics of the centrality of GDP growth in economic policy throughout the postwar lifetime of modern national accounting, their critiques seem to have been gaining fresh traction (Coyle,

---

[3] ICT's explicit network externalities function to alter the correlation between innovations and institutional systems. A new correlation creates new features of the innovation, which lead to an exponential increase in its outcomes such as sales and profits (Watanabe and Hobe, 2004; Watanabe et al., 2004). Schelling (1998) portrayed an array of logistically developing and diffusing social mechanisms stimulated by these interactions.

2016). Recently, questions about the effect of digital technologies on the understanding and measurement of the economy have also become more prominent (Bean, 2016; Coyle, 2016).

2.1.3 Hedonic pricing approach

Accurate price indices are crucial for preparing true estimates of GDP and corresponding productivity measures. The price index must capture price changes for so-called "relevant" market basket goods while also controlling for changes in the characteristics and/or quality of these goods (Wasshausen and Moulton, 2006).

Traditional price indices are well suited for capturing price change for goods that exhibit little or no changes in quality over time; however, for products whose characteristics or quality change rapidly (e.g., ICT goods) or are heterogeneous by nature (e.g., custom software), hedonic methods may be more suitable and practical (Wasshausen and Moulton, 2006).

Hedonic prices were introduced by Griliches (1961). While some prior attempts to apply hedonic techniques to price statistics existed (e.g., Waugh, 1928; Court, 1939; Stone, 1954, 1956), Griliches took an unconventional method, which was at the time on the periphery of price statistics, and demonstrated to the economics and statistics community its use in addressing critical quality adjustment problems that had previously been considered intractable (Wasshausen and Moulton, 2006).

Following Griliches, hedonic methods quickly grew to be a new branch of economic research (e.g., Griliches, 1971; 1990; Triplett, 1975; 1987; 1990; Berndt, 1983).

Hedonic prices attempt to measure the deflated monetary price of a good by considering changes in quality. As identified by Stone in the 1950s, assessing changes in the quality of goods is problematic and quite subjective. This is the ultimate cause of the limited influence of that methodology.

The shift in hedonic prices brought about by ICT is significantly stronger than the shift that took place in previous decades (Wasshausen and Moulton, 2006; BLS, 2011; Byrne and Corrado, 2015; Corrado and Ukhaneva, 2016; Cavallo and Rigobon, 2016; Wasshausen, 2017). As a result, the digital economy has exacerbated this measurement problem (Ahmad and Schreyer, 2016).

2.1.4 Integration of national statistical accounts with accurate price index efforts

Although digitalization has increased the size of the problem, it may also be part of the solution. There is a considerable scope to complement traditional methods of price measurement with new data sources and data-gathering techniques, including scanner data and web-scraping, that provide the capacity to collect large samples of prices at high frequency (Ahmad and Schreyer, 2016). The advancement of big data technology supports this.

Griffith and Nesheim (2013) demonstrated the significance of the scanner data approach in assessing consumers' willingness to pay for the organic characteristics of food products. These pioneer challenges explore a complex approach to hedonic pricing methods by using the advancement of digital innovation. The evidence suggests that the more timely collection of data and information using digitalized sources can provide more robust and efficient alternatives (Ahmad and Schreyer, 2016).

Contrary to such successive efforts toward an appropriate analysis of the changes in product quality, there has been a lack of sufficient attempts in national statistical accounts to integrate their sources with these efforts.[4]

Given that the shift in hedonic prices brought about by ICT is stronger than the shift that took place in the previous decades, this integration is a crucial subject to the digital economy. In addition, given the significant shift in people's preferences from economic functionality to suprafunctionality beyond economic value to encompass social, cultural, and emotional values (McDonagh, 2008), measuring changes in the quality of goods and services that correspond to people's satisfaction will certainly become complicated. Thus, the integration of this new measurement data with that of existing sources becomes crucial for measuring GDP in the digital economy.

The noteworthy coevolution among a shift in people's preferences from economic functionality to suprafunctionality, advances in ICT and subsequent changes in digital product quality, and the accompanying paradigm change to uncaptured GDP as reviewed earlier (see details of this coevolution in 2.4.2) may provide insight into the integration of national accounts with the above product-oriented microanalysis efforts.

---

[4] Hedonic price indices used to deflate a number of GDP final demand components in recent years remain at a level equal to 20% of nominal GDP (Wasshausen and Moulton, 2006).

2.2 From "computer-initiated" to "internet-initiated" productivity paradox

2.2.1 Computer-initiated productivity paradox

Following the "productivity paradox" postulated by Nobel Laureate Robert Solow (Solow, 1987), a significant number of studies have discussed the social and economic effects of ICT advancement. The reaction to the productivity paradox by Brynjolfsson (1993), as well as several other analyses, was an attempt to understand the relationship between ICT and its productivity (Kraemer and Dedrick, 1994; Lichtenberg, 1995; Brynjolfsson and Hitt, 1996).

Brynjolfsson and Hitt (1996) disproved the productivity paradox and attributed it to problems with productivity measurement and a long lag between technology investments and productivity gains. Later, Brynjolfsson et al. found a significant positive relationship between ICT investments and productivity (Brynjolfsson and Hitt, 1998; Brynjolfsson and Yang, 1999). In the late 1990s, some signs emerged that productivity in the workplace had improved, especially in the United States, thus encouraging the popular consideration that there was no paradox (Triplett, 1999).

2.2.2 Internet-initiated productivity paradox

A new productivity paradox appeared late in the first decade of this century, and it was largely attributed to the third industrial revolution initiated by the dramatic development of the Internet (Rifkin, 2011). In 2 decades, the Internet grew from being a network of researchers to become the day-to-day reality of billions of people (McKinsey Global Institute, 2011). Undoubtedly, the Internet has transformed how people live, work, and socialize and how countries develop and grow. Consequently, the computer-initiated ICT world has become more interactive, integrated, and seamless, and this interconnectedness is creating many new opportunities.

However, Cowen (2011) argued the following: "Contrary to the dramatic advancement of the Internet and subsequent ICT advancement, we were living through the consequence of a dramatic decrease in the rate of innovation." He claimed that the consequence of reduced innovation was fewer new industries, less creative destruction, and thus fewer new jobs. He stressed that, historically, technological progress had brought a large and predictable stream of growth to most of the economy. However, these assumptions turned out to be wrong or misleading when applied to the

Internet. He then suggested this result was the possible consequence of the two-faced nature of ICT.

Brynjolfsson, who first reacted to Solow's production paradox in 1993, raised the following question: "Could technology be destroying jobs?" (Brynjolfsson and McAfee, 2011). Using the music industry as an example, he contended, "Because you and I stopped buying CDs, the music industry has shrunk according to revenues and GDP. But we're not listening to less music. There's more music consumed than before." He further suggested that rather than growth, it was the yardstick that might be deficient, and he thus postulated the limitations of GDP statistics in reflecting the true picture of digital consumption (Brynjolfsson and McAfee, 2014).

Lowrey (2011) has maintained that the Internet promotes a free culture, the consumption of which provides utility and happiness to people (e.g., Tapscott, 1994), but that these aspects of its value cannot be captured through GDP data, which measure revenue.

Following these arguments, the authors stressed the significance of the two-faced nature of ICT as a structural source of the Internet-initiated productivity paradox (Watanabe et al., 2015b). They stressed that while the advancement of ICT generally contributes to enhancing technology prices through the development of new functionalities, the dramatic advancement of the Internet has resulted in a decline in ICT prices because digital content is characterized by the provision of freebies, easy replication, and mass standardization. When firms seek to maximize profits in a highly competitive market, their ICT prices correspond to marginal productivity, resulting in a productivity decline (Watanabe et al., 2015b).

2.3 New spin-off business strategies in the transition to an Internet of Things society

2.3.1 New stream toward an Internet of Things society

The Internet of Things (IoT)[5] has the potential to change the basis of competition and drive new business models (McKinsey Global Institute, 2015), thus propelling the next phase of the digitization of our society (EU, 2017).

---

[5] Internet Society (2015) defines IoT as scenarios in which network connectivity and computing capability extend to objects, sensors, and everyday items not normally considered by computers, allowing these devices to generate exchanges and consume data with minimal human intervention.

Aside from discussing the opportunities, some studies have indicated the possibility of another productivity paradox. According to McKinsey Global Institute (2015), the economic effect of IoT could, by 2025, reach USD 3.9 trillion to 11.1 trillion per year, which is roughly equivalent to 11% of global GDP. However, McKinsey Global Institute (2015) also saw the possibility of another productivity paradox in the context of IoT because of a possible lag between technology investments and productivity gains being reflected at a macroeconomic level.

With the rapid advancement of the Internet and the IoT, our world is becoming an IoT-based society (Bharadwaj et al., 2013; Internet Society, 2016). The IoT has changed the traditional meaning of the word "product" introduced in the Product of Things (PoT) era. In the IoT era, a product can be a technology, device, service (powered by software), flow of data, software application, or any combination of the above.

The transformation of the traditional Internet, in which data are "created by people," into the IoT, in which data are "created by things" (Madakam et al., 2015), generates data at a much larger scale. To capitalize on the highly promising business opportunities of the IoT, global ICT firms must restructure their business models and embrace sophisticated digital solutions (Bharadwaj et al., 2013).

The importance of business models and digital business strategies (DBS) cannot be overemphasized because of the challenges and tremendous interest in the IoT. Bharadwaj et al. (2013) and Kahre et al. (2017) stressed the significance of DBS and discussed the fundamental role of digital technologies in transforming business strategies, business processes, firm capabilities, and the nature of products and services.

They also highlighted the significance of DBS as (1) the significant role of ICT pervading digital resources in other functional areas, such as operations, purchasing, the supply chain, and marketing; (2) going beyond systems and technologies; and (3) explicitly linking DBS to create differential business value, thereby elevating the performance implications of the ICT strategy beyond efficiency and productivity.

Bharadwaj et al. (2013) also suggested that the role of ICT strategy should be reconsidered from the perspective of a functional-level strategy that subordinates the business strategy in the DBS, which fuses the ICT and business strategies.

2.3.2 Spin-off dynamism toward a new coevolution

The authors previously analyzed the business strategies of 500 global ICT firms in 2007 and 2010 (before and after the Lehman shock in 2008) and identified the following strategies for resilient market value creation in the digital economy (Watanabe et al., 2014):

(1) Dependence on high R&D profitability while restraining its elasticity

(2) Effective utilization of external resources in innovation

(3) Hybrid management of technology between indigenous R&D and assimilation of spillover technology

In their subsequent studies, the authors attempted to compare the spin-off dynamism from traditional computer-initiated ICT innovation in the era of the PoT with Internet-initiated ICT innovations using their coevolutional framework, which combines the advancement of ICT, a paradigm change, and a shift in people's preferences, as illustrated in Fig. 1.9 (see Chapter 1).

The authors found that people's preferences have shifted from economic functionality to suprafunctionality consistent with the shift from computer-initiated innovation to the new stream of Internet-initiated innovations. The economic effect of innovation has increasingly shifted from captured GDP (monetized consumption) to uncaptured GDP (non-monetized consumption) because of its digital nature, the free availability of products, and new business models (Watanabe et al., 2015a,b, 2016a,b, 2017a; Naveed et al., 2017).

This concept of spin-off dynamism toward a new coevolution may shed light on the current critical issues related to measuring GDP in the digital economy.

While an increasing number of studies have attempted to analyze this dynamism (e.g., see work by Brynjolfsson and McAfee, 2014; Ahmad and Schreyer, 2016), none have elucidated the inside the black box of this dynamism from the viewpoint of the possible consequences of the transformation of the development trajectory toward an IoT-based society as reviewed earlier.

The research studies of Sussan and Acs (2017) and Gestrin and Staudt (2018) are important exceptions. These researchers attempted to identify the transformation from the nondigital to the digitalizing state by analyzing the process of becoming an increasingly digital economy. Their attempts provide inspiring suggestions for practical analysis of this transformation dynamism (see 7.2 I Chapter 7).

As reviewed earlier, a possible solution to this critical issue in the digital economy can be obtained by analyzing the dynamism of this coevolution (Watanabe et al., 2016a).

Inspired by this expectation, this book attempts to draw a perspective on this critical issue.

2.4 Limitations of GDP data for measuring the digital economy

2.4.1 Emergence of a free culture

Several analyses and debates have attempted to understand the sources of the so-called free culture promoted by the Internet.

2.4.1.1 Unique functions derived from online intermediaries

Online intermediaries play a core role in how the Internet functions, and the Internet relies on the efficient operation of these online intermediaries in providing platforms to facilitate the exchange of goods, services, or information online. Copenhagen Economics (2013) examined the effect of online intermediaries[6] on the GDP of 27 EU countries in 2012. Its report estimated (1) direct GDP contribution through consumption (EUR 220 billion, 1.7% of GDP), (2) indirect GDP contribution through productivity increase (EUR 210 billion, 1.65% of GDP), and (3) beyond-measurement GDP contribution (EUR 640 billion, 5.0% of GDP) derived from B2B platforms by e-commerce, online advertising, and consumer benefits of free services such as Google search, among others. The report also pointed out that these estimates were understated because they did not include the direct contribution of investments (which are hard to measure) and the sociocultural value created by social network development.

2.4.1.2 Consumer surplus

In the digital economy, the economic gain to be had by increasing consumer surplus is another source of uncaptured GDP. Brynjolfsson et al., 2017) analyzed online booksellers and found that the increased product variety available through electronic markets could be the significantly larger source of consumer surplus when compared with efficiency gains through increased competition and lower average prices. Their analysis indicated that the increased product variety of online bookstores enhanced consumer welfare by USD 731 million to 1.03 billion in the year 2000. This value is 7 to 10 times larger than the consumer welfare gain created by increased competition and lower product prices in this market.

Brynjolfsson et al. (2017) also pointed to the possibility of large welfare gains in other stock-keeping unit (SKU)-intensive consumer goods, such as

---

[6] Online intermediaries provide platforms for the exchange of goods, services, or information over the Internet.

music, movies, consumer electronics, and computers. A white paper by Japan's Ministry of Internal Affairs and Communication (2016) demonstrated similar results when it analyzed consumer surplus in music and audio-visual services. Analyzing the economics of the IoT, McKinsey (2015) estimated that consumer surplus derived from the IoT could represent more than 10% of the global economy by 2025.

2.4.1.3 New goods and services derived from disruptive innovations
New goods are at the heart of economic progress, but this realization is only the beginning of an understanding of the economics of new goods (Brynjolfsson et al., 2017).

The US Council on Competitiveness (2016) has noted that the apparent slowdown in productivity in industrialized countries (see Fig. 1.7) could simply be due to the lack of resource capacity in statistical offices to properly measure the massive quality gains and hard-to-measure benefits of relatively new goods and services (e.g., Google, Facebook, and Twitter) that are radical breaks with previous products or in some cases are provided to users for free. According to this report, some evidence suggests that statistical agencies are now better able to understand the economics of new goods and services, but adjustment issues related to previous gains remain a problem for accurately measuring productivity growth.

Current estimates for the nonmarket benefits of free goods and services, such as Google, Wikipedia, and Facebook, do not make up for the shortfall in productivity growth (The US Council on Competitiveness, 2016). Moreover, these estimates may understate the nonmarket benefits, but it would be difficult to determine the extent to which this is true.

The Economist (2016) raised similar concerns by claiming that "GDP is a bad gauge of material well-being. Time for a fresh approach."

2.4.1.4 Online piracy
Another difficult issue, in addition to the beyond-measurement difficulties inherent in disruptive innovations caused by the dramatic advancement of the Internet, is the corresponding increase in online piracy.

2.4.2 Emergence of uncaptured GDP

Analyzing the economic effects of the advancement of technology in the digital economy, Watanabe et al. (2015a) discussed the two-faced nature of ICT and the emergence of uncaptured GDP, which is fatal to the advancement of the Internet (Watanabe et al., 2015a, 2015b, 2016a, 2016b,

2018a). As mentioned earlier, they indicated that although ICT advances generally contribute to the enhancing of technology prices through new functionality development, the dramatic advancement of the Internet contributes to decreasing technology prices resulting from the unique inherent characteristics of freebies, easy replication, and mass standardization. With this understanding, they supported Lowrey (2011) supposition that the Internet promotes a free culture, the consumption of which provides utility and happiness to people, but that it cannot be accurately captured through current GDP statistics, which measure revenue. They defined this added value of free culture as uncaptured GDP. It is this type of GDP that this book attempts to operationalize.

2.5 Conclusion

The productivity paradox created by the introduction of information technology has generated many long-lasting concerns. With a focus on contemporary implications for the digital economy, a chronology of the paradox was reviewed, while the consequent productivity decline and the limitations of GDP accounting in the digital economy were investigated.

Noteworthy findings include the following:

(1) This issue is related to the mismatch between the quality of products and statistical sources that has hung over macroeconomics for years.

(2) The digital economy, due to its unique features, has exacerbated this issue because it has created a much stronger change than that of previous decades.

(3) The hedonic pricing approach has made a significant contribution to overcoming this mismatch.

(4) The integration of national accounts with an accurate price index supported by the advancement of digital innovation could lead to a solution for these long-lasting constraints.

(5) While the popular assertion of no productivity paradox was encouraged in the late 1990s in response to the computer-initiated productivity paradox, a new productivity paradox appeared late in the first decade of this century.

(6) This new productivity paradox can be attributed to the emergence and advancement of the Internet, which promotes a free culture, the consumption of which provides utility and happiness to people but the value of which cannot be captured through GDP data, which measure revenue.

(7) This postulate suggests the concept of uncaptured GDP, which creates a new coevolution between the advancement of the Internet and the shift in people's preferences from economic functionality to supra-functionality that goes beyond economic value.

(8) This new coevolution has been spun off from traditional coevolution, which consists of traditional ICT, captured GDP, and economic functionality.

(9) This new spin-off coevolution leads to innovation emergence dyna-mism in the digital economy.

(10) The limitation of GDP data in measuring the digital economy can be attributed largely to a new stream of innovation derived from increasing dependence on uncaptured GDP.

(11) Therefore, a possible solution to this critical issue in the digital econ-omy can be obtained by analyzing the dynamism of this new coevolution.

These findings give rise to the following suggestions for overcoming the limitations of GDP as well as the productivity decline in the digital economy:

(1) The unique indigenous nature of the Internet, which incorporates free-bies, easy and free replication, and mass standardization, should be recognized.

(2) The two-faced nature of ICT concerning price formation, which is derived from the Internet's indigenous nature, should be analyzed.

(3) The coevolutionary dynamism among Internet advancement, increasing dependency on uncaptured GDP, and the shift in people's preferences to suprafunctionality that goes beyond economic value, which has spun off from traditional coevolution, should be traced.

(4) GDP accounting should be systematically reviewed, taking into ac-count the above points.

(5) An attempt should be made to measure uncaptured GDP by analyzing the dynamism of new spin-off coevolution.

References

Ahmad, N., Schreyer, P., 2016. Measuring GDP in a Digital Economy. OECD Statistics Working Papers, 2016/07. OECD Publishing, Paris.

Baranzini, M., Marangoni, G., 2015. Richard Stone: An Annotated Bibliography. University of Lugano, Lugano.

Brynjolfsson, E., Hitt, L., 1996. Paradox lost? Firm-level evidence on the returns to in-formation systems spending. Management Science 42, 541–558.

Bean, C., 2016. Independent Review of UK Economic Statistics. https://www.gov.uk/government/publications/independent-review-of-uk-economic-statisticsfinal-report. retrieved 06.06.2018.

Berndt, E.R., 1983. Quality adjustment, hedonics, and modern empirical demand analysis. In: Diewert, W.E., Montemarquette, C. (Eds.), Price Level Measurement. Statistics Canada, Ottawa.

Bharadwaj, A., Sawy, O.A.E., Pavloyu, P.A., Venkatraman, N., 2013. Digital business strategy: toward a next generation of insights. MIS Quarterly 37 (2), 471–482.

BLS, 2011. Hedonic Models in the Producer Price Index (PPI). U.S. Bureau of Labor Statistics, Washington. http://www.bls.gov/ppi/ppicomqa.htm. retrieved 07.06.2018.

Brynjolfsson, E., 1993. Productivity paradox of information technology. Communications of the Association for Computing Machinery 36 (12), 66–77.

Brynjolfsson, E., Hitt, L., 1998. Beyond the productivity paradox. Communications of the ACM 41 (8), 49–55.

Brynjolfsson, E., Yang, S., 1999. The intangible costs and benefits of computer investments: evidence from financial markets. Atlanta, Georgia. Proceedings of the International Conference on Information Systems.

Brynjolfsson, E., McAfee, A., 2011. Race against the Machine. Digital Frontier, Lexington, MA.

Brynjolfsson, E., McAfee, A., 2014. The Second Machine Age: Work, Progress, and Prosperity in a Time of Brilliant Technologies. W.W. Norton & Company, New York.

Brynjolfsson, E., Hu, Y., Smith, M., revised, 2017. Consumer surplus in the digital economy: estimating the value of increased product variety at online booksellers. Management Science. https://doi.org/10.2139/ssrn.400940 retrieved 07.06.2018.

Byrne, D., Corrado, C., 2015. Prices for Communications Equipment: Rewriting the Record. Board of Governors of the Federal Reserve System Finance and Economics Discussion Series. http://papers.ssrn.com/sol3/papers.cfm?abstract_id=2662599##. retrieved 07.06.2018.

Corrado, C., Ukhaneva, O., 2016. Hedonic Prices for Fixed Broadband Services: Estimation across OECD Countries. OECD Science, Technology and Industry Working Papers, 2016/07. OECD Publishing, Paris.

Cavallo, A., Rigobon, R., 2016. The billion prices project: using online prices for measurement and research. The Journal of Economic Perspectives 30 (2), 151–178.

Chipman, J.S., 1959. Book reviews: quantity and prices Indexes in national accounts, Richard Stone. The Journal of Political Economy 67 (3), 317–318.

Copenhagen Economics, 2013. The Impact of Online Intermediaries on the EU Economy.

Court, A.T., 1939. Hedonic price Indexes with automotive examples. In: The Dynamics of Automotive Demand. General Motors Corporation, New York, pp. 99–117.

Cowen, T., 2011. The Great Stagnation: How America Ate All the Low-Hanging Fruit of Modern History, Got Sick, and Will (Eventually) Feel Better. A Penguin eSpecial from Dutton, Penguin, New York.

Coyle, D., 2016. The Political Economy of National Statistics. Economics Discussion Paper Series EDP-1603. The University of Manchester, Manchester.

Economist, 2016. How to Measure Prosperity. https://www.economist.com/news/leaders/21697834-gdp-bad-gauge-material-well-being-time-fresh-approach-how-measure-prosperity. retrieved 30.04.2016.

EU, 2017. The Internet of Things: Digital Single Market. EU, Brussels.

Gestrin, M.V., Staudt, J., 2018. The Digital Economy, Multinational Enterprises, and International Investment Policy. OECD, Paris.

Griffith, R., Nesheim, L., 2013. Hedonic methods for baskets of goods. Economics Letters 120, 284–287.

Griliches, Z., 1961. Hedonic price indexes for automobiles: an econometric analysis of quality change. In: The Price Statistics of Federal Government. NBER, New York, pp. 173–196. NBER Staff Report No. 3, General Series No. 73.

Griliches, Z., 1971. Price Indexes Quality Change: Studies in New Methods of Measurements. Harvard University Press, Cambridge.

Griliches, Z., 1990. Hedonic price indices and the measurement of capital and productivity: some historical reflections. In: Berndt, E.R., Triplett, J.E. (Eds.), Fifty Years of Economic Measurement: The Jubilee of the Conference on Research in Income and Wealth. NBER Studies in Income and Wealth. University of Chicago Press, Chicago, pp. 185–206.

Internet Society, 2015. The Internet of Things: An Overview. Internet Society, Reston. https://www.internetsociety.org/doc/iot-overview. retrieved 05.08.2017.

Internet Society, 2016. Global Internet Report 2016. Internet Society, Reston. https://www.internetsociety.org/globalinternetreport/2016/wp-content/uploads/2016/11/ISOC_GIR_2016-v1.pdf. retrieved 05.08.2017.

Japan Ministry of Internal Affairs and Communication (MIC), 2016. White Paper of Japan's ICT. MIC, Tokyo.

Kahre, C., Hoffmann, D., Ahlemann, F., 2017. Beyond business-IT alignment-digital business strategies as a paradigmatic shift: a review and research agenda. Proceedings of the 50th Hawaii International Conference on System Sciences 4706–4715.

Kraemer, K.L., Dedrick, J., 1994. Payoffs from investment in information technology: lessons from the Asia-Pacific region. World Development 22 (12), 1921–1931.

Lichtenberg, F.R., 1995. The output contributions of computer equipment and personnel: a firm-level analysis. Economics of Innovation and New Technology 3, 201–217.

Lowrey, A., 2011. Freaks, geeks, and GDP. Slate. http://www.slate.com/articles/business/moneybox/2011/03/freaks_geeks_and_gdp.html. retrieved 20.06.17.

Madakam, S., Ramaswamy, R., Tripathi, S., 2015. Internet of Things (IoT): a literature review. Journal of Computer and Communications 3 (5), 164–173.

McDonagh, D., 2008. Satisfying needs beyond the functional: the changing needs of the silver market consumer. In: Proceedings of the International Symposium on the Silver Market Phenomenon. Business Opportunities and Responsibilities in the Aging Society, Tokyo.

McKinsey Global Institute, 2011. Internet Matters: The Net's Sweeping Impact on Growth, Jobs, and Prosperity. McKinsey & Company, San Francisco.

McKinsey Global Institute, 2015. The Internet of Things: Mapping the Value Beyond the Hype. McKinsey & Company, San Francisco.

Moss, M., 1958. Book reviews: quantity and prices indexes in national accounts by Richard Stone. The American Economic Review 48 (3), 475–477.

Naveed, K., Watanabe, C., Neittaanmäki, P., 2017. Co-evolution between streaming and live music leads a way to the sustainable growth of music industry — lessons from the US experiences. Technology in Society 50, 1–19.

Pesaran, M.H., Harcourt, G.C., 2000. Life and work of John Richard Nicholas Stone 1913–1991. The Economic Journal 110, 146–165.

Rifkin, J., 2011. The Third Industrial Revolution: How Lateral Power Is Transforming Energy, the Economy, and the World. Macmillan, New York.

Schelling, T.C., 1998. Social mechanisms and social dynamics. In: Hedstrom, P., Swedberg, R. (Eds.), Social Mechanisms: An Analytical Approach to Social Theory. Cambridge Univ. Press, Cambridge, pp. 32–43.

Solow, R., 1987. We'd Better Watch Out, Review of Cohen, S.S., and Zysman, J., Manufacturing Matters: The Myth of the Post-industrial Economy. New York Times Book Review, p. 36.

Stone, R., 1954. The Measurement of Consumer Behavior and Expenditure in the United Kingdom, 1920—1938. In: Studies in the National Income and Expenditure of the United Kingdom, vol. 1. Cambridge University Press, Cambridge.

Stone, R., 1956. Quantity and Price Indexes in National Accounts. OEEC, Paris.

Stone, R., 1984. The Accounts of Society. Nobel Memorial Lecture, Cambridge, UK.

Sussan, F., Acs, Z.J., 2017. The digital entrepreneurial ecosystem. Small Business Economics 49 (1), 55—73.

Tapscott, D., 1994. The Digital Economy: Promise and Peril in the Age of Networked Intelligence. McGraw-Hill, New York.

Triplett, J.E., 1975. The measurement of inflation: a survey of research on the accuracy of price Indexes. In: Paul, E.L. (Ed.), Analysis of Inflation. D.C. Heath and Company, Lexington, pp. 19—82.

Triplett, J.E., 1987. Hedonic functions and hedonic Indexes. In: Eatwell, J., Milgate, M., Newman, P. (Eds.), The New Palgrave: A Dictionary of Economics. Macmillan, London, pp. 630—634.

Triplett, J.E., 1990. Hedonic methods in statistical agency environments: an intellectual biopsy. In: Berndt, E.R., Triplett, J.E. (Eds.), Fifty Years of Economic Measurement: The Jubilee of the Conference on Research in Income and Wealth. NBER Studies in Income and Wealth. University of Chicago Press, Chicago, pp. 207—233.

Triplett, J., 1999. The solow productivity paradox: what do computers do to productivity? Canadian Journal of Economics 32 (2), 309—334.

US Council on Competitiveness, 2016. No Recovery: An Analysis of Long-Term U.S. Productivity Decline. US Council on Competitiveness, Washington, D.C.

Wasshausen, D., 2017. BEAs ICT Prices: Historical Analysis and Future Plans. BEA, Washington. http://bea.gov/about/pdf/acm/2017/ICT-Deflators.pdf. retrieved 09.06.2018.

Wasshausen, D., Moulton, B.R., 2006. The Role of Hedonic Methods in Measuring Real GDP in the United States. BEA Papers 0067. Bureau of Economic Analysis, Washington.

Watanabe, C., Hobo, M., 2004. Creating a firm self-propagating function for advanced innovation-oriented projects: lessons from ERP. Technovation 24 (6), 467—481.

Watanabe, C., Kondo, R., Ouchi, N., Wei, H., Griffy-Brown, C., 2004. Institutional elasticity as a significant driver of IT functionality development. Technological Forecasting and Social Change 71 (7), 723—750.

Watanabe, C., Naveed, K., Zhao, W., 2014. Institutional sources of resilience in global ICT leaders: harness the vigor of emerging power. Journal of Technology Management for Growing Economies 5 (1), 7—34.

Watanabe, C., Naveed, K., Zhao, W., 2015a. New paradigm of ICT productivity: increasing role of un-captured GDP and growing anger of consumers. Technology in Society 41, 21—44.

Watanabe, C., Naveed, K., Neittaanmäki, P., 2015b. Dependency on un-captured GDP as a source of resilience beyond economic value in countries with advanced ICT infrastructure: similarities and disparities between Finland and Singapore. Technology in Society 42, 104—122.

Watanabe, C., Naveed, K., Neittaanmäki, P., Tou, Y., 2016a. Operationalization of un-captured GDP: the innovation stream under new global mega-trends. Technology in Society 45, 58—77.

Watanabe, C., Naveed, K., Neittaanmäki, P., 2016b. Co-evolution of three mega-trends nurtures un-captured GDP: uber's ride-sharing revolution. Technology in Society 46, 164—185.

Watanabe, C., Naveed, K., Neittaanmäki, P., 2017. Consolidated challenge to social demand for resilient platforms: lessons from uber's global expansion. Technology in Society 48, 33—53.

Watanabe, C., Moriya, K., Tou, Y., Neittaanmäki, P., 2018a. Structural sources of a productivity decline in the digital economy. International Journal of Managing Information Technology 10 (1), 1—20.

Watanabe, C., Tou, Y., Neittaanmäki, P., 2018b. A new paradox of the digital economy: structural sources of the limitation of GDP statistics. Technology in Society 55, 9—33.

Watanabe, C., Naveed, K., Tou, Y., Neittaanmäki, P., 2018c. Measuring GDP in the digital economy: increasing dependence on uncaptured GDP. Technological Forecasting and Social Change 137, 226—240.

Waugh, F.W., 1928. Quality factors influencing vegetable prices. Journal of Farm Economics 10 (2), 185—196.

CHAPTER 3

Increasing dependence on uncaptured GDP and ways to measure it

Contents

Transforming the Socio Economy with Digital Innovation
ISBN 978-0-323-88465-5
https://doi.org/10.1016/B978-0-323-88465-5.00006-4

3.1 Structural sources of productivity decline in the digital economy

3.1.1 Scheme for measuring the digital economy

This section examines an approach to measuring the digital economy. Fig. 3.1 presents a scheme for measuring the digital economy with a focus on the dramatic advancement of the Internet.

New and unique but identical services include (1) e-commerce as initiated by Alibaba, Amazon, and Rakuten, with selling efficiency and inexpensive services; (2) search engines with online advertising such as Google and Yahoo, with reduced costs for information search services; (3) free search engines such as Wikipedia, Linux, and R, with free information, search, and dissemination; (4) social networks such as Twitter, Facebook, LinkedIn, and YouTube, with services for finding and exchanging information efficiently; and (5) cloud computing platforms such as those offered by Amazon, Apple, Cisco, IBM, Google, and Microsoft, with services to convert fixed costs into marginal costs.

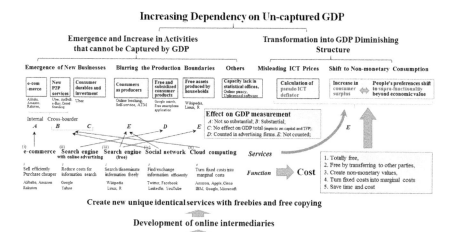

Figure 3.1 Measuring scheme for the digital economy. *(Sources: OECD, 2010. The Economic and Social Role of Internet Intermediaries. OECD, Paris; Copenhagen Economics, 2013. The Impact of Online Intermediaries on the EU Economy, Are GDP and Productivity Measures Up to the Challenges of the Digital Economy? (Ahmad, N., Schreyer, P., 2016. Measuring GDP in a Digital Economy. OECD Statistics Working Papers, 2016/07. OECD Publishing, Paris.; OECD, 2016. Tax Challenges in the Digital Economy. OECD, Paris.), Watanabe, C., Naveed, K., Neittaanmäki, P., Tou, Y., 2016. Operationalization of un-captured GDP: the innovation Stream under new global mega-trends. Technology in Society 45, 58—77.)*

These services are provided free of charge by transferring costs to other parties, creating nonmonetary value, turning fixed costs into marginal costs, and saving on time and cost.

This scheme identifies sources that lead to the digital economy's increasing dependence on uncaptured GDP. It clarifies the factors derived from the emergence and increase in activities and the transformation into a GDP-diminishing structure.

3.1.2 Increasing dependence on beyond-GDP measurements

3.1.2.1 Emergence of and increase in activities that cannot be captured by GDP

Services creation increasingly leads to the emergence of activities whose values cannot be captured by GDP. These activities are as follows: (1) emergence of new businesses such as e-commerce-based transactions, new P2P services (e.g., Uber, Airbnb, e-Bay, and crowd-funding), and consumer durables and investment (e.g., Uber); (2) blurring of production boundaries, such as consumers as producers, free and subsidized consumer products, and free assets produced by householders; and (3) Widening knowledge gaps of statistics staff, and increasing online piracy and unlicensed software.

3.1.2.2 Transformation into a GDP-diminishing structure

The transformation into a GDP-diminishing structure cannot be overlooked. It can be derived from (1) misleading information and communication technology (ICT) prices that result from calculating a pseudo-ICT deflator in evaluating the real value of the ICT-driven digital economy, and (2) the shift to nonmonetary consumption. This type of consumption results in increased consumer surplus (to be reviewed in Section 3.2) and stems from a shift in people's preferences to suprafunctionality, which is beyond economic value and encompasses social, cultural, and emotional values.

3.1.3 Effect on GDP accounting

As reviewed earlier, as GDP is considered the most fundamental yardstick in devising economic policy, the identification of loopholes in GDP measurement and the extent of the resultant bias has become a crucial subject in studying the digital economy. The Organisation for Economic Co-operation and Development has taken a leading role in this identification and has classified the above effects into (A) not so substantial, (B) substantial, (C) no effect on the GDP total, (D) counted in certain parties, and (E) not counted by the GDP framework, as illustrated in Fig. 3.1 (Ahmad and Schreyer, 2016).

Although we expect people to enjoy the well-being enabled by the digital economy, the value of that marginal increase in well-being is excluded from GDP accounting and considered at odds with the conceptual basis for measuring GDP. Such treatment causes fear, which leads to the pseudo optimization of a nation's trajectory management.

The above overview of the structural sources of the digital economy's declining productivity reveals that the two-sided nature of ICT (which leads to a decline in ICT prices) (Watanabe et al., 2015b) on the supply side and the shift to nonmonetary consumption on the demand side are critical sources of productivity declines in the digital economy. The succeeding sections focus on the analysis of these issues.

3.2 The two-sided nature of information and communication technology

3.2.1 Calculation of the pseudo—information and communication technology deflator

This section analyzes the dynamism inspired by the preceding review of the structural sources of the digital economy's declining productivity triggered by decreases in ICT prices.

As reviewed in Chapter 2, the Internet promotes a free culture, the consumption of which provides utility and happiness to people but cannot be captured through the GDP data, which measure revenue (Lowrey, 2011; Rifkin, 2011). These unmeasured services are called uncaptured GDP (Watanabe et al., 2015a). The value of these services compensates for the productivity declines resulting from the decreased prices that are caused by ICT's two-sided nature, as reviewed previously. Fig. 3.2 illustrates this dynamism.

The right-hand side of Fig. 3.2 presents the consequence of "a great stagnation in the digital economy" (Cowen, 2011) derived from technology's (primarily ICT's) decreased contribution to growth. Given that firms pursue profit maximization in a competitive market, their marginal ICT productivity corresponds to the relative price of ICT, and the contribution of ICT to the growth rate can be attributed to the product of this productivity and R&D intensity (R&D expenditure per sales). Therefore, decreased ICT prices result in the stagnation of growth.

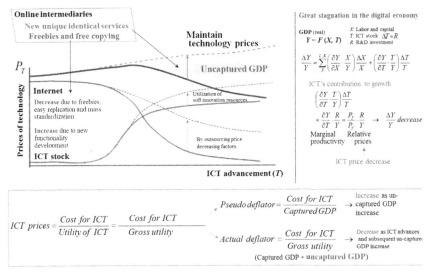

Figure 3.2 Calculating the pseudo—information and communication technology deflator scheme. *(Source: Watanabe, C., Naveed, K., Zhao, W., 2015a. New Paradigm of ICT productivity: increasing role of un-captured GDP and growing anger of consumers. Technology in Society 41, 21—44.)*

Under this dynamism, the ICT deflator calculated without including uncaptured GDP is in fact a pseudo deflator. The actual deflator should be calculated by using gross utility, which accounts for uncaptured GDP in addition to traditional GDP. This deflator decreases with ICT advances, and subsequently, uncaptured GDP grows. This decrease reacts to higher real ICT prices as their denominator decreases (Watanabe et al., 2018c). The bottom portion of Fig. 3.2 explains the confusion. This confusion often misleads to the miscalculation of the ICT deflator.

3.2.2 Two sides of the information and communication technology (ICT) of the world's ICT leaders

To further demonstrate the above supposition of the two-sided nature of ICT, Fig. 3.3 illustrates the trends in declining ICT prices and its sources, namely, the Internet dependency and ICT stock increases of global ICT leaders Finland and Singapore[1] in the period from 1994 to 2011 (see the details on the analytical framework and the empirical results in Appendix A2.1).

[1] Finland and Singapore shared the first and second position in world ICT rankings (WEF, 2013a, 2016) (see Figs. 1.2 and 1.3 and Table 3.3).

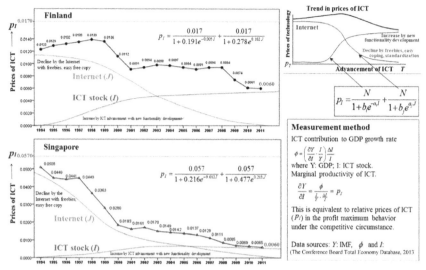

Figure 3.3 *Trends in the information and communication technology (ICT) prices of global ICT leaders: Finland and Singapore* (1994—2011). *Data sources: I:* ICT stock (Conference Board Total Economy Database, 2013), *J:* Internet dependency— Percentage of individuals using the Internet (ITU, 2014). *(Source: Watanabe, C., Naveed, K., Zhao, W., 2015a. New Paradigm of ICT productivity: increasing role of un-captured GDP and growing anger of consumers. Technology in Society 41, 21—44.)*

Both ICT leaders demonstrated clear evidence of the two-sided nature of ICT. That is, the advancement of ICT (represented by ICT stock increases) leads to increased ICT prices, whereas the advancement of the Internet leads to decreased ICT prices.

3.2.3 Two-sided polarization of the information and communication technology (ICT) of 500 global ICT firms

The preceding analysis demonstrates clear evidence of the two-sided nature of ICT, but the magnitude of the polarization depends on a national-level macroanalysis using aggregated data. To confirm this result using microdata, which represent actual competitive behavior in the digital market, Fig. 3.4 illustrates the trends in ICT price decreases due to ICT advancement among 500 global ICT firms between 2005 and 2016[2] (see the details of the analytical framework and the empirical results in Appendix AI-1).

---

[2] Over 50,000 primary data (500 firms by seven items by 11 years + 14,438 scientific paper data) were used.

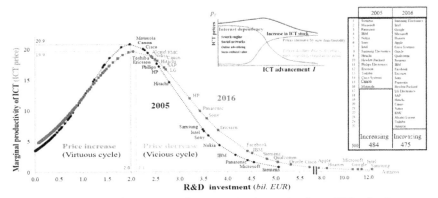

Figure 3.4 Bilateral information and communication technology (ICT) price increases and decreases for 500 global ICT firms (2005, 2016). *(Sources: European Union (EU), 2017. Economics of Industrial Research and Innovation. EU, Brussels, and each firm's annual reports.)*

Provided that global ICT firms pursue a profit maximization strategy in the competitive global market, their ICT prices are represented by the marginal productivity of ICT. Their ICT advancement efforts are then represented by their gross ICT stock (incorporating all ICT advancement facilities including Internet-relevant facilities) in proportion to their overall R&D investments (see Figs. A1-1 and A1-2 in Appendix AI-1).

Fig. 3.4 shows the polarization between highly R&D-intensive firms and relatively non-R&D-intensive firms (see also Fig. 1.8 of Chapter 1). The former experienced price decreases as a consequence of ICT advancement through increases in R&D investment, and the latter maintained a virtuous cycle as prices increased with increases in R&D investment.

This polarization can be attributed to the logistic growth nature of the ICT-driven trajectory (Schelling, 1998; Watanabe et al., 2004). The behavior of highly R&D-intensive firms demonstrates declining productivity as ICT advances, a consequence of the digital economy.

Fig. 3.4 demonstrates that the two-sided nature of ICT continues as digitization proceeds. In 2005, price-decreasing firms made up only 16 of the 500 global ICT firms, but by 2016, their number had increased to 25. Furthermore, highly R&D-intensive firms are confronting sales stagnation while relatively non-R&D-intensive firms are enjoying sales increases, as indicated in Table 3.1.

All of these results support the supposition of a two-sided nature for ICT, which is a critical structural source of productivity decline in the digital economy.

Table 3.1 Contrast in sales growth rate between highly R&D-intensive and non-R&D-intensive global information and communication technology firms (2005–16)—average sales growth rate (% p.a.).

Highly R&D-intensive firms

	Samsung	Google	Microsoft	Apple	Amazon
2005–8	14.5	72.6	13.3	38.5	25.5
2009–12	14.2	27.5	8.8	53.5	38.7
2013–16	9.7	24.0	8.7	27.5	28.0

Relatively non-R&D-intensive firms

	Electronic arts	Taiwan semiconductor	Accenture	Kyocera	Free scale
2005–8	1.9	9.7	0.8	0.1	−1.5
2009–12	7.4	15.9	5.8	12.4	0.8
2013–16	8.0	21.6	14.6	18.6	4.0

Data sources: Same as those of Fig. 3.4.

Confronting such circumstances in the digital economy, highly R&D-intensive global ICT firms have been attempting to activate latent self-propagating functions (Tou et al., 2019) based on their explicit network externality functions, which alter the correlation between innovations and institutional systems and create new features of innovation and in turn leads to exponential increases in growth (Watanabe and Hobo, 2004). The activated self-propagating function induces new functionality development leading to suprafunctionality beyond economic value, which corresponds to shifts in people's preferences in the digital economy. The transformative strategy that matches the productivity decline derived from the supply side in the digital economy with the structural change on the demand side is thus a crucial part of the survival strategy in the digital economy (Naveed et al., 2018; Watanabe et al., 2018a, 2018b, 2018c).

The next section analyzes the shift in people's preferences on the demand side of the digital economy.

3.3 Shift from monetary to nonmonetary consumption

3.3.1 Shift from economic functionality to suprafunctionality

As illustrated in Fig. 3.1, the digital economy's shift to nonmonetary consumption has become significant in the economy's transformation to a GDP-diminishing structure.

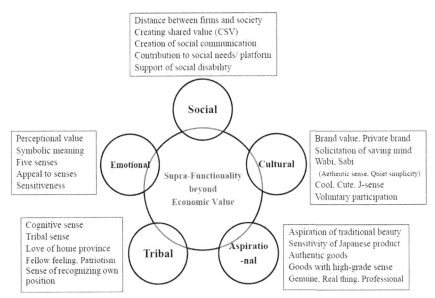

Figure 3.5 Basic concept of suprafunctionality beyond economic value. *(Source: Watanabe, C., Naveed, K., Zhao, W., 2015a. New Paradigm of ICT productivity: increasing role of un-captured GDP and growing anger of consumers. Technology in Society 41, 21–44.)*

As a consequence of the historical change in the experience of nations and under the general shift from a commodity-oriented to service-and information-oriented society, consumer preference is generally assumed to steadily shift from one driven by economic functionality (captured by GDP) to one driven by suprafunctionality beyond economic value.[3] Here, suprafunctionality beyond economic value encompasses social, cultural, aspirational, tribal, and emotional values, as illustrated in Fig. 3.5, and these values are not necessarily captured in the measurement of GDP (McDonagh, 2008). This shift seems to have significant relevance to consumer surplus, as reviewed in Fig. 3.1, and the economy's increasing dependence on uncaptured GDP.

This shift can be clearly observed in Japan, which is extremely sensitive to institutional innovation against external shocks and crises (Hofstede, 1991; Watanabe, 2009). Fig. 3.6 illustrates this shift as demonstrated by

---

[3] Watson and McDonagh (2004a,b) observed users' needs for products and pointed out that responding to the suprafunctional needs of users, such as their emotional and cultural requirements is fundamental to the success of a product.

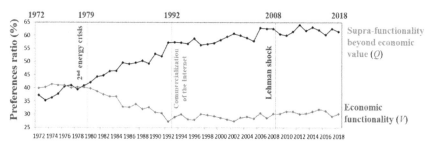

Figure 3.6 Trends in shifts in preferences in Japan *(1972–2018). (Source: Japan Cabinet Office (JCO), 2019. National Survey of Lifestyle Preferences. JCO, Tokyo.)*

Japan's *Public Opinion Survey Concerning People's Lifestyles,*[4] which are conducted annually by Japan's Cabinet Office.

As shown in Fig. 3.6, in contrast to the steady decline in people's preferences in economic functionality (*V*), suprafunctionality beyond economic value (*Q*) steadily increases and exceeds *V* in 1979, the year of the second energy crisis. Whereas *Q* continues to increase steadily, *V* declines to its lowest level in 1992, the year immediately after the commercialization of the Internet in 1991. It has remained at the same level since then. A decline in *Q* due to the Lehman shock in 2008 is followed by a sharp recovery. Consequently, the shifting trend from *V* to *Q* can be classified into the four phases just described: *Phase 1* (1972–9), *Phase 2* (1980–2), *Phase 3* (1993–2008), and *Phase 4* (2009–18).[5]

This shift in people's preferences induces the advancement of the Internet (Tapscott, 1994; OECD, 2010), which in turn accelerates the shift in people's preferences. Therefore, the advancement of the Internet and the shift to suprafunctionality lead to a coevolutionary dynamism, as illustrated in Fig. 1.9 in Chapter 1.

Under this coevolutionary dynamism, a conflict occurs between captured and uncaptured GDP during this shift. This conflict leads to

---

[4] In this survey, personal preference for future life is chosen from three options: (1) Richness of the heart-spiritual happiness (*since a reasonable level of material affluence has been achieved, future emphasis should be put on spiritual happiness and a comfortable life.*), (2) Wealth of Things—material affluence (*emphasis should still be put on material affluence for future life.*), or (3) Cannot identify explicitly. While the second option corresponds to a preference for economic functionality, the first option corresponds to that of suprafunctionality beyond economic value (Watanabe et al., 2011).

[5] See the details in Chapter 4 (4.2.1.3 Shifting Consumers' Preferences from Economic to Suprafunctionality).

growing anger among consumers (Watanabe et al., 2015a), thus resulting in declines in consumption. This situation can be considered a source of "the great stagnation in the digital economy" (Cowen, 2011) from the demand side.

During "the great stagnation in the digital economy" (Cowen, 2011) due to this conflict in ICT advancement, and with ICT's two-sided nature on the supply side, the only option possible for sustainable growth comes from enhancing utility (satisfaction of consumption) through Internet inducement of ICT stock (see the mathematical demonstration and empirical results in Appendix AI-3). Consequently, effective enhancement of utility as a function of the Internet and ICT stock can be the key to sustainable growth under "the current great stagnation in the digital economy." Furthermore, because consumption makes up a major part of GDP, how effectively this utility is reflected in consumption would be a key measure for assessing the state of the economy's dependence on uncaptured GDP.[6]

3.3.2 Shifts in consumer preferences

Measurement of the elasticity of utility to consumption

Utility is governed by ICT stock and Internet dependence in the digital economy. The elasticity of utility to consumption[7] can be measured by the sum of the elasticity of ICT stock to consumption and that of Internet dependency to consumption. Table 3.2 compares the elasticity of consumption[8] in six countries in 2013.

Fig. 3.7 suggests a contrast in this elasticity between the two global ICT leaders, Finland and Singapore. Singapore demonstrates conspicuously high

---

[6] Lower level of utility reflection to consumption suggests higher level of uncaptured GDP dependence.

[7] Elasticity is the measurement of how responsive an economic variable (X) is to a change in another (W). The elasticity of X to W (X elasticity to W) ε_{WX} implies a 1% increase in X increases ε_{WX} % increase in W and represents the efficiency of X inducement of W.

[8] This elasticity is computed by using a consumption function governed by I and J as follows: $C = C(I,J) = $ Taylor expansion to the secondary term.

$$\ln C = a + b \ln I + c \ln J + d \ln I \cdot \ln J$$

$$\varepsilon_{cj} = \frac{\partial \ln C}{\partial \ln J} = c + d \ln I + (b + d \ln J) \cdot \frac{\partial \ln I}{\partial \ln J} = c + d \ln I + (b + d \ln J) \cdot \varepsilon_{ji} \text{ where } a - d\text{:}$$

coefficients (see Watanabe et al., 2015a).

Table 3.2 Elasticity of utility to consumption in six countries *(2013).*

	Finland	Singapore	USA	UK	Germany	Japan
Efficiency of J inducement of I 1. J elasticity to I (ε_{ji})	0.75	0.39	0.55	0.39	0.22	0.21
Efficiency of J inducement of C 2. J elasticity to C (ε_{cj})	0.23	0.49	0.37	0.15	0.10	0.10
Efficiency of I inducement of C 3. I elasticity to C $(\varepsilon_{ci} = \frac{\varepsilon_{cj}}{\varepsilon_{ji}})$ [2/1]	0.30	1.27	0.68	0.40	0.47	0.48
Extent of reflection of U to C 4. U elasticity to C (ε_{cu}) [2+3]	0.53	1.76	1.05	0.55	0.57	0.58

$$U = U(V, Q) \quad V = V(I, J), Q = Q(I, J)$$
$$U = U(I, J) = \frac{\partial U}{\partial I} \cdot I + \frac{\partial U}{\partial J} \cdot J = \frac{\partial U}{\partial C} \left(\frac{\partial C}{\partial I} \cdot I + \frac{\partial C}{\partial J} \cdot J \right)$$
$$\frac{\partial C}{\partial U} \frac{U}{C} = \frac{\partial C}{\partial I} \frac{I}{C} + \frac{\partial C}{\partial J} \frac{J}{C}$$
$$(\varepsilon_{cu}) \quad (\varepsilon_{ci}) \quad (\varepsilon_{cj})$$

U: Utility,   C: Traditional consumption
V: Economic functionality,   Q: Supra-functionality
J: Internet dependency,   I: ICT stock

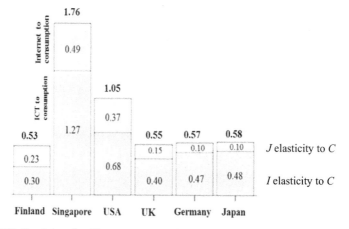

Figure 3.7 Elasticity of utility to consumption in six countries *(2013). (Source: Watanabe, C., Naveed, K., Zhao, W., 2015a. New Paradigm of ICT productivity: increasing role of un-captured GDP and growing anger of consumers. Technology in Society 41, 21–44.)*

elasticity, whereas Finland demonstrates the opposite—it has the lowest level of elasticity among the six countries compared.

With this observation in mind, Fig. 3.8 illustrates this contrast in the development trajectories between these global ICT leaders.

This figure demonstrates the difference in development trajectories between Finland and Singapore. Finland effectively utilizes the Internet to induce ICT stock, as demonstrated by its high Internet elasticity to ICT stock. Its induced ICT stock contributes significantly to satisfying the consumer preference for suprafunctionality beyond economic value rather than solely economic functionality. Consequently, increased ICT does not

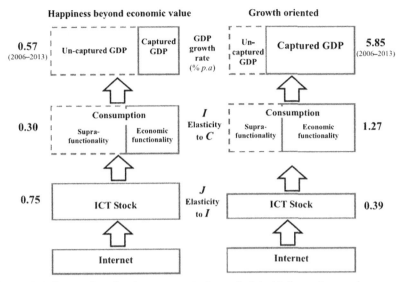

Figure 3.8 *Contrasting development trajectory of global information and communication technology leaders Finland and Singapore (2013). J: Internet dependence, I: ICT stock, C: consumption; GDP growth rate is the average for 2006–13. (Source: Watanabe, C., Naveed, K., Zhao, W., 2015a. New Paradigm of ICT productivity: increasing role of un-captured GDP and growing anger of consumers. Technology in Society 41, 21–44.)*

reflect increased consumption, which is measured by the value of GDP, thus resulting in a low GDP growth rate. Although Finland's ICT significantly contributes to suprafunctionality beyond economic value, that contribution cannot necessarily be captured by GDP.

Singapore's behavior is contrary to that of Finland. Although Singapore's ICT inducement due to the Internet is smaller than that of Finland, it contributes largely to consumer preferences for economic functionality. This is captured by GDP value, thus leading to a high GDP growth rate (5.85% in Singapore vs. 0.57% in Finland on average for 2006–13).

This analysis suggests the significance of the elasticity of utility to consumption in inducing spin-off coevolution from the demand side.[9]

---

[9] While this is for macro national-level analysis, see Brynjolfsson et al. (2019) for the measurement of new and free goods that are not well-measured in the current national accounts in the digital economy.

3.4 Emergence of uncaptured GDP and its measurement

3.4.1 Measuring uncaptured GDP

To date, several attempts have been made to measure uncaptured GDP in the context of *beyond GDP*, which includes "true wealth and the well-being of nations" (Wesselink et al., 2007), "quality of human life while living within the carrying capacity of the supporting ecosystems" (Costanza et al., 2009), "quest for a measure of social welfare" (Fleurbaey, 2009), "well-being, economic welfare and sustainability" (Bleys, 2012), and "global genuine progress" (Kubiszewski et al., 2013). However, there has been no attempt thus far to measure uncaptured GDP as a consequence of the new coevolution in the digital economy. To link this issue to the uncaptured GDP problem driven by digital innovation, Brynjolfsson and McAfee (2014) have pointed out that "the rise in digital innovation means we need innovation in our economic metrics." Prompted by this understanding, a practical method to measure uncaptured GDP was developed from the follow-up to earlier efforts to determine a new method for measuring the magnitude of uncaptured GDP (Watanabe et al., 2015b). Consequently, the state of the shifting trend in the coevolution of three megatrends was identified.

As illustrated in Fig. 1.9 of Chapter 1, coevolution of the Internet, uncaptured GDP, and suprafunctionality beyond economic value are created by spin-off dynamism. In this dynamism, the stimulation from ICT advancement (the supply side) and inducement from a shift in people's preferences (the demand side) drive the dependence on uncaptured GDP. The equilibrium of both inertias leads to rising power that emerges as uncaptured GDP, as illustrated in Fig. 3.9 (see Appendix AI-4).

This understanding helps measure the uncaptured GDPs of Finland and Singapore. Here, the inducement of the shift in people's preferences depends on the elasticity of utility to consumption (see the details of the analytical framework and the empirical result in Appendix AI-4).

Uncaptured GDP

Supply-side stimulation   Demand-side inducement

Primary impacts

Secondary impacts

Induced consumption by Uncaptured GDP

$$W = A_s J^\alpha \cdot e^{\lambda E^m} = A_d E^\beta \cdot e^{\kappa J^n}$$

Primary Secondary   Primary Secondary
Supply-side   **Demand-side**

J: Internet dependence; E: elasticity of utility to consumption.
$A, \alpha, \beta, \lambda, \kappa$: coefficient; m, n: power factor.

Figure 3.9 Equilibrium creates a lift as uncaptured GDP rises.

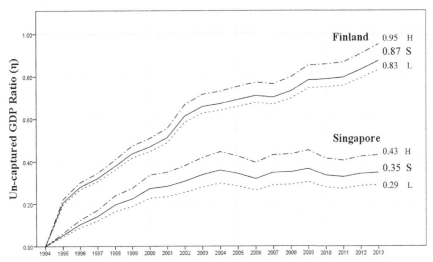

Figure 3.10 Trends in the uncaptured GDP ratios in Finland and Singapore *(1994—2013)*. Uncaptured GDP ratio (η) = uncaptured GDP/captured GDP. *H,* higher possible estimate, *L,* lower possible estimate; *S,* standard estimate. *(Source: Watanabe, C., Naveed, K., Neittaanmäki, P., Tou, Y., 2016. Operationalization of un-captured GDP: the innovation Stream under new global mega-trends. Technology in Society 45, 58—77.)*

Fig. 3.10 demonstrates an estimate of the possible trends in the uncaptured GDP ratio (uncaptured GDP/captured GDP) in both countries over the period 1994—2013 with three possibilities (standard, high, and low estimates).

As anticipated by Fig. 3.8, Finland demonstrates higher dependence on uncaptured GDP than Singapore does.

Based on this estimate (standard estimate), Fig. 3.11 compares the trends in captured and uncaptured GDP between the two countries from 1994 to 2013.

As shown in the figure, although Finland's captured GDP is lower than that of Singapore after 2010, Finland has a higher gross GDP (the sum of captured and uncaptured GDP) than Singapore. This result is in line with the previous estimate comparing the elasticity of utility to consumption and suggests that Finland has shifted largely to uncaptured GDP dependence, whereas Singapore has maintained its traditional GDP dependence.

3.4.2 Differences in the shift to the new coevolution

People's preferences have been shifting to suprafunctionality beyond economic value, which cannot be measured by GDP. A great difference

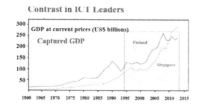

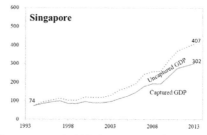

Figure 3.11 Comparison of captured and uncaptured GDP between Finland and Singapore (1994–2013). *(Source: Watanabe, C., Naveed, K., Neittaanmäki, P., Tou, Y., 2016. Operationalization of un-captured GDP: the innovation Stream under new global mega-trends. Technology in Society 45, 58–77.)*

exists between Finland and Singapore—Finland experiences happiness and well-being amidst "the great stagnation," whereas Singapore undergoes economic growth amidst its more stifling society (Table 3.3). This difference can be explained by the contrasting uncaptured GDP trends between the two countries.

Given the above estimation of uncaptured GDP, the correlation between Internet advancement and the uncaptured GDP ratios in Finland and Singapore over the period of 1996–2013 was analyzed to identify the possible shift from the traditional coevolution to the new coevolution. Fig. 3.12 demonstrates the difference in the correlation between the two ICT leaders (see details of the analysis in Appendix AI-4).

As shown in the figure, Finland's tendency is toward coevolution of ICT advancement through increases in Internet productivity, and its increased dependence on uncaptured GDP occurred in 2002, which is immediately after the bursting of the Internet bubble in 2000 and the emergence of the substantial digital economy. Since then, Finland has shown higher elasticity of ICT advancement to uncaptured GDP ratio, thereby suggesting its active coevolution.

Singapore's experience is in sharp contrast to the noticeable coevolution in Finland. Singapore's traditional captured GDP has increased even though

Table 3.3 Differences between the institutional systems of Finland and Singapore (2013).

	Finland	Singapore	References
Population (million)	5.5	5.4	The Global Competitiveness Report 2014 WEF (2014a)
ICT (rank out of 148)	1	2	The Global Information and Technology Report 2014 WEF (2014a)
Global competitiveness (rank out of 148)	3	2	The Global Competitiveness Report 2014 WEF (2014b)
GDP per capita (US$ 1000)	47.1	54.8	The Global Competitiveness Report 2014 WEF (2014b)
GDP growth rate (2006–13) (% p.a. at fixed price)	0.57	5.85	World Economic Outlook Database (IMF (2014))
Happiness (rank out of 156)	7	30	World Happiness Report 2013 The Earth Institute Colombia University (2013)
Inequality (GINI index)*2010	19	45	Distribution of Household Income by Source ILO (2012)
Gender parity (rank out of 136)	2	58	The Global Gender Gap Report 2013 WEF (2013a,b)

it reacted earlier than Finland did to its Internet productivity immediately after the bursting of the Internet bubble in 2000. Therefore, Singapore still clings to the traditional coevolutionary cycle that depends on traditional captured GDP.

As reviewed earlier, significant coevolution occurs among the advancement of the Internet, uncaptured GDP dependence, and coevolution of the shift in people's preferences with advancement of the Internet. The contrasting coevolution of the advancement of the Internet and uncaptured GDP dependence between the two countries suggests that Finland has shifted from the "traditional coevolution of computer-initiated ICT, captured GDP, and economic functionality" to the "new coevolution of the advancement of the Internet, uncaptured GDP, and supra-functionality beyond economic value," whereas Singapore has maintained a more traditional coevolution.

This finding supports the following view: "The well-being of the Finnish people has developed in a more positive direction than one might

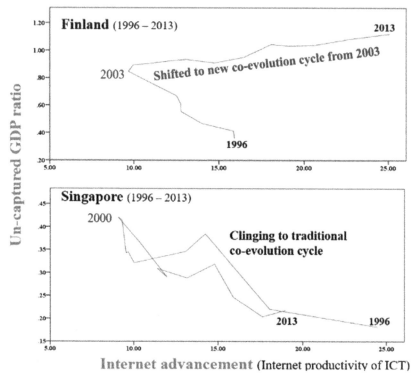

Figure 3.12 Correlation between internet advancement and shifts uncaptured GDP in Finland and Singapore. *(Original source: Watanabe, C., Naveed, K., Neittaanmäki, P., Tou, Y., 2016. Operationalization of un-captured GDP: the innovation Stream under new global mega-trends. Technology in Society 45, 58–77.)*

conclude based on the economic development of recent years indicated by GDP data" (Ylhainen, 2017).

These results remind us of the limitations of GDP for measuring the digital economy and the significance of uncaptured GDP to represent the real state of the digital economy.

3.4.3 The consequence of the trajectory option

Fig. 3.13 compares the development trajectory between ICT leaders in 2013–6 as a consequence of the above trajectory—increasing dependence on uncaptured GDP in Finland and on captured GDP in Singapore.

Worth noting here is Finland's resurgent trend in GDP growth, as illustrated in Fig. 3.14 (OECD, 2017), together with increasing human capital and happiness. This can be attributed to the hybrid role of soft innovation resources (*SIRs*) (see Chapter 4).

Figure 3.13 Comparison of the development trajectory in Finland and Singapore (2013–16). *(Sources: Updates of Watanabe, C., Naveed, K., Neittaanmäki, P., Tou, Y., 2016. Operationalization of un-captured GDP: the innovation Stream under new global mega-trends. Technology in Society 45, 58–77.; Watanabe, C., Naveed, K., Tou, Y., Neittaanmäki, P., 2018c. Measuring GDP in the digital economy: increasing dependency on uncaptured GDP. Technological Forecasting and Social Change 137, 226–240.)*

Another noteworthy contrast is the GNI/GDP ratio (GNP/GDP ratio). This ratio demonstrates the interactive return gain structure by comparing the state of profits gained from abroad (value higher than 1) and the state of lost domestic gains (value lower than 1).[10]

It seems surprising that regardless of its higher level of GDP growth, Singapore is losing its domestic gains while Finland is gaining profits from abroad despite lower GDP growth (Watanabe et al., 2016). Considering that both countries depend highly on exports (Jacobs, 2013), this contrast demonstrates that the world trade market has been shifting to corresponding to an economy that depends on uncaptured GDP.

3.4.4 Insights into activating a new coevolutionary dynamism

Fig. 3.9 suggests the formation of a tornado, which is a vortex that has grown in the updraft caused by a huge cumulonimbus cloud (Schmitter, 2010). As illustrated in Fig. 3.15, this tornado can be activated by spin-off coevolutionary dynamism.

---

[10] GNI (GNP) − GDP = Balance on income + Balance stemmed from the terms of tradeBalance on income has close relevance to Income balance in the international trade structure, asCurrent balance = Trade balance + Service balance + Income balance + Current transfers.

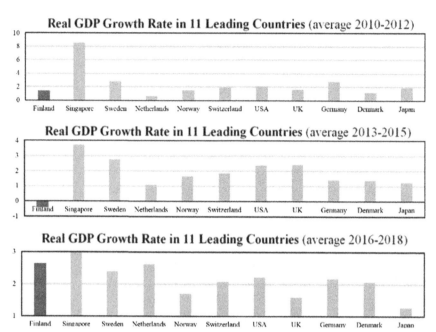

Figure 3.14 GDP growth rate for 11 leading countries (2010–18). *(Source: IMF (annual issues).)*

Figure 3.15 Formation of a tornado.

Recalling the dilemma between R&D (centered on ICT) expansion and declining productivity, this "tornado-forming dynamism" that activates spin-off coevolutionary dynamism, without directly depending on the expansion of R&D, may provide a possible solution to the central issue of the digital economy—dilemma-free sustainable growth.

For this purpose, the formation of a "cumulonimbus cloud" by activating spin-off coevolutionary dynamism plays a crucial role.

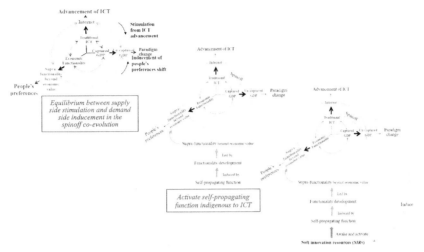

Figure 3.16 Scheme of the investigation of sustainable growth dynamism.

As reviewed earlier, the empirical analysis of the development trajectory of 500 global ICT firms in the digital economy (Fig. 3.4) identified how R&D-intensive firms have confronted the fear of this dilemma between increased R&D investment and declining productivity. These firms have attempted to maintain sustainable growth while avoiding the dilemma by activating the latent self-propagating function indigenous to ICT, which can be awoken and activated through network externalities (Watanabe and Hobo, 2004). The activated self-propagating function induces new functionality development that leads to suprafunctionality beyond economic value, generating a kind of economic "cumulonimbus cloud."

Based on this finding, the next chapter investigates this activation dynamism. An empirical analysis of six remarkable disruptive business models in the digital economy was conducted. The results of the analysis suggest that activation of this self-propagating function can be enabled by harnessing the vigor of *SIRs*. *SIRs* are latent innovation resources that are awoken and activated by the digital platform ecosystem and are considered condensates and crystals of the advancement of the Internet.

Fig. 3.16 illustrates the scheme of this investigation.

3.5 Conclusion

As measuring GDP in the digital economy becomes more significant, concern over the limitations of traditional GDP also grows. This chapter explored a practical new solution to this challenge through intensive empirical analyses of national, industrial, and individual behaviors in the digital economy.

Given the two-sided nature of ICT and the shift in people's preferences to functionality extending beyond economic value, the concept of uncaptured GDP was proposed, along with a potential way to measure it. The significance of dependence on uncaptured GDP was demonstrated by identifying the transformative direction of leading global ICT firms. A scheme was proposed to examine sustainable development that avoids the critical dilemma of ICT productivity in the digital economy.

The following findings are noteworthy:

(1) ICT prices have continued to decline because of the trap in ICT advancement derived from the two-sided nature of ICT. That is, the advancement of ICT generally contributes to enhanced technology prices through new functionality development, whereas the dramatic advancement of the Internet leads to decreases in technology prices because of certain characteristics: the provision of freebies, easy replication, and mass standardization. Therefore, declines in marginal productivity occur at the leading ICT firms.

(2) To compensate for decreased technology prices, new unique and identical services have been provided that are not necessarily captured by GDP, which measures economic value, thus leading to increased dependence on uncaptured GDP.

(3) Mismeasurement of ICT prices (dependence on the pseudo deflator) can be attributed to this phenomenon.

(4) These services correspond to people's preferences to shift from economic functionality to suprafunctionality beyond economic value, which encompasses social, cultural, and emotional values.

(5) This shift induces further advancement of the Internet, which intensifies the increasing dependence on uncaptured GDP. Therefore, a new spin-off coevolution has emerged and is occurring among Internet advancement, increasing uncaptured GDP, and shifts in people's preferences.

(6) This coevolution provides insight into the integration of national accounts with efforts at product-oriented microanalysis and leads the way to measuring uncaptured GDP.

(7) In this coevolutionary dynamism, the equilibrium of the inertia between the advancement of ICT (the supply side) and shifts in people's preferences (the demand side) plays a role in the spin-off that leads to

increases in uncaptured GDP, and this equilibrium can in turn be used to measure uncaptured GDP.

(8) Since 2002, Finland has shifted from the traditional computer-initiated ICT and captured GDP coevolution to the Internet and the new coevolution initiated by uncaptured GDP, but Singapore has retained its traditional coevolution.

(9) Singapore, in contrast to its notable GDP growth, is losing its domestic gains. This can be attributed to a worldwide shift from captured to uncaptured GDP.

(10) Under such circumstances in the digital economy, notwithstanding a fear of the dilemma of R&D expansion coupled with declining productivity, leading global ICT firms have been endeavoring to create suprafunctionality by harnessing *SIRs*.

(11) This trajectory is a way to achieve sustainable growth through gross GDP, including uncaptured GDP.

(12) The survival strategy of global ICT firms depends on the construction of a platform that demonstrates the above dynamism.

These findings give rise to the following suggestions for optimal trajectory management in the digital economy:

(1) A spin-off should be realized to the new coevolution occurring among the advancement of the Internet, increasing dependence on uncaptured GDP, and the shift in people's preferences to suprafunctionality beyond economic value.

(2) Further efforts should be made to transfer the insight of this dynamism to the integration of national accounts with efforts at product-oriented microanalysis.

(3) Sustainable growth by gross GDP, including uncaptured GDP, should be targeted.

(4) Management systems that harness *SIRs* should be further explored.

(5) Optimal national accounting based on gross GDP and a corresponding taxation system should be developed.

(6) Broadly applicable comprehensive uncaptured GDP measurement should be further developed.

(7) The higher well-being that the nation enjoys should be demonstrated rather than merely assessed through captured GDP.

This chapter offers a perspective on a current critical issue and explores new insights for measuring the digital economy. However, the analysis is still at a macro level and thus needs further development through the exploration and integration of micro investigations.

Future works should focus on in-depth microlevel international and historical reviews of success stories of gross GDP management at both national and industrial levels.

The development of public policies based on the gross GDP concept should be prioritized with a view to identifying optimal trajectories in the overall system that account for both captured and uncaptured GDP. In this context, the transformative direction of leading global ICT firms should be carefully analyzed, and possible opportunities created by the pioneering endeavors of such firms should be identified.

References

Ahmad, N., Schreyer, P., 2016. Measuring GDP in a Digital Economy. OECD Statistics Working Papers, 2016/07. OECD Publishing, Paris.

Bleys, B., 2012. Beyond GDP: classifying alternative measures for progress. Social Indicators Research 109 (3), 355—376.

Brynjolfsson, E., McAfee, A., 2014. The Second Machine Age. W.W. Norton & Company, New York.

Brynjolfsson, E., Collis, A., Diewert, W.E., Eggers, F., Fox, K.J., 2019. GDP-B: Accounting for the Value of New and Free Goods in the Digital Economy. NBER Working Paper 25695. NBER, Cambridge.

Copenhagen Economics, 2013. The Impact of Online Intermediaries on the EU Economy.

Costanza, R., Hart, M., Posner, S., Talberth, J., 2009. Beyond GDP: The Need for New Measures of Progress. Pardee Paper 4. Pardee Center for the Study of the Longer-Range Future, Boston.

Cowen, T., 2011. The Great Stagnation: How America Ate All the Low-Hanging Fruit of Modern History, Got Sick, and Will (Eventually) Feel Better. A Penguin eSpecial from Dutton, Penguin, New York.

European Union (EU), 2017. Economics of Industrial Research and Innovation. EU, Brussels.

Fleurbaey, M., 2009. Beyond GDP: the quest for a measure of social welfare. Journal of Economic Literature 47 (4), 1029—1075.

Hofstede, G., 1991. Cultures and Organizations. McGraw-Hill International, London.

International Labor Organization (ILO), 2012. Distribution of Household Income by Source. ILO, Geneva.

International Monetary Fund (IMF), 2014. The World Economic Outlook Database. IMF, Washington, DC.

International Telecommunication Union (ITU), 2014. World Telecommunication/ICT Indicators Database, 2014. ITU, Geneva.

Jacobs, M., May 14, 2013. Social Innovation: Lessons from Singapore, South Korea, and Taiwan. The Guardian.

Japan Cabinet Office (JCO), 2019. National Survey of Lifestyle Preferences. JCO, Tokyo.

Kubiszewski, I., Costanza, R., Franco, C., Lawn, P., Talberth, J., Jackson, T., Aylmer, C., 2013. Beyond GDP: Measuring and achieving global genuine progress. Ecological Economics 93 (C), 57—68.

Lowrey, A., 2011. Freaks, Geeks, and GDP. Slate. http://www.slate.com/articles/business/moneybox/2011/03/freaks_geeks_and_gdp.html (retrieved 20.06.17).

McDonagh, D., 2008. Satisfying needs beyond the functional: the changing needs of the silver market consumer. In: Proceedings of the International Symposium on the Silver Market Phenomenon - Business Opportunities and Responsibilities in the Aging Society, Tokyo.

Naveed, K., Watanabe, C., Neittaanmäki, P., 2018. The transformative direction of innovation toward an IoT-based society — increasing dependency on uncaptured GDP in global ICT firms. Technology in Society 53, 23—46.

OECD, 2010. The Economic and Social Role of Internet Intermediaries. OECD, Paris.

OECD, 2016. Tax Challenges in the Digital Economy. OECD, Paris.

OECD, 2017. OECD Review of Innovation Policy: Finland Assessment and Recommendation. OECD, Paris.

Rifkin, J., 2011. The Third Industrial Revolution: How Lateral Power Is Transforming Energy, the Economy, and the World. Macmillan, New York.

Schelling, T.C., 1998. Social mechanisms and social dynamics. In: Hedstrom, P., Swedberg, R. (Eds.), Social Mechanisms: An Analytical Approach to Social Theory. Cambridge Univ. Press, Cambridge, pp. 32—43.

Schmitter, E.D., 2010. Modeling tornado dynamics and the generation of infrasound, electric, and magnetic fields. Natural Hazards and Earth System Sciences 10, 295—298.

Tapscott, D., 1994. The Digital Economy: Promise and Peril in the Age of Networked Intelligence. McGraw-Hill, New York.

The Conference Board Total Economy Database, 2013. http://www.conference-board.org/data/economydatabase (retrieved 10.01.14).

The Earth Institute, Colombia University, 2013. World Happiness Report 2013. The Earth Institute, Colombia University, New York.

Tou, Y., Watanabe, C., Moriya, K., Neittaanmäki, P., 2019. Harnessing soft innovation resources leads to neo open innovation. Technology in Society 58, 101114.

Watanabe, C., 2009. Managing Innovation in Japan: The Role Institutions Play in Helping or Hindering How Companies Develop Technology. Springer Science & Business Media, Berlin.

Watanabe, C., Hobo, M., 2004. Creating a firm self-propagating function for advanced innovation-oriented projects: lessons from ERP. Technovation 24 (6), 467—481.

Watanabe, C., Kondo, R., Ouchi, N., Wei, H., Griffy-Brown, C., 2004. Institutional elasticity as a significant driver of IT functionality development. Technological Forecasting and Social Change 71 (7), 723—750.

Watanabe, C., Nasuno, M., Shin, J.H., 2011. Utmost gratification of consumption by means of supra-functionality leads a way to overcoming global economic stagnation. Journal of Services Research 11 (2), 31—58.

Watanabe, C., Naveed, K., Zhao, W., 2015a. New Paradigm of ICT productivity: increasing role of un-captured GDP and growing anger of consumers. Technology in Society 41, 21—44.

Watanabe, C., Naveed, K., Neittaanmäki, P., 2015b. Dependency on un-captured GDP as a source of resilience beyond economic value in countries with advanced ICT infrastructure: similarities and disparities between Finland and Singapore. Technology in Society 42, 104—122.

Watanabe, C., Naveed, K., Neittaanmäki, P., Tou, Y., 2016. Operationalization of un-captured GDP: the innovation Stream under new global mega-trends. Technology in Society 45, 58—77.

Watanabe, C., Moriya, K., Tou, Y., Neittaanmäki, P., 2018a. Structural sources of a productivity decline in the digital economy. International Journal of Managing Information Technology 10 (1), 1—20.

Watanabe, C., Tou, Y., Neittaanmäki, P., 2018b. A new paradox of the digital economy: structural sources of the limitation of GDP statistics. Technology in Society 55, 9—33.

Watanabe, C., Naveed, K., Tou, Y., Neittaanmäki, P., 2018c. Measuring GDP in the digital economy: increasing dependency on uncaptured GDP. Technological Forecasting and Social Change 137, 226—240.

Watson, B., McDonagh, D., 2004a. Design and emotion: supra-functionality for engineers. In: Proceedings of the 4th Design and Emotion International Conference (July 2004), Ankara, Turkey.

Watson, B., McDonagh, D., 2004b. Supra-functionality: responding to users needs beyond the functional. The Journal of the Institution of Engineering Designers 30 (5), 8—11.

Wesselink, B., Bakkes, J., Hinterberger, F., Brink, P., 2007. Measurement beyond GDP. In: Background Paper for the International Conference beyond GDP: Measuring Progress. True Wealth, and the Well-being of Nations, Brussels.

World Economic Forum (WEF), 2013a. The Global Information Technology Report 2013. WEF, Geneva.

World Economic Forum (WEF), 2013b. The Global Gender Gap Report, 2013. WEF, Geneva.

World Economic Forum (WEF), 2014a. The Global Information Technology Report, 2014. WEF, Geneva.

World Economic Forum (WEF), 2014b. The Global Competitiveness Report, 2014. WEF, Geneva.

World Economic Forum (WEF), 2016. The Global Information Technology Report 2016. WEF, Geneva.

Ylhainen, I., 2017. Challenges of Measuring the Digital Economy. https://www.sitra.fi/en/articles/challenges-measuring-digital-economy/.

CHAPTER 4

The emergence of soft innovation resources

Contents

Transforming the Socio Economy with Digital Innovation
ISBN 978-0-323-88465-5
https://doi.org/10.1016/B978-0-323-88465-5.00004-0

4.1 The new stream of the digital economy and beyond

4.1.1 The new stream of the digital economy under spin-off dynamism

In the previous chapter, the concept of uncaptured GDP was proposed by comparing the spin-off dynamism from traditional computer-initiated information communication and technology (ICT) innovation with Internet-initiated ICT innovation (see Fig. 1.9 in Chapter 1). It was based on (1) the two-sided nature of ICT and the shift in people's preferences for functionality defined by more than simply economic value and (2) the coevolutionary framework comprising the advancement of ICT, a paradigm change, and a shift in people's preferences.

The significance of dependence on uncaptured GDP was demonstrated by identifying the transformative direction of leading global ICT firms as they have attempted to create suprafunctionality by harnessing new innovation resources identical to the advancement of digital innovation initiated by the Internet. This chapter analyzes these innovation resources in light of the increasing significance of management systems that harness them.

An in-depth microlevel analysis of the unique features of Internet-driven ICT was conducted alongside international and historical reviews of noteworthy disruptive innovation from which new innovation resources have emerged.

4.1.2 Digital innovation with a unique nature

The spin-off from the coevolution of traditional computer-initiated ICT innovation to that of Internet-initiated innovation produces and broadly disseminates digital innovation. The coevolutionary nature is unique in that while simultaneously disseminating innovation, it creates digital solutions that meet social demand. Computer-initiated solutions are substitutes for traditional functions, just as mobile phones are substitutes for a broad array of functions, now performing the same functions as watches, cameras, calculators, TVs, music devices, maps, compasses, translators, newspapers, books, and games.

4.1.2.1 Simultaneous dissemination

The digitalization of economic activity can be broadly defined as the incorporation of data and the Internet into production processes and products, new forms of household and government consumption, fixed capital formation, cross-border flows, and finance (International Monetary Fund (IMF), 2018).

Consequently, this activity is subject to the unique features of ICT, which are centered on advancement of the Internet with simultaneous dissemination.

The simultaneous dissemination features of ICT can be attributed to the Internet's functional features of self-propagating permeation, homogeneous ICT stock creation (see the details in A1.1 in Appendix I), and coevolutionary advancement with new functional devices.

(1) Self-propagating permeation

The dramatic advancement of the Internet has created the digital economy, which has changed the way business and daily life are conducted (Tapscott, 1994). The further progression of digitized innovation over the last 2 decades, such as cloud services, mobile services, and artificial intelligence, has augmented this change significantly. This has accelerated the permeation of the Internet into ICT in general (Watanabe et al., 2018a,b,e,f) (see Fig. A1-1 in the Appendix) and has provided us with unprecedented services and conveniences (DBCDE, 2009).

(2) Homogeneous information communication and technology stock creation

Such permeation creates homogeneous ICT stock that acts as locomotive power for the Internet of Things (IoT) society.

By means of a bibliometric approach, the authors have traced the trend in the transforming factor of R&D into ICT stock[2] in 27 ICT-related key scientific research articles consisting of (1) Internet R&D, (2) Internet-related peripheral R&D, and (3) other ICT R&D for the period from 1980 to 2015 (see Fig. A1-2 in the Appendix and the details in Watanabe et al., 2018a,e). The above analysis demonstrated that while the values of the transformation factor had diverged by 2005, they were converging during the period from 2010 to 2015. For this reason, the technology stock of both the Internet and other broad ICT can be treated as the sum of the respective R&D that leads to homogeneous ICT stock creation.

---

[2] ICT stock, T, can be approximated by the ratio of R&D expenditure, R, and the transforming factor, χ, as $T \approx R/\chi$ in the long term, where $\chi = \rho$ (rate of the obsolescence of technology) $+ g$ (growth rate of R at the initial state).

(3) Coevolutionary advancement with new functional devices

The dramatic advancement of the Internet and the further progression of digitized innovation have augmented the Internet's permeation of not only broad ICT but also all production factors leading to an IoT society (Watanabe et al., 2012a,b, 2018a,e).

In this permeation process, digital innovation is mutually stimulating, leading to coevolutionary dynamics, and creates a new social ecosystem (OECD, 2016a,b).

Figs. 4.1 and 4.2 demonstrate the correlation between the ratio of GDP per capita and Internet use and the ratio of smartphone ownership in 40 countries in 2015—11 countries with advanced economies and 29 countries with emerging and developing economies (EDEs).

Figs. 4.1 and 4.2 demonstrate that ICT simultaneously permeates 40 countries regardless of each country's stage of economic development. Previously, a delay in economic development was a fundamental impediment for EDEs, resulting in a vicious cycle between economic development and technological advancement. However, Figs. 4.1 and 4.2

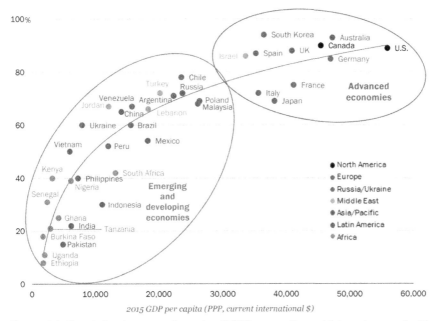

Figure 4.1 Correlation between the ratio of GDP per capita and internet usage in 40 countries (2015). *(Source: Pew Research Center, 2016. Smartphone Ownership and Internet Usage Continues to Climb in Emerging Economies. Pew Research Center, Washington, D.C.)*

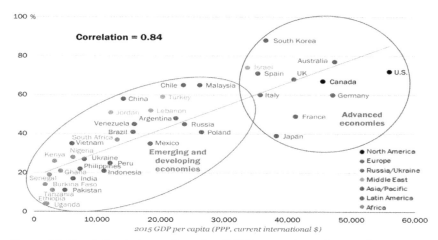

Figure 4.2 Correlation between the ratio of GDP per capita and smartphone owner-ship in 40 countries (2015). *(Source: Pew Research Center, 2016. Smartphone Ownership and Internet Usage Continues to Climb in Emerging Economies. Pew Research Center, Washington, D.C.)*

demonstrate that countries with EDEs enjoy Internet and smartphone usage notwithstanding their low levels of economic development.

Moreover, Fig. 4.3 demonstrates that contrary to traditional technology, the discrepancy between high- and low-income countries in the dissemi-nation speed of advanced IT—e.g., for the Internet and mobile phones—has narrowed dramatically.

Such simultaneous worldwide dissemination creates a new ICT-driven social ecosystem (UNESCO, 2015). In this dissemination process, digita-lized innovation is mutually stimulating, leading to coevolutionary

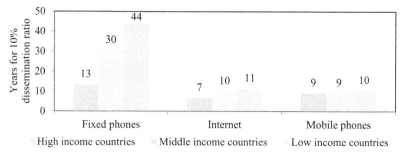

Figure 4.3 Years of a 10% dissemination ratio for fixed phones, internet, and mobile phones by income level. *(Source: Ministry of Internal Affairs and Communication (MIC), 2011. White Paper on Japan's Information and Communication. MIC, Tokyo.)*

dynamics, and creates a new social ecosystem. Fig. 4.4 and Table 4.1 demonstrate a strong correlation between Internet use and smartphone ownership in 40 countries regardless of economic level. Such a strong correlation stimulates the coevolutionary development of ICT advancement, leading to the creation of a new social ecosystem.

All of these factors demonstrate ICT's simultaneous dissemination crossover to a technoeconomy, which can be seen as one of the unique features of ICT (Tou et al., 2019a.b).

4.1.2.2 The digital solution to social demand

Such unique features of ICT with simultaneous dissemination can be attributed to the coevolutionary development of the following enablers of a digital solution for social demand:

(1) Advancement of a social networking service and online retailers have given way to trends to be identified, marketed, and sold immediately. Styles and trends are easily conveyed online to attract trendsetters. Posts on Instagram or Facebook can easily increase awareness about new trends in customer preference.

(2) IoT improves customer experiences and digital capabilities of the retailer that can open communication between retailers and customers.

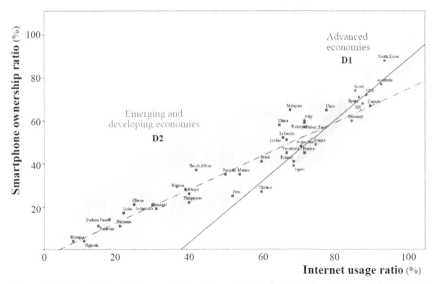

Figure 4.4 Correlation between internet usage and smartphone ownership in 40 countries (2015).

Table 4.1 Correlation between internet usage and smartphone ownership in 40 countries (2015).

$\ln SP = -0.941 + 1.153\, D_1 \ln ID + 1.147 \ln D_2\, ID$ $adj.\ R^2\ 0.933$

        (-4.31) (22.66) (19.81)

D, dummy variables—D_1: $AE = 1$, $EDE = 0$; D_2: $AE = 0$, $EDE = 1$; ID, Internet usage ratio; SP, smartphone ownership ratio.Figures in parentheses are t-statistics; all are significant at the 1% level. AE, advanced economy; EDE, emerging and developing economy

Retailers interact with the customer to collect data that helps retailers understand needs and concerns, and implement it to create a more personalized experience (McKinsey Global Institute, 2015).

(3) **3D printing technology** has enabled customers to realize their wish to manufacture their visions with their own hands.

(4) **Artificial intelligence (AI)** and its applications to **machine learning (ML)** provide systems with the ability to automatically learn and improve from experience.

(5) **Mobile commerce** enables customers to enjoy a seamless mobile-friendly shopping experience by clicking on the item they like and be redirected to the product page, effectively reducing search time. Businesses can provide their customers with a simple way to discover products and shop, all through their handy smartphones.

(6) **Virtual reality (VR)/augmented reality** merges the physical and online worlds of retail. They enable shoppers to try outfits on an avatar, customized to the correct measurements, before purchasing an item. These platforms change the online shopping experience for the better as avatars and virtual platforms engage and retain customers for longer periods.

Thus, as a consequence of spin-off from the coevolution of traditional computer-initiated ICT innovation to Internet-initiated innovation, digital innovation emerges, and in its unique coevolutionary nature, it simultaneously disseminates digital solution while satisfying social demand (Watanabe et al., 2018e,f). This coevolution is also subject to coevolution with shifts to a new socioeconomic stream that includes eco-conscious smart consumer society, the sharing economy, and the circular economy. The noncontact socioeconomy that has emerged in the wake of the COVID-19 pandemic would provide similar inducement.

4.1.3 The shift to new socioeconomic trends

4.1.3.1 Shift to an eco-conscious smart consumer society

Triggered by the energy crises of 1973 and 1979, people's codes of conduct began to shift to energy-saving behavior, with an attitude that small is beautiful and an overall eco-friendly approach. The paradigm shift from an industrial society to an information society started at the beginning of the 1990s, and the subsequent new economy of the 1990s accelerated a shift in peoples' preferences from economic functionality to suprafunctionality beyond economic value (Japan Cabinet Office (JCO), 2010; Japan Cabinet Office (JCO), 2012, 2018; McDonagh, 2008; McDonagh and Thomas, 2010; Watanabe, 2013; Watanabe and Hobo, 2004; Weightman and McDonagh, 2004). The global economic stagnation that ensued from the financial crisis of 2008 resulted in so-called smart consumers who engaged in less excessive consumption and reinforced the shift in preferences (Watanabe et al., 2015a).

Thus, over the last half-century, people's general attitudes have moved away from "great is good and consuming is a virtue" to a more eco-conscious code of conduct, as illustrated in Fig. 4.5.

Such a socioeconomic stream makes up the foundation for the evolution of disruptive business models. These models in turn enable the awakening and *utilization of suprafunctionality beyond economic value* as well as *utmost gratification ever experienced* (an unprecedented level of gratification) (Watanabe et al., 2011).

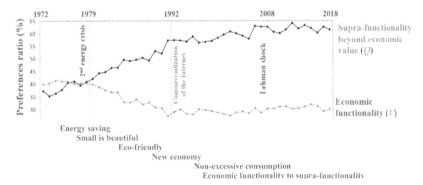

Figure 4.5 Shifting trends in customer preferences and codes of conduct over the last half-century in Japan.

4.1.3.2 Shift to a sharing economy

Cohen and Kietzmann (2014) highlighted how some altogether new and different business models has emerged in the first decade of this century. These developments have started to challenge traditional thinking about how resources can and should be offered and consumed. This way of thinking supports the arguments that incremental improvements in our existing production and consumption systems are insufficient to make our global economy more sustainable (Lovins and Cohen, 2011; Stead and Stead, 2013). Consequently, a new business model that emphasizes the sharing economy inevitably emerges. Cohen and Kietzmann (2014) also noted that shared mobility solutions, as reviewed earlier, can be attributed to multiple agents, including public and private providers. These can also seek to develop business models that address deficiencies in public infrastructure and public transit systems, historically the exclusive purview of local and regional governments. They also warned that the common interest in sustainability among these different types of agents does not always lead to harmony, instead giving rise to agency conflicts that can reduce the positive sustainability impact of their individual and collective initiatives. Watanabe et al. (2016b, 2017a) demonstrated the conflict of Uber's global expansion. The emergence of the sharing economy and its rapid shift, accelerated by the digital economy, have created significant impacts on traditional business. This has led to the shift to new disruptive business models driven by growing consumer desire for variety, sustainability, and affordability. In recognition of this consumer shift, the sharing economy can be expected to appear in broad areas as the sharing of mobility, space, human skills, and goods, as illustrated in Table 4.2.

Consequently, this socioeconomic stream also builds a foundation for the evolution of disruptive business models, particularly for the effective utilization of so-called *sleeping-capable resources* as well as of *memories and future dreams* (Watanabe et al., 2016c, 2017b; Naveed et al., 2017). In line with the increasing trend in this stream, consumers are choosing to rent

Table 4.2 Sharing economy in four business areas.

Share of movement	Share of space
Ridesharing (e.g., Uber) **Carsharing** (e.g., Grab)	**Vacant space** (e.g., airbnb) **Coworking space** (e.g., WeWork)
Sharing of human skills	**Sharing of goods**
Cloudsourcing (e.g., Amazon Web Services) **Task-sharing** (e.g., Cloud works)	**Reuse** (e.g., Mercari) **Fashion** (e.g., Air closet)

rather than own goods outright. This trend is partly driven by the younger generation's hunger for newness and simultaneous embrace of sustainability (Matsuda, 2010, 2012). Consequently, the lifespans of products, particularly of fashion products, are being extended as preowned, refurbished, repaired, and rental business models continue to evolve. Across many categories, consumers have demonstrated an appetite to shift away from traditional ownership to newer ways to access products, including the preowned and rental markets. Additionally, the circular nature of this partnership bolsters the corporate and social responsibility of the fashion brand (McKinsey and Company, 2019).

Thus, this shift has corresponded to increasing concern to shift to a circular economy, and it has been accelerated by advancement of the digital economy. Moreover, the unexpected consequences of the COVID-19 pandemic have been reflected in the contrasting popularity of the four business areas in Table 4.2. In contrast to the growing popularity of sharing human skills and goods, dependency on movement and spatial sharing have been declining.

4.1.3.3 Shifting to a circular economy

Given the increasing dependence on the foregoing new socioeconomy as an eco-conscious smart consumer society and sharing economy, the global consequences of environmental concerns and the subsequent shift from a fossil economy to a circular economy will inevitably boost the circular economy.

The world is already using approximately 1.6 planets' worth of resources every year. There is an urgent need to shift from "take-make-waste" production and consumption models to a new model called "circular fashion" where resource loops are tightened and valuable materials are recovered (McDonough, 2020).

Contrary to the current fossil economy where manufacturers extract resources from the earth to make products that will soon be discarded in landfills, circular fashion requires the production of goods and services to operate like systems in nature, where the waste and demise of a substance becomes the food and source of growth for something new.

The shift in people's preferences to suprafunctionality beyond economic value and to the sharing economy corresponds to this requirement. Advancement of ICT centered on Internet-driven digital innovation enables this requirement to be met by constructing a platform ecosystem—all stakeholders (company, employee, user, and government) work together to meet social demand. Thus, shifting to this economy induces such disruptive business models as activating and utilizing *trust by overdrawing past information* along with *untapped resources and vision.*

4.1.3.4 Shifting to a noncontact socioeconomy after COVID-19
Covid-19 influences the above trends and changes the current socioeconomic environment to the following new normal. This inevitably affects the inducement of disruptive business models.

(1) Transformation of lifestyle
The response to the COVID-19 crisis calls for curbing outside activities, social distancing, and significant reductions in contact opportunities with others. Consequently, people's lifestyle will change.

There is a possibility that a new normal will emerge. It will include such practices as telework; greater than ever business use of the Internet; reduced contact during daily life, work, education, leisure and with family and friends; and community formation. "Self" would be the keyword for consumption. Business models and commodities that support "do it yourself" will become popular.

A cultural shift in working and the consumption of goods will also occur. The understanding of individual preparedness and the way of working in classic settings has shifted. Individual responsibility for work outcomes is emphasized. Social contact over the Internet has increased, even among the aging population. New technology will become easier to use. At the same time, the proficiency of older users will go up. The consumption of entertainment will shift to be massively online.

(2) Reconsideration of the concepts of central and local
Along with lifestyle changes, or as an incentive for it, the conventional concepts of central and local districts need to be reconsidered.

It becomes critical to understand the importance of an individual in society regardless of central or local, and one's responsibility in the chain of goods and services provided to and/or from the local community.

(3) Rebuilding the significance of internationalization
It is inevitable that international supply chains will be restructured, while offshore business activities, daily remote education, and reconsideration of the necessity of air travel will be reconsidered. Understanding the importance of securing critical goods and their supply chain, with the role of locally produced goods will be the basis of the significance of internationalization.

The sharing of manufacturing will become more prevalent. In this practice, manufacturing facilities capable of variable use according to supply and demand conditions are mutually interchanged among producers.

(4) The new social contract between the state and citizens

In the post—COVID-19 era, economies as well as societies and democracies may change. For example, it is undeniable that when a nation is taken for granted by those tasked with protecting it, its people may choose to take over its protection.

In other words, the state does not protect the people, so the people become the parties that protect society, and each person's choice of action determines the future of society.

(5) Reestablishment of public—private boundaries

In such a situation, it is implied that the conventional idea of public and private cannot function properly and that a new form of social partnership or a new type of relationship between the state and citizens is required.

In the post—COVID-19 economy, the possibility for blurring public—private boundaries will be high. If Boeing is nationalized or airlines and automobile companies are nationalized, today's capitalism will be transformed into a "new national capitalism" because the boundary between the public and private sectors will become unrecognizable.

(6) Rethinking free market fundamentalism

As a result of pursuing efficiency based solely on market universalism, a supply chain that relies heavily on China and that ignores national interests has been formed. The result is an economic culture that impairs a country's own economic security and neglects its workers. As a result, the solidarity of the people has been damaged.

After the COVID-19 pandemic subsides, economic principles will be pursued with more consideration for national security and the benefits of countries' own citizens.

(7) Exfoliation from the myth of GDP

It seems that the myth of GDP will be a watershed that fluctuates from the bottom. The 2008 financial crisis curbed excessive consumption, but the current crisis may also have the side effect of excessive hospitalization, unnecessary health care, and overmedication. Excessive entertainment and interaction at night are also possible. Post—COVID-19 contactless economic societies may have the effect of greatly reducing such components of consumption. This is true for both consumption and investment regardless of whether the sector is public or private. On the contrary, it will become possible to recognize and enhance the "joy of consumption" (utility), which does not necessarily involve financial expenditure. This can be considered an inevitable dependence on uncaptured GDP (Watanabe et al., 2015b, 2016a).

(8) Disruptive innovation that coevolves with pandemic
Elucidation of the behavior of the new coronavirus does not rule out the possibility of progressive and disruptive innovation that produces a unique effect while controlling toxic intoxication similar to that of cooking pufferfish, extracting medicine from poisonous snakes, and making beautiful lacquerware using lacquer, which has a high risk of rashes.

(9) Accelerated change in history
It is recognized that all of the above is not necessarily a new evolutional change but rather the unavoidable change accelerated as an inevitable consequence of the digital and postdigital economies.

4.1.4 Emergence of disruptive business models

The foregoing "great coevolution" due to the new stream of the digital economy under the spin-off dynamism (4.1.1), digital innovation with unique nature (4.1.2), and the shift to new socioeconomic trends (4.1.3) induce remarkable disruptive business models in the digital economy from which new innovations emerge as illustrated in Fig. 4.6.

4.2 Remarkable disruptive business models from which new innovations emerge

4.2.1 Suprafunctionality beyond economic value - Driving force in a shift in people's preferences[3]

4.2.1.1 Evolution of disruptive business model toward utilization of suprafunctionality

With the immense diffusion of digital technologies and smart devices, consumer preferences and the ways to tackle their preferences have been

---

[3] See the details of the analysis in the authors' previous works (Watanabe et al., 2011, 2015a) as this analysis was based on them.

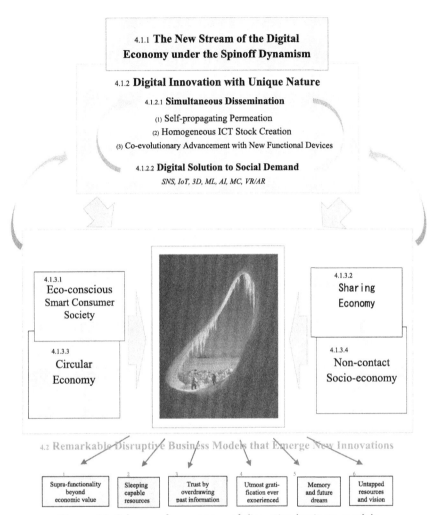

Figure 4.6 Scheme of emergence of disruptive business models.

also changing. As the consumer is no longer a passive recipient of information or a sidelines spectator, modern consumers are actively engaged in the buying process. They are more proactive, demanding, knowledgeable, tech-savvy, and have more information available than any previous generations in history (Watanabe et al., 2015a).

As a consequence of these historical changes in the consumer experiences, in line with the general shift in commodity-oriented society to service and information-oriented society, it is generally postulated that consumer's preferences have been steadily shifting from economic functionality driven preferences to suprafunctionality that goes beyond economic value-driven preferences (McDonagh, 2008). Businesses must engage and communicate with consumers to develop an understanding of their needs and desires.

Recent decreasing willingness to consume can be considered a protest by consumers against producers unable to satisfy their requirements. The dissatisfaction has frustrated consumers for being consumers and unable to produce the goods and services they desire by themselves resulting in the growing anger of consumers. The necessary resolve to this anger may transform into a springboard for new innovation. This builds the foundation for the evolution of disruptive business models that awaken and utilize **"suprafunctionality beyond economic value."**

This section attempts to analyze such a remarkable business model.

4.2.1.2 Transforming the shift in people's preferences into innovation—a new approach

As a consequence of historical changes in experiences with the rapid and widespread diffusion of digital technologies and smart devices, people's preferences and the ways to tackle their preferences have been changing.

It is generally postulated that people's preferences have been steadily shifting from preferences driven by economic functionality to suprafunctionality beyond economic value-driven preferences (McDonagh, 2008; JCO, 2012). Here suprafunctionality beyond economic value encompasses social, cultural, aspirational, tribal, and emotional values. Fig. 3.5 in the preceding chapter (Section 3.3.1) demonstrates the basic concept.

A novel concept of suprafunctionality was postulated by Weightman and MacDonagh (2004). They stressed that "In main stream industrial/product design it is now recognized that the most successful products are combined with good functionality and the effective satisfaction of suprafunctional needs, including establishing positive emotional relationships between users and the products that they use and buy."

They further explained that "It is also important to understand that people buy products for a mix of rational and irrational reasons. Consumer purchases may involve replacements for existing products due to the product failure or due to the costly repairs of their existing products. Other potential reasons could be the obsolescence of the existing product, improved functionality, or performance of the new product as compared to the existing one. The other reasons could be the improved supra-functionality of the new products in terms of looks, aesthetics, brand image, symbolic, social, and cultural associations, or are just cooler."

McDonagh and Thomas (2010) pointed that "People relate to the products and services in their individual and interesting ways. Material possessions often serve as symbolic expressions of who we are. The clothes we wear, the household items we buy, and the cars we drive all enable us to express our personality, social standing, and wealth."

These pioneer works have convinced us of a shift to suprafunctionality beyond economic value. The shift in people's preferences from economic functionality to suprafunctionality can be observed clearly in the "Public Opinion Survey Concerning People's Lifestyles," conducted annually by Japan's Cabinet Office, as illustrated in Fig. AIII-1.1 in Appendix III.

Looking at this figure we note that contrary to the steady decline in people's preference for economic functionality (V), suprafunctionality beyond economic value (Q) steadily increased and exceeded V in 1979, the year of the second energy crisis. While Q continues to increase steadily, V declined to its lowest level in 1992, the year immediately after the commercialization of the Internet in 1991. It has stayed at a similar level since then. A decline in Q due to the financial crisis in 2008 was followed by a sharp recovery. Consequently, a shifting trend from V to Q can be classified into four phases: *Phase 1* (1972—9), *Phase 2* (1980—92), *Phase 3* (1993—2008), and *Phase 4* (2009—12).

Table AIII-1.1 demonstrates that GDP (Y) elasticity to supra-functionality beyond economic value (Q) (which cannot necessarily be captured by GDP) exhibits a slight successive increasing trend. At the same time, economic functionality (V) (which can be captured by GDP by its nature) has dramatically decreased after Phase 3 (after commercialization of the Internet at the beginning of the 1990s), showing a shift away from economic functionality in the digital economy.

These results demonstrate that while people's preferences have shifted in line with increased GDP, their inducement has shifted to uncaptured GDP suggesting the prelude of the new paradox due to an Internet-initiated ICT world.

Such an increasing people's initiative accelerates a shift in their prefer-ences from economic functionality to suprafunctionality beyond economic value encompassing social, cultural, aspirational, tribal, and emotional value (Weightman and McDonagh, 2004; McDonagh, 2008; Watanabe, 2009, Watanabe et al., 2011).

4.2.1.3 Growing consumer anger

As postulated by the economist Franco Modigliani, people never forget the utmost gratification of consumption ever experienced (the most satisfying consumption experiences they have) that has memorized in their brain and affects their preferences in consumption (Modigliani, 1965). In light of the changing people's preferences together with the general shift in our socioeconomic paradigm from commodity-oriented society to service and information-oriented one (see Fig. 4.5), it is generally postulated that the consumer's preferences have steadily been shifting from economic functionality to suprafunctionality beyond economic value.

In light of technological change and shifting consumer preferences, it has been observed that the hatred of consumption particularly among young consumers, has been increasing due to the nonexistence of suitable goods and services corresponding to their requirements (Matsuda, 2010, 2012; Watanabe et al., 2012a). The decreasing willingness to consume can be considered a protest by consumers against producers unable to satisfy their requirements. The dissatisfaction has frustrated consumers for being consumers and unable to produce the goods and services they desire by themselves as illustrated in Fig. 4.7.

Fig. 4.7 demonstrates this phenomenon.

4.2.1.4 Emerging conflict in transition as a springboard for new innovation

Together with the shifting preferences of consumers, the focus of businesses has also been shifting. Traditionally the priority of businesses has been to

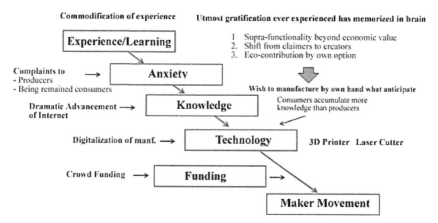

Figure 4.7 The growing anger of consumers and a maker movement.

find as many consumers as possible, and convert some of them into loyal customers by establishing a long-term relationship. With the widespread diffusion and availability of digital technologies, finding and approaching customers has become comparatively easier but the larger challenge is how to retain them. Accordingly, businesses devote significant resources to develop and maintain a relationship with loyal customers.

Today's consumers have the power to reject businesses, brands, and institutions unresponsive to their shifting needs and preferences. The extent of understanding and responsiveness to consumers' shifting lifestyle preferences, aspirations, needs, changing working environments, and buying behavior will determine the winners and losers in the future marketplace. As a result, businesses must engage and communicate with consumers to develop an understanding of their needs and preferences.

The real-time responsiveness and convenience can be a key competitive advantage for the firms in designing their products and services. However, convenience alone does not automatically lead to success because consumers do not waste time on bad design either. If the content or the layout of a site is unattractive, consumers will immediately leave that site or app and switch to something else. Consumers also remember their good and bad experiences for a long into the future. This means businesses have a short window of opportunity in which capture the attention of consumers and influence their buying decisions.

Transition from a commodity-oriented society to a service and information-oriented society, which includes changing technologies and shifting socioeconomic value, produces conflicts. These occur due to the mismatch between the producer and consumer preferences and expectations that resulted in the growing anger of consumers and the possibility of a post-excessive-consumption society.

In light of the above discussion, Fig. 4.8 demonstrates the emerging phenomenon of ICT advancement, shifting socioeconomic value, the emergence of conflict in transition, consumer anger, and the necessary resolve to transform the growing anger of consumers into a springboard for new innovation.

This suggests the significance of harnessing the vigor of broad hidden innovation resources that have emerged from disruptive business models in the digital economy as illustrated in Fig. 4.6 in the preceding section.

The resilience of any system depends on its capacity to use a shock as a trigger for renewal and improvement (Ilmola and Casti, 2013). This means it is essential to transform consumer anger into a springboard for new

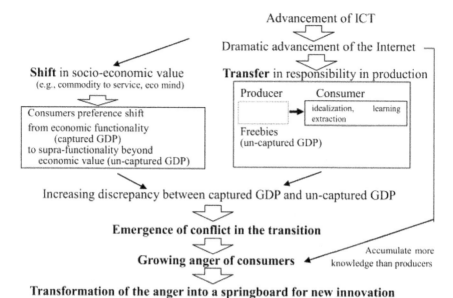

Figure 4.8 Transition dynamism in new paradox of productivity and its impact on consumers.

innovation and a successful transformation of the coemergence of innovation and consumption is crucial. The innovation-consumption coemergence corresponds to coevolutionary acclimatization by harnessing the vigor of hidden counterparts, consumers.

4.2.1.5 Discussion

The increasing anger of consumers has had significant consequence. An empirical analysis of the preference shift from economic functionality to suprafunctionality beyond economic value demonstrates the conflict between captured GDP and uncaptured GDP.

Noteworthy findings include the following:

(1) The recent great stagnation can largely be attributed to a consumer preference shift from economic functionality to suprafunctionality beyond economic value, which produces conflicts between producers and consumers.

(2) This conflict has led to emerging anger of consumers demonstrated by declining marginal propensity to consume (Table AIII-1.2).

(3) This anger can be transformed into a springboard for new innovation leading to innovation-consumption coemergence.

These findings provide the following policy suggestions:

(1) Provided that suprafunctionality beyond economic value plays a governing role for consumers, a similar dynamism of encompassed values should be traced.

(2) The relationship between these two streams should be analyzed.

(3) In this context, the strategy for innovation–consumption coemergence should be developed on a priority basis.

(4) While a way to appease consumer's growing anger may provide a constructive suggestion for this coemergence, given that this anger remains intangible, the way to conceptualize the voiceless voice of the consumer anger should be taken seriously.

(5) The vigor of broad hidden innovation resources that have emerged from disruptive business models in the digital economy should be utilized by awaking and activating it.

This analysis is thus expected to explore significant insight in elucidating the institutional sources of resilience in the transition from the paradigm of captured GDP to that of uncaptured GDP. This exploration is expected to emerge a remarkable business model that transforms consumer anger into a springboard for new innovation.

Points of future works are summarized as follows:

(1) To generalize the foregoing findings and policy suggestions, analyses of additional countries should be conducted.

(2) An interdisciplinary approach exploring a way to analyze innovation–consumption coemergence should be attempted by integrating economics, psychophysiology, and engineering.

(3) Given the significance of harnessing the vigor of broad hidden innovation resources that have emerged from disruptive business models in the digital economy, such resources should be explored extensively.

4.2.2 Sleeping capable resources - Uber's ridesharing revolution[4]

4.2.2.1 Evolution of disruptive business model toward utilization of sleeping resources

Given the significance of harnessing the vigor of hidden innovation resources that have emerged from disruptive business models in the digital economy, this section attempts to explore such resources by awaking

---

[4] See the details of the analysis in the authors' previous works (Watanabe et al., 2016b, 2017a) as this analysis was based on them.

"**sleeping-capable resources**" by examining a pioneer of the sharing economy—Uber's ridesharing revolution.

Uber is a ridesharing digital platform company. It has disrupted the traditional taxi industry by effectively utilizing digital technologies and an innovative business model.

This section presents the impact of Uber on the New York City (NYC) taxi industry by comparing the coexisting development trajectories of Uber and taxis. It further analyzed the institutional factors that contributed to the success of Uber. It is found that Uber has successfully utilized sleeping capable resources through managing to pull costs down and improving the quality of service by innovative utilization of modern digital technologies.

Thus, Uber has accomplished rapid worldwide deployment and shed light on the ICT-driven sharing economy. As of June 2016, Uber offers its service in over 479 cities worldwide as demonstrated in Fig. AIII-2.1 in Appendix III-2.

At the same time, such rapid expansion has resulted in confronting legal battles and raised a long-term question over the coexistence, or coevolution, of new innovation and traditional institutional systems.

In light of such a question, this section also examined the institutional sources contrasting success and failure in Uber's global expansion.

Based on these analyses, this section suggests the significance of the ICT-driven disruptive business model (IDBM) with a consolidated challenge to social demand (CCSD) as a remarkable business model that creates a springboard for new innovation in the digital economy.

4.2.2.2 Uber's ridesharing revolution—a new approach

With the advancement of digital technology and the Internet, we are in the midst of a transformative shift in business design, where business models have been moving from pipes to platforms.

The platform business models create value through the exchange of products or services between producers and consumers enabled by certain technologies. These platforms provide services such as content sharing, cloud computing, data analytics, and even the exchange of physical products and services. Platforms allow participants to cocreate and exchange value with each other. External developers can extend platform functionality and contribute to the infrastructure of the business. Platform users acting as producers can create value on the platform for other users to consume. Uber, Airbnb, and YouTube are some of the successful companies using such multisided platform business models.

Isaac and Davis (2014) considered Uber one of the most disruptive, successful tech-startup companies. It has severely disrupted the taxi service industry with its efficient and innovative use of digital technologies. Horpedahl (2015) highlighted that smartphone apps have enabled consumers to bypass traditional taxicabs (Fig. AIII-2.2). Uber leverages the sharing economy revolution (Belk, 2014), leading to the transformation of the market for taxi cabs and limousines. The ridesharing revolution triggered by Uber was also postulated by Koopeman et al. (2014), King (2015), and Ehret (2015).

Isaac and Davis (2014) appreciated Uber as one of the most disruptive, successful tech startup companies, one that has severely disrupted the taxi service industry. They pointed out that much of the success Uber has generated so quickly relies on (1) its ability to classify itself as a "technology company" instead of as a transportation company, (2) the ability to classify their drivers as independent contractors instead of as employees, and (3) a depressed market in which workers are willing to assume the burden of risks and costs associated with driving for the company.

4.2.2.3 Information communication and technology–driven disruptive business model

Uber is perceived by passengers as a better service with cost and time savings in reaching a location. Its system is also convenient for drivers because they can work flexible hours and have the choice to reject unwanted clients. Through their cashless, credit card-based system, Uber can trace and choose highly rated drivers. Reliance on digital technology provides passengers with a transparent view of quality and prices. Similarly, drivers can give feedback on passengers' behavior.

Fig. AIII-2.3 compares trends in Uber and taxi trips and prices in NYC.

The contribution of trips increase can be attributed to the effects of learning and economy of scale (Watanabe et al., 2009a,b), whereas the contribution of smartphones increase can be attributed to ICT's self-propagating function, which is based on the acceleration of learning and economy of scale effects (Watanabe et al., 2004, 2009b).

Fig. AIII-2.3A demonstrates that while the number of taxi trips kept declining, the number of Uber trips sharply increased. Fig. AIII-2.3B shows that while the taxi prices have increased, the Uber prices have sharply declined.

The discrepancy between actual medallion prices and estimated medallion prices without Uber can be considered uncaptured GDP as demonstrated in Fig. AIII-2.4A. The uncaptured GDP that has emerged due to Uber can be captured by measuring the discrepancy between taxi prices and the magnitude of their decline effect derived from Uber.

Therefore, the magnitude of the declining effect can be measured by the balance of taxi prices and the aggregated prices of taxis and Ubers with a respective share of trips. Fig. AIII-2.4B presents uncaptured GDP per trip induced by Uber since the beginning of 2015. It has been increasing significantly.

Uber's IDBM can be appreciated as a forerunner in the transformation of a new business design that consolidates new technoeconomic streams. These include the sharing economy, ICT advancement, and increasing anger of passengers (see 4.2.1). In this way, the company orchestrates potential spin-off dynamism from traditional coevolution to uncaptured GDP coevolution as illustrated in Fig. 4.9.

4.2.2.4 Rapid growth and legal battle - consolidated challenge to social demand

Uber's rapid expansion provides constructive insights regarding the significance of IDBM not only in transportation but also in nearly all business fields. While at the same time Uber's legal battles in some cities around the world raise a serious question regarding the rationale of IDBM (Fig. AIII-2.5).

The comparative empirical analysis of Uber's expansion and its legal battles in 16 countries in the early stage (around 2016) found that the legal conflict of Uber can be attributed to its coevolution or disengagement with

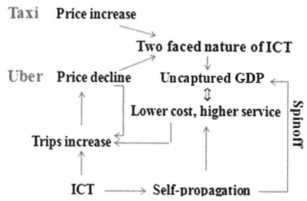

Figure 4.9 The dynamism of Uber's information communication and technology—driven disruptive business model.

institutions depending on the velocity of the company's expansion (its growth rate) and the institutional elasticity of the host city or country. Fig. AIII-2.6 illustrates the scheme of adaption of Uber in institutional systems in different host cities or countries.

The rapid growth of technological development significantly enhances its functionality level, but it does not give sufficient time for the host to develop necessary routinization. It can restrict the necessary interaction with institutions that should be developed in a self-propagating manner, and it is a necessary condition for the successful adaption of ICT-driven innovations similar to Uber, so the optimal velocity of growth is very crucial.

The other important factor is the institutional elasticity of the host because nonelastic institutions are prone to internal regulations and to protect the vested interests of incumbent organizations. There exists a certain threshold that resists innovation (Oreg and Goldenberg, 2015). Fig. AIII-2.7 illustrates this contrast.

Nowadays, a key factor in creating a business opportunity is the ability to solve a social problem and fulfill a social demand. Uber has developed a digital platform supported by an innovative business model and managed to disrupt the traditional taxi industry. It has created a social demand by providing better user experience for comparatively affordable prices, and been denoted as IDBM. Uber has managed to create a social demand successfully, but as is evident through the analysis of Uber's global expansion, it has faced challenges and legal battles. Through our empirical analyses, we found that the diffusion velocity and institutional elasticity of the host determined the adaption of Uber.

Notably, those countries or cities without legal battles have constructed a coevolutionary acclimatization system by starting a consolidation dialogue with a broad range of stakeholders to develop mutual trust. One successful example is the tripartism framework introduced by Singapore. The objective of this forum is to forge consensus in strategies for the development of benefits for employers, workers, and society and to take action to achieve sustainable national growth. Such frameworks facilitate the consolidation dialogue among a broad group of stakeholders including companies, employers, users, and governments to discuss their concerns and challenges in solving a social problem or in fulfilling a social demand as demonstrated in Fig. 4.10. This suggests a significance that IDBM with CCSD would be critical for resilient IDBM.

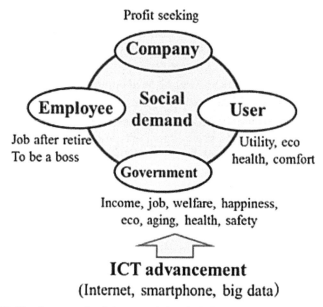

Profit seeking

ICT advancement
(Internet, smartphone, big data)

Figure 4.10 The framework of the consolidated challenge to social demand. *(Source: Watanabe, C., Naveed, K., Neittaanmäki, P., 2017a. Consolidated challenge to social demand for resilient platforms: lessons from Uber's global expansion. Technology in Society 48, 33–53.)*

4.2.2.5 Discussion
The secret of Uber's success

In light of the disruptive digital-technology driven business model that Uber has used to trigger a ridesharing revolution, the institutional sources of the company's platform ecosystem architecture were analyzed. Noteworthy findings include the following:

(1) The coexisting development trajectory corresponds to the two–sided nature of the ICT behind the emergence of uncaptured GDP.

(2) This emergence can be attributed to the strong substitution of taxi by Uber, which was accelerated by the contrast between the vicious cycle between the increase in price and decrease in trips by taxi and the virtuous cycle between price decline and trips increase in Uber.

(3) Uber's virtuous cycle can be attributed to ICT's self-propagating function, which enhances the level of functionality as its diffusion proceeds.

(4) This self-propagating function plays a vital role in spin–offs from traditional coevolution to new coevolution between ICT advancement, paradigm change to increasing dependence on uncaptured GDP, and people's preferences shift to suprafunctionality beyond economic value.

(5) This spin-off further accelerates lower cost and higher services, which also accelerates the foregoing virtuous cycle.

(6) Uber's success can be attributed to constructing such IDBM.

Sources of legal battles

Notwithstanding such a sophisticated business model, legal battles in several cities around the world were observed as Uber rapidly expanded globally. Sources of the contrast of success and failure can be attributed to its coevolution or disengagement with host institutions as follows:

(1) This contrast can be subject to Uber's growth rate and the institutional elasticity of the host.

(2) Countries/cities without battles have constructed a coevolutionary acclimatization system and harnessed the vigor of counterparts.

(3) This system induces CCSD, which consolidates the broad stakeholders including companies, employers, users, and governments, based on trust among them, for social demands.

(4) Thus, IDBM with CCSD would be critical for resilient IDBM coevolving with the institutional systems of the host.

Because Uber can be recognized as incorporating the inherent potential of IDBM with CCSD, its success in global expansion depends on the optimal balance of timing, pace, and selection of the host with indigenous institutional systems suitable enough to constructing coevolutionary acclimatization.

Implications

Given Uber's global expansion, the company has had coevolutionary success with institutional systems in some host countries/cities and legal battles in others. Due to these different outcomes, the sources of these contrasts resulting from business strategy, platform ecosystem design, and institutional systems in the host country/city should be further studied. It is important to recognize that optimal trajectory leading to coevolution with institutional systems should be considered flexible and dynamic manner depending on the extent of the dissemination of the business model, increasing impacts on traditional/competing customs and businesses.

The vigor of broad hidden innovation resources that have emerged from disruptive business models in the digital economy should be utilized by awaking and activating. This emerges a remarkable business model that transforms sleeping capable resources into a springboard for new innovation.

Given the significance of ICT and trust in IDBM with CCSD in the digitally rich environment, trust-based education in digitally rich learning environments would be further relevant area for further study.

4.2.3 Trust from overdrawing past information - Trust-based digitally rich learning environments[5]

4.2.3.1 Evolution of the disruptive business model that results in overdrawing of past information

The quality of higher education is crucial for innovation in the digital economy (Fig. AIII-3.1 in Appendix III-3). Such quality, in turn, is subject to a trust in teachers to deliver good education and the advancement of ICT (Fig. AIII-3.2). With these aspects in mind, this section attempts to analyze the dynamism of the coevolution between them.

Using a unique dataset representing the above system, an empirical numerical analysis of 20 countries was attempted. This analysis consisted of the rate of trust in teachers to provide good education in the context of quality of education and their social status, the level of higher education, and the state of ICT advancement toward digitally rich learning environments (Figs. AIII-3.3—3.6). These countries can be divided into three groups: ICT-advanced countries (*IACs: Finland, Singapore, Netherlands, Switzerland, UK, USA, Korea, Germany, Israel, Japan*), ICT-semiadvanced countries (*ISCs: Portugal, Spain*), and ICT-growing countries (*IGCs: Czech Republic, Turkey, Italy, China, Brazil, Greece*).

It was found that while *IACs* have embarked on the coevolution of ICT, higher education, and trust, *IGCs* have not been successful in this due to a vicious cycle between ICT and trust. Finland's educational success can be attributed to coevolution, which corresponds to the emergence of uncaptured GDP similarly to the leading edge of an IDBM. The paradox of education productivity in *IGCs* can be attributed to disengagement.

It is suggested that steady ICT advancement fully utilizing external resources in digitally rich learning environments may be essential for *IGCs* in achieving high quality of higher education. On the other hand, continuing innovation to transform learning environments into new, digitally rich learning environments should be maintained in *IACs*.

---

[5] See the details of the analysis in the authors' previous work (Watanabe et al., 2016c) as this analysis was based on it.

This section attempts to analyze a business model that creates a springboard for new innovation in the digital economy by activating ICT-driven **"trust by overdrawing past information"** in digitally rich learning environments.

4.2.3.2 Trust-based digital learning inducing innovation—a new approach

In the preceding section, we found that IBDM with CCSD explores new innovation resources in the digital economy. This section takes a new approach to constructing this dynamism based on Luhmann's postulate (1997) that trust is a consequence of "overdrawing" past information, as illustrated in Fig. 4.11.

Good quality higher education is crucial for economies that want to move up the value chain beyond simple production processes and products (World Economic Forum: WEF, 2013a). Quality is subject to trust in teachers to deliver good education (OECD, 2014a,b; Varkey Gems Foundation: VGF, 2014; Sahlberg, 2010; Stehlik, 2016) and the advancement of ICT leading to digitally rich learning environments (UNESCO, 2003). As a result, coevolution between higher education, trust in teachers, and the advancement of ICT has been gaining increasing significance.

This section aims to explore a new approach for systematically constructing the above-mentioned coevolution by using a unique dataset. This dataset represents the above system, which consists of the rate of trust in teachers to provide good education in the Global Teacher Status Index (VGF, 2014), which analyzes teacher's impact on educational performance,

Figure 4.11 Coevolution between information communication and technology, trust in teachers, and higher education.

together with statistics on higher education level (WEF, 2013a) and ICT advancement (WEF, 2013b). Using this dataset, we undertook an empirical numerical analysis of 20 countries consisting of *IAC, ISC,* and *IGC* with this coevolution dynamism.

Given the significant shift from traditional teaching practice to blended learning in which a student learns through delivery of content via digital media, and digitally rich innovative learning environments (DILEs), alongside the significant effect of the learner's ability to "overdraw" past information on trust (Luhmann, 1979), the state of a country in this shift has become crucial for its performance.

IACs have shifted to DILEs and constructed a coevolutionary dynamism between ICT, higher education, and trust. This corresponds to emerging uncaptured GDP, as observed in the IDBM (Watanabe et al., 2016b, 2017a).

ISCs are in transition from traditional teaching and learning environments (TTLEs) to DILEs and are experiencing an unsuccessful coevolution due to a vicious cycle between ICT advancement and higher educational level enhancement.

IGCs remain in traditional learning environments and suffers from disengagement due to a mismatch between ICT advancement and trust in teachers.

These findings give rise to suggestions for the respective countries concerning their successful coevolution, which depends on the state of their ICT advancement.

4.2.3.3 The effect of blended learning and teacher resistance
Prompted by the empirical findings above, the effect of the shift to blended learning and teacher's resistance to this shift was reviewed because this shift demonstrates the concave educational level in the transition from traditional technical practice. Of particular interest was the peculiar behavior of *ISC* in the transition from being an *IGC* to *IAC*, which brings a decline in higher educational level with the advancement of ICT.

The use of the Web and other Internet technologies in education has exploded in the last couple of decades (Chen et al., 2010), leading to the creation of digitally rich learning environments.

Blended learning, which introduces digital and online media to the education system by harnessing the vigor of the advancement of the Internet, is certain to increase the speed of this trend (Jeffrey et al., 2014). Under these circumstances, the contribution of ICT advancement to higher education can be developed in a hybrid manner through traditional teaching practice and blended learning.

While strong resistance by teachers to the use of new technology in education can impede the dependence on blended learning (Anderson and van Weert, 2002), once a certain higher education level has been attained, increasing dependence on blended learning will overcome such resistance (Jeferry et al., 2014), leading to coevolution between the advancement of ICT and further dependence on blended learning.

However, before such coevolution can be realized, the transition to blended learning results in a decline in higher education at its transition period.

An *ISCs* are in transition from being an *IGC* to an *IAC*, which is contrary to a normal trajectory as demonstrated by *IGCs,* and *IACs* shows a slightly negative coefficient. This corresponds to the decline in the transition period.

Based on this observation, Fig. 4.12 identifies the state of hybrid development of 20 countries in three groups.

Fig. 4.12 demonstrates that the concave trend of *ISCs* is a consequence of the transition from traditional teaching practice to blended learning. This reveals the unexpected behavior of the advancement of ICT that results in a decline in higher education level in the transition from *IGC* to *IAS*.

4.2.3.4 Coevolution and disengagement reassessed

These findings urges us to reassess the coevolution and disengagement dynamism between ICT, higher education level, and trust in teachers in the 20 countries.

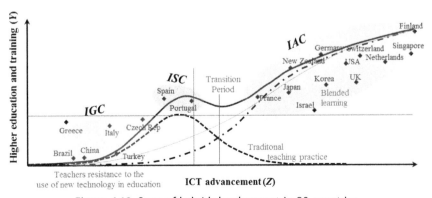

Figure 4.12 State of hybrid development in 20 countries.

It is revealed that contrary to general understanding, the advancement of ICT decreases higher education levels in *ISCs* as a result of their transition from traditional teaching practice to blended learning.

This reassessment identifies the state of digitally rich learning environments and subsequent coevolution and disengagement for the 20 countries, which depend on the state of their ICT advancement. This identification will provide insights into the respective countries regarding their priority countermeasures for coevolution between ICT advancement, higher education enhancement, and trust in teachers increase as suggested in Fig. AIII–3.7. This figure compares state of digitally rich learning environments, subsequent coevolution, and priority countermeasures among *IASs*, *ISCs*, and *IGCs*.

4.2.3.5 Discussion

There is a strong notion that the quality of higher education is crucial for the innovation of the digital economy. In addition, this quality is subject to a sophisticated system with trust in teachers and advancement of ICT. With these in mind, the dynamism of coevolution between them was analyzed.

An empirical numerical analysis of 20 countries was attempted with the help of a unique dataset representing the above-described system. This system consists of the rate of trust in teachers for providing good education in the context of the quality of the education system and the social status of teachers, the level of higher education and the state of ICT advancement toward digitally rich learning environments.

The following findings are noteworthy:

(1) ICT-driven trust-based higher education is becoming crucial for nations' competitiveness in DILEs.

(2) In such environments, ICT advancement, higher education, and trust in teachers are closely interweaved with each other.

(3) Given the significant shift from traditional teaching practice to blended learning toward DILEs, the state of a country in this shift has become crucial for its performance.

(4) *IACs* have shifted to DILEs and constructed coevolutionary dynamism between ICT, higher education, and trust.

(5) This coevolution corresponds to emerging uncaptured GDP as observed in the leading edge of IDBM.

(6) *ISCs* are in the transition from TTLEs to DILEs and unsuccessful coevolution due to a vicious cycle between ICT advancement and higher educational level enhancement.

(7) *IGCs* remain in TTLEs and suffer from disengagement due to a mismatch between ICT advancement and trust in teachers.

These findings led to the following suggestions for the respective countries about their successful coevolution being dependent on their state of ICT advancement:

(1) For *IACs*, transcending innovation, which transforms learning environments into digitally rich new learning environments, should be maintained.

(2) Timely transfer of coevolutionary resources to *IGCs* is needed to harness their vigor in a programmatic way.

(3) Inspired by the emergence of uncaptured GDP, IDBM that leads to digitally rich learning environments should be explored.

(4) For *ISCs*, a clear understanding of the state of transition from being an *IGC* to being an *IAC* should be maintained.

(5) Given that the advancement of ICT creates a decline in higher education, optimal supplement compensating this decline should be taken.

(6) Effective utilization of external resources for accelerating the shift to DILEs should be provided.

(7) For *IGCs*, effective utilization of external resources for the steady advancement of ICT should be made a priority.

(8) The consistent effort for a steady shift to DILEs should be made in a programmatic manner while maintaining an optimal balance with TTLEs.

This section explored a new systematic approach for coevolution between ICT advancement, higher education enhancement, and an increase in trust in teachers. This coevolution emerges a remarkable business model that transforms trust into a springboard for new innovation.

Further work should focus on in-depth analysis of institutional systems that accelerate or impede this coevolution and on a detailed microanalysis of specific initiatives including vision, leadership, and curriculum.

A further analysis of peculiar behavior at the transition to DILEs is another important subject to be undertaken. For that, a wider empirical analysis covering more countries should be considered. Furthermore, with the notion that trust depends on overdrawing of past information, a business model constructing coevolutionary acclimatization through harnessing the "vigor of time," as governing past memory ever experienced and decisive to consumers' behavior when shopping, should be envisioned.

4.2.4 Utmost gratification ever experienced - The commodification of past experiences[6]

4.2.4.1 Evolution of disruptive business model toward utilization of utmost gratification

As discussed in the previous section, the transition to a post-excessive-consumption society has included a shift in the preferences of consumers from economic functionality to suprafunctionality beyond economic value. Due to the nonavailability of desired products and services, consumer anger has increased and their urge to design and produce products has also increased. Consequently, to better understand consumer needs and desires, the coemergence of innovation-consumption has become critical. As pointed out in the preceding section, conceptualization of the consumer anger is a key subject for this coemergence.

Following this point, this analysis focused on the identification of how to conceptualize the voiceless voice of consumer anger. With this understanding, a new approach was attempted that integrates technometrics, psychophysiology, and engineering for advanced monitoring techniques.

Pilot experiments at supermarkets in both Japan and Finland have been conducted. The results demonstrate the significance of this approach. They also highlight the importance of commodifying learning experiences when reconstructing a virtuous cycle between ICT advancement and increased productivity. This cycle also helps coevolutionary acclimatization that harnesses the vigor of counterparts in nations and firms as well as at the consumer level.

The shift to a new socioeconomic trend, particularly to smart eco-conscious customer society establishes the foundation for the evolution of disruptive business models that leads to the awakening and utilization of **"utmost gratification ever experienced."**

This section attempts to analyze such a remarkable business model that creates a springboard for new innovation in the digital economy.

4.2.4.2 Harnessing utmost gratification for innovation—a new approach

Given the increasing initiative among consumers to innovate toward a post-excessive-consumption society (Matsuda, 2010, 2012; McDonagh, 2008; McDonagh et al., 2010; Watanabe, 2009; Watanabe et al., 2011),

---

[6] See the details of the analysis in the authors' previous works (Watanabe, 2010, 2013; Watanabe et al., 2011, 2012a) as this analysis was based on them.

development trajectory can be expected to be initiated by innovation and consumption coemergence (Watanabe et al., 2012a; Watanabe, 2013).

As the preceding analysis showed, while consumer anger has been growing, it remains intangible. Therefore, the key to innovation-consumption coemergence depends on how to conceptualize the "voice-less voice" of consumer anger.

Gibson (1977, 1979) postulated that the perception of the environment inevitably leads to some course of action. He stressed that "Affordances, or clues in the environment that indicate possibilities for action, are perceived in a direct, immediate way with no sensory processing." This postulate suggests that innovative goods emit tempting signals to consumers while consumers also emit signals anticipating an exciting function to be heroes/heroines in a drama (Kondo et al., 2007; Watanabe, 2009, 2010) as illustrated in Fig. AIII-4.1 in Appendix III-4.

The correspondence of consumer demand and innovative goods triggered by the foregoing resonance produces new value, which in turn enhances demand and innovation and leverages the spirally developing virtuous cycle as a consequence of the coemergence of innovation and consumption as illustrated in Fig. AIII-4.2 (Polanyi, 1969; Ishii, 2009).

Innovation-consumption coemergence is triggered by resonance between signals emitted by both innovative goods/services and consumers, and resonance is induced by learning both by consumers and innovative goods/services (Watanabe, 2009; Watanabe et al., 2012b).

4.2.4.3 Consumers psychophysiology behavior

Motivation is considered a basis of consumers psychophysiology behavior. This is a condition that energizes behavior and gives it direction. It is experienced subjectively as a conscious desire (Baudrilard, 1998; Hilgard et al., 1999). Toates (1986) explained this behavior that "An external stimulus, such as the sight of food, is compared to the memory of its past reward value. At the same time, physiological signals of hunger and satiety modulate the potential value at the moment. These two types of information are integrated to produce the final incentive motivation for the external stimulus, which is manifested in behavior and conscious experience."

These postulates suggest that while consumers' communicative functions in response to attractive goods include changes in heartbeat and skin temperature (Levenson et al., 1990), emotional expressions by the face demonstrates their experience of emotions most vividly. This is called the facial feedback hypothesis (Tompkins, 1962, Rutledge and Hupka, 1985).

There exist two body temperature regulation pathways. While sympathetic body temperature regulation pathway against a stress burden due to surprise or gratification decreases facial temperature through vasoconstriction, the metabolic body temperature regulation pathway in response to an increase in brain activity increases in facial temperature. Consumers' facial temperature change when met with innovative goods is subject to the consequence of these two pathways.

In addition to Modigliani (1965), Maslow (1954) and Katahira (1987, 2003) demonstrated that people's utmost gratification ever experienced is memorized in the brain. When consumers are confronted with innovative goods, it collates with the utmost gratification they have ever experienced, and they search for an existing learning record in the brain. Because this search activity elevates brain temperature, to maintain homeostasis, the heat in the brain accumulated by elevated brain temperature should be released from the face, leading to elevated facial temperature (Collaborative Research Center of Meisei University, 2010). This can be attributed to the metabolic control system. At the same time, in the process of searching, upon confronting surprise or gratification, vasoconstriction that narrows blood vessels and decreases blood flow emerges, resulting in descending facial temperature. This can be attributed to the sympathetic nervous system

This reaction by consumers when they encounter innovative goods represents the degree of resonance between affordance emitting tempting signals from innovative goods incorporating supreme functionality (Gibson, 1977, 1979) and aura emitting anticipating signals from consumers anticipating an exciting function (Collaborative Research Center of Meisei University, 2010). For this reason, consumers' facial temperature can be considered to represent the degree of the resonance between innovative goods and consumers. Fig. AIII-4.3 illustrates this postulate.

To understand the resonance between innovative goods and consumers, pilot experiments measuring the facial temperature of consumers encountering attractive goods were conducted at leading supermarkets both in Tokyo (February 2011) and Jyväskylä, Finland (March 2012).

Fig. AIII-4.4 demonstrates the advanced thermography used for the experiments. This thermography enables examinees' facial temperatures to be monitored in a spot at a 0.01-degree level without notifying the examinees. Monitoring records are automatically transferred to a PC, whereby actual states of consumers' reaction against innovative goods can be monitored and analyzed.

Figs. AIII–4.5 and 4.6 demonstrate the general arrangements of the pilot experiments in Tokyo and Finland. Fig. A_{III}–4.5 shows the target product in Tokyo, melon bread, which has been gaining in popularity among Japanese. In Finland (Fig. AIII–4.6), this target was cosmetics, due to their strong interest and attractiveness.

The typical results of the experiments are demonstrated in Fig. 4.13 (Tokyo) and AIII.4.7 (Finland).

These results demonstrate the effects of attractive goods in changing consumers' facial temperature, the influence of sales promoters' recommendations on such change, and a significant effect of learning on facial temperature change.

4.2.4.4 The commodification of learning experiences

Pilot experiments demonstrate the significance of learning experiences in inducing the decision on purchase in consumers by promoting them to recall their positive instances of utmost gratification. Because innovation-consumption coemergence is triggered by resonance between signals emitted by both innovative goods/services and consumers, this resonance is induced by coevolutionary learning between consumers and innovative goods/services (Watanabe, 2009; Watanabe et al., 2011, 2012b). Thus, the

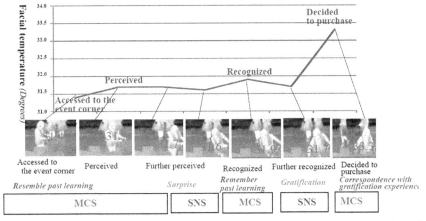

Figure 4.13 Standard pattern of facial temperature change in purchased (Tokyo). (*Source: Watanabe, C., 2013. Innovation-consumption co-emergence leads a resilience business. Innovation and Supply Chain Management 7 (3), 92–104.*)

commodification of learning experiences would be essential for innovation-consumption coemergence.

Based on such understanding, Fig. 4.14 proposes a platform for the commodification of learning experiences that contributes to activating innovation-consumption coemergence.

4.2.4.5 Discussion

The increasing significance of the effective utilization of soft innovation resources (*SIRs*) against the trap of ICT advancement in the digital economy, alongside growing anger among consumers toward a post-excessive-consumption society, highlight the critical role of innovation-consumption coemergence. For this, conceptualization of the voiceless voice of consumer anger has left as a key subject to be undertaken. This suggests the significance of a new approach integrating technometrics, psychophysiology, and engineering for advanced monitoring techniques.

Pilot experiments at supermarkets in both Japan and Finland demonstrated the significance of this approach and have highlighted the importance of the commodification of learning experiences.

Noteworthy findings include the following:

(1) The dramatic advancement of the Internet alongside a post-excessive-consumption society has accelerated a shift in the preferences of consumers from economic functionality to suprafunctionality beyond economic value.

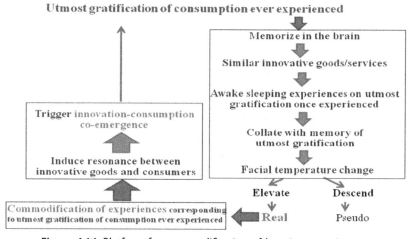

Figure 4.14 Platform for commodification of learning experiences.

(2) Due to the nonavailability of desired products and services, consumer anger has increased.

(3) Consequently, the coemergence of innovation-consumption has become critical.

(4) This coemergence is triggered by resonance between innovative goods/services and consumers, which is induced by coevolutionary learning between consumers and innovative goods/services.

(5) The key subject for this coemergence is conceptualization of the voiceless voice of consumer anger.

(6) Facial temperature hypothesis can lead a way to this conceptualization.

(7) The advanced psychophysiological measuring approach provides constructive elucidation of this dynamism.

(8) This dynamism explores the way to the commodification of learning experiences.

These findings supply the following policy suggestions:

(1) Both partner (e.g., producers vs. consumers; advanced vs. growing economies) should realize the limits to individual strength and the significance of fusion with global best practices.

(2) Both partners should make every effort in constructing a coevolutionary acclimatization trajectory.

(3) Such a trajectory can be expected to accelerate from stimulation of innovation-consumption coemergence.

(4) The commodification of learning experiences contributes to constructing this coemergence.

This commodification emerges as a remarkable business model that transforms trust into a springboard for new innovation.

The points of anticipated future works are summarized as follows:

(1) Further exploration of the possible applicability of advanced thermography.

(2) Development of analytical methods enabling an explicit link between consumers' prior learning experiences and facial temperature change.

(3) Elimination of the biases for the sufficient use of thermography.

(1) Development of experimental sectors (e.g., apparel, home electric appliances, mobile phones).

(2) Comparative analysis with more institutional systems, particularly with emerging markets.

(3) The treatment of personal data obtained through the experiment must be carefully addressed.

4.2.5 Memories and future dreams - Coevolution of streaming and live music[7]

4.2.5.1 Evolution of disruptive business model toward utilization of memories and future dreams

As the digitization of music has gained popularity, there is strong fear about an impending collapse of the music industry as occurring in other print media industries such as newspapers and book publishing.

However, recent changes in the music industry initiated by a resurgence of the live music industry are giving rise to expectations for the survival and growth of the music industry. The parallel paths of the increasing popularity of streaming services and a resurgence of live music suggest the significance of their coevolution for the sustainability of the music industry.

Aiming to demonstrate this hypothetical view, this section attempts to elucidate the coevolution dynamism between the increasing popularity of streaming music and the resurgence of live music.

An empirical analysis of monthly trends in the US music industry by its sectors revealed that (1) the coevolution between streaming and live music industries have functioned well over the last few years, (2) the live music industry has incorporated a self-propagating function by assimilating innovations previously initiated by digital music, (3) given the above coevolution, the recent resurgent trend in the music industry can be sustained, (4) the advancement of digital innovations has transformed the live music industry into a "live-concert-streaming music industry" (*LCSM*) that further enables the participative creativity (Choi and Burnes, 2013) of its stakeholders.

This analysis suggests that *LCSM* induces IDBM with CCSD by activating "**memories and future dreams**" and explores a new business model for the development of cultural industries in the digital economy.

This section attempts to analyze such a remarkable business model.

4.2.5.2 Coevolution of streaming and live music—a new approach

Digital music, which emerged in 2004, is considered the premier example of digital innovation. It has provided the music industry with new disruptive business models and new digital music products and services for consumers. The United States plays a leading role in the global music industry and has taken the locomotive role in the development and

---

[7] See the details of the analysis in the authors' previous works (Watanabe, 2017; Naveed et al., 2017) as this analysis was based on them.

consumption of digital music as demonstrated in Fig. AIII-5.1 in Appendix III-5.

Fig. AIII-5.2 overviews the development trajectory of the US music industry from 1950 to 2015 by revenues of its different sectors: live music and recorded music.

In 2010, the continued decline in the music industry revenues suddenly changed and turned upward largely due to the renaissance of the live music industry. Music revenues increased by 15% between 2010 and 2013 and reached 30% by 2015.

Fig. AIII-5.3 reviews the details of the actors supporting this resurgence, which also suggests that streaming music has been gaining popularity and demonstrating sustainable growth by replacing music downloading services.

A clear shift has been observed in the number of consumers who select streaming as a primary source of their music consumption contrary to all other formats of recorded music. With every other format of the recorded music industry declining, it seems that streaming music could be the potential driving force behind the growth of the live music industry (Fly, 2016).

This pattern suggested that there could be parallel paths of sustainable growth in which the resurgence of live music may have a coevolutionary dynamism.

This resurgence can also be attributed to the assimilation of the preceding digital innovations, particularly those initiated by streaming services and those introduced by downloading services.

Furthermore, the general trend in the shift of people's preferences from economic functionality to suprafunctionality beyond economic value, as reviewed in the preceding sections, may further accelerate our higher dependence on live music while maintaining streaming as a complement of this radical shift, because of its comparative advantages of discoverability, accessibility, and portability.

These observations convince us that streaming, accompanied by live music sales, may be the driving force behind the survival and new growth of the music industry (Fly, 2016).

These trends suggest that live music will transform music into the new music industry. Fly (2016) suggested that "It is likely that a combined industry consisting of both streaming and live music will continue to grow shortly." He also anticipated that to take advantage of this trend, the artists would likely find the most success in promoting their music through streaming services and by conducting live tours.

However, all these analyses remain phenomenological observations or conceptual analyses, and none of the studies have analyzed the structural dynamism that may enable a resurgence of the music industry.

Inspired by this state, an empirical numerical analysis analyzing this structural dynamism is attempted in this section.

With a hypothetical view that the coevolution of the increasing popularity of streaming music and the subsequent assimilation of the preceding innovations in digital music are sources of the resurgence of live music, based on econometric modeling, an empirical analysis to demonstrate this view is undertaken.

The dynamism analysis was conducted by using the monthly development trajectories of different sectors of the US music industry for the last 3 decades, with special attention given to the era of digital music.

4.2.5.3 Self-propagating function incorporated in live music industry

It was anticipated that the coevolution between streaming and live music might enable live music to assimilate the preceding digital innovation accumulated in streaming music. This set of innovations also assimilated the preceding innovation (Watanabe et al., 2001, 2002) from downloading music. We expect to see that this assimilation would be a driving force for the resurgence of live music.

Fig. AIII-5.4 illustrates the concept of assimilation of spillover technology in this dynamism and demonstrates the trend in the assimilation capacity of the live music industry.

Fig. A_{III}-5.4 shows that while the assimilation capacity of live music continued to decline particularly after the economic recession in 2009, this changed to an upward trend from late 2010 and dramatically increased from the middle of 2013.

This significant assimilation of digital innovation from digital music through the coevolution with streaming music enabled live music to incorporate a self-propagating function that enhances the functionality of live music. This contributes to the increase in its revenues and assets as illustrated in Fig. 4.15.

4.2.5.4 Transformation into a "live-concert-streaming music industry"

These analyses demonstrate that the recent noteworthy stream in the resurgence of the US music industry can be attributed to the coevolution

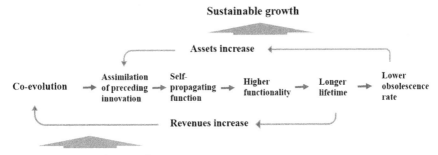

Figure 4.15 Scheme for sustaining the resurgent trend of the music industry.

between the streaming music and live music industries and their assimilation of preceding innovations.

To address this concern, the structure governing the future trends in the respective music industries and the tasks to be carried out to maintain the coevolution of live music and digital music initiated by streaming music were analyzed. by using the hybrid logistic growth model. Fig. 4.16 demonstrates monthly trends in revenues of physical music, digital music, and live music for January 1985 to December 2015. Prospects to 2030 thereon are also illustrated in the figures.

Table AIII-5.1 tabulates the results of the hybrid logistic growth regression for three music industry segments, which demonstrates an extremely high level of statistical significance.

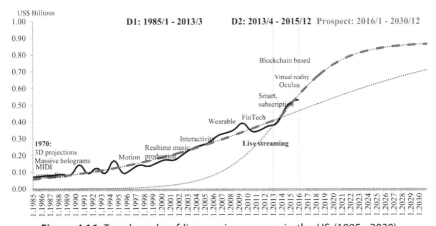

Figure 4.16 Trends and pof live music revenues in the US (1985–2030).

4.2.5.5 Discussion

This analysis identified a resurgent trend in the US music industry that is on the brink of an impending collapse due to diminishing revenues as a consequence of digitization. Based on this identification, structural sources enabling such a resurgence were analyzed.

This analysis shows that the recent resurgence of live music in parallel with the increasing popularity of streaming services could effectively save the music industry. The analysis was based on the possibility that live music has effectively assimilated digital innovation from digital music through its coevolution with streaming music.

An empirical analysis of monthly trends in the US music industry by sectors over the last 3 decades was conducted and revealed the following noteworthy features:

(1) A coevolution between the streaming and live music industries has functioned well over the last few years.

(2) The live music industry has incorporated a self-propagating function by assimilating its preceding innovations initiated by digital music.

(3) The recent resurging trend in the music industry can be attributed to the coevolution between the streaming and live music industries.

(4) This coevolution has enabled the live music to assimilate digital innovation initiated by digital music.

(5) The advancement of digital innovation such as AI, ML, fintech, VR, and big data has enabled the sustainability and activation of this coevolution while leading the live music industry to transform into the "live-concert-streaming music industry" (*LCSM*), which enables participative creativity for all stakeholders,

(6) *LCSM* corresponds to the historical demand of consumers as *a)* consumers' propensity has shifted from viewership to physical ownership, digital ownership, access to viewership and access, *b)* consumers' preferences have shifted from passive listening or viewing to access to widening choice, participation, integration, cocreation, and participative creativity, *c)* emergence of the collaborative cultural landscape, *d)* collaboration of live entertainment and digital distribution, and *e)* transformation of the complex chain of live music with multiple stakeholders into a more straightforward productive chain.

(7) In this collaborative cultural environment, the importance of trust among participating stakeholders (e.g., artists, music providers, ticket sellers, consumers) has become even more crucial.

(8) The importance of trust together with the above points, suggests the significance of a trust-based IDBM with CCSD for the successful development of the cultural industries.

These findings give rise to the following insights about the sustainable growth of the music industry:

(1) The establishment of a platform where streamed music services would participate with live music to construct a coevolutionary relationship between them.

(2) Participative creativity of stakeholders should be nourished.

(3) Experiences of the preceding trust-based IDBM with CCSD initiatives in the sharing economy such as Uber's ridesharing revolution provide many learning opportunities.

(4) The digitization of music and the coevolution of streaming and live music is a crucial step for the resurgence of the music industry.

(5) Active introduction of advanced digital innovations should be initiated by providing a testbed for the advancement of such innovations.

(6) Next-generation of the "live-concert-streaming music industry" (*LCSM*) should be envisioned.

This section explored a blueprint for the future of the music industry and provided a prototype of a dynamic system called trust-based IDBM with CCSD for the further development of cultural industries. The historical demand for these systems can be applied not only to the music industry but also to other broader cultural industries, and lessons from the music industry can provide helpful guidelines.

LCSM awakens memories and future dreams from which emerges a remarkable business model that transforms trust into a springboard for new innovation.

Further research should focus on the following subjects:

(1) In-depth analysis of country-specific institutional systems, accelerating the coevolution between the live and streaming music industries.

(2) The optimal introduction of advanced digital innovations.

(3) A wider empirical analysis covering more countries.

4.2.6 Untapped resources and vision - Harnessing the vigor of untapped resources of women's potential[8]

4.2.6.1 Evolution of disruptive business models toward harnessing untapped resources and vision

The harnessing of untapped resources has become essential for inclusive growth in digital economies. The harnessing of women's potential is an

---

[8] See the details of the analysis in the authors' previous work (Watanabe et al., 2017b) as this analysis was based on it.

urgent subject in this context, and successive initiatives have been flourishing in many countries.

However, given the institutional complexity of the issue, uniformed nonsystematic approaches are hardly satisfactory in achieving a timely solution.

Against this backdrop, this section attempts to analyze a new ICT-driven disruptive innovation that may nurture uncaptured GDP by harnessing untapped resources such as women's economic potential.

Using a unique dataset representing the state of gender balance improvement, an empirical numerical analysis of 44 countries was attempted. The 44 nations were classified as emerging countries (EMCs), industrialized countries (INCs), and countries with specific cultures (CSCs), particularly cultures based on the traditions of male-dominated societies (see Fig. AIII-6.1 in Appendix III-6).

It was found that while INCs have achieved high performance in coevolution between "ethnocultural development," ICT advancement, and gender balance improvement, EMCs have been constrained by low ICT advancement. Also, despite their high economic level, CSCs have been constrained by a traditionally male-dominated culture.

This section attempts a new practical approach exploring a remarkable business model by harnessing **"untapped resources and vision"** for sustainable growth.

4.2.6.2 Harnessing the vigor of women's potential—a new approach

Bridging the gender divide is a matter not only of fairness but also of effective governance and inclusive growth (OECD, 2016a,b). It has been demonstrated that companies with more women board directors experienced higher financial performance (Catalyst, 2005). The growing participation of women in the labor market has been a major engine of global growth and competitiveness (ILO, 2015).

However, despite growing awareness of the benefits of gender equality in decision-making, the pace of progress in achieving this has been slow and varies considerably across countries (UNWomen, 2015; OECD, 2016a,b; FINNCHAM, 2016).

To date, several studies have identified sources that impede gender balance improvement. The OECD (2014a,b) pointed to the presence of a range of external and internal barriers in all areas of the public domain, including cultural barriers, structural barriers, lack of gender-disaggregated evidence and accountability mechanisms, and self-imposed barriers. The UNDP (2010) revealed that while there is explicit evidence regarding a virtual cycle between economic growth and gender balance improvement, emerging countries cannot afford to overcome the constraints of low incomes. UNESCO and Institute of Statistics (2014) noted the limits of scientific resources with women's initiatives.

Moreover, a few papers have noted the significance of cultural dimensions in activating untapped female resources (Wiles et al., 1995; Stedham and Yamamura, 2004; Daechun and Kim, 2007; Carrasco et al., 2012). Hofstede (1991) postulated that a nation's culture can be classified into five dimensions: "power distance" (inequality), "individualism" (the degree to which individuals are integrated into groups), "masculinity" (the distribution of roles between the genders), "uncertainty avoidance" (the extent to which a culture programs its members to feel either uncomfortable or comfortable in unstructured situations), and "long-term orientation."

Wiles et al., (1995), Stedham and Yamamura (2004), Daechun and Kim (2007), and Carrasco et al. (2012) identified the significance of cultural dimensions, particularly of "masculinity" and "individualism" in gender balance improvement (see Table AII-14 in Appendix II-4 for details on these concepts and survey results).

4.2.6.3 Gender-balanced leadership in the digital economy

This section analyzed the trilateral coevolution between "ethnocultural development," gender balance improvement, and ICT advancement. The Gender Balance Index (GBI) and intensity of male-dominated society (*IMS*: the ratio of "masculinity" and "individualism") based on the cluster of EMCs, INCs, and CSCs were used. Fig. AIII-6.2 illustrates the dynamism inducing this trilateral coevolution.

(1) Contribution of the gender balance index to economic growth

Fig. AIII-6.3 illustrates the correlation between the GBI and GDP per capita. EMCs demonstrate an extremely low elasticity of gender balance improvement to GDP per capita, followed by INCs and CSCs. This suggests that the EMCs pursue avenues toward economic growth other than through gender balance improvement. The higher income level of CSCs despite the lowest level of the GBI can be attributed to their highest elasticity and reveals the structural impediment blocking gender balance improvement.

(2) Contribution of economic growth to information communication and technology advancement

Fig. AIII-6.4 illustrates the correlation between GDP per capita and ICT advancement. EMCs, INCs, and CSCs share a similar level of elasticity, which suggests that all nations' ICT grows uniformly with income growth in the digital economy.

(3) Gender balance improvement induced by information communication and technology and blocked by male-dominated society

While ICT advancement contributes to gender balance improvement, this improvement is blocked by cultural dimensions. Fig. 4.17 illustrates these multiple correlations.

CSCs demonstrate an extremely high negative elasticity of the intensity of male-dominated society to gender balance improvement. This can be a substantial source of the lowest level of gender balance improvement despite high levels of both income and ICT. EMCs represent the highest elasticity of ICT to this balance, which provides expectation that their gender balance could be improved once they achieve ICT advancement.

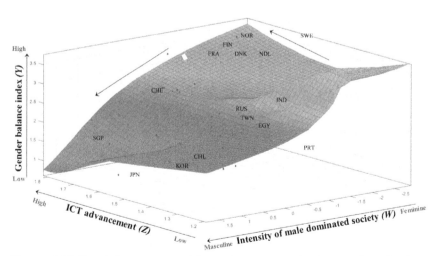

Figure 4.17 Correlation among information communication and technology advancement, intensity of male-dominated society, and GBI in 44 countries (2013).

$$\ln Y = -1.19 + 2.63\, D_1 \ln Z + 2.12\, D_2 \ln Z \quad \textbf{\textit{adj.R}}^2 \quad 0.734$$
$$(-1.30)^{**}(3.93)(3.70)$$
$$-0.41\, D_1 \ln W - 0.37\, D_2 \ln W - 2.49 D_3 \ln W + 1.64 D$$
$$(-1.96)^* \quad (-4.01) \quad (-4.26) \quad (3.55)$$

Y: Gender Balance Index; W: intensity of male-dominated society (M/I); Z: ICT advancement (NRI); all are logarithmic values. D_1, D_2, and D_3: coefficient dummy variables corresponding to EMC, INC, and CSC, respectively; D: dummy variable (SGP = 1, others = 0) Figures in parentheses are t-statistics; all are significant at the 1% level except *5% and **15%.

(4) Gender balance improvement supported by income growth and blocked by male-dominated society

While income increase contributes to gender balance improvement, this improvement is blocked by cultural dimensions. Fig. AIII-6.5 illustrates this multiple correlation.

Similar to Fig. 4.17, CSCs demonstrate an extremely high negative elasticity of the intensity of male-dominated society to gender balance improvement, as this is considered a substantial source of their lowest level of gender balance improvement, despite the high level of income and ICT. EMCs record the highest elasticity of income to this balance, which provides expectation that their gender balance could be improved once they achieve growth.

(5) Information communication and technology contribution to income growth

Fig. AIII-6.6 illustrates a correlation between ICT advancement and GDP per capita. INCs demonstrate the highest elasticity of ICT advancement to GDP per capita increase, followed by CSCs. EMCs lag behind the two groups, suggesting that they require further improvement in the introduction and utilization of ICT.

(6) Information communication and technology advancement stimulated by gender balance improvement

Fig. AIII-6.7 illustrates a correlation between the GBI and ICT advancement. INCs record the highest elasticity of gender balance improvement to ICT advancement, followed by CSCs and EMCs. This suggests EMCs need dramatic advancements in women's ICT involvement and an increase in women's contribution to ICT advancement through effective ICT utilization and development.

4.2.6.4 Consequences of coevolutionary dynamism

Fig. 4.18 illustrates trilateral coevolutionary dynamism induced by the foregoing six coevolutions.

Table AIII-6.1 summarizes the elasticities of the trilateral coevolution. Looking at this table, we note that while EMCs demonstrate the highest level of elasticity of GDP per capita to gender balance improvement … due to an extremely low level of elasticity of gender balance improvement to ICT advancement $(Y \rightarrow Z)$ and elasticity of ICT to GDP per capita $(Z \rightarrow X)$, their performance regarding the trilateral coevolution results in a low level. Contrary to this low performance by EMCs, INCs demonstrate explicit performance in their trilateral coevolution. This can be attributed to their outperformed elasticity of gender balance improvement to ICT advancement $(Y \rightarrow Z)$, supported by the lowest impediment of IMS. $(W \rightarrow Y)$.

4.2.6.5 Discussion

In light of the increasing significance of harnessing the vigor of women's potential in digital economies, an empirical numerical analysis focusing on the trilateral coevolution between "ethnocultural development," gender balance improvement, and ICT advancement in 44 countries was attempted.

Noteworthy findings include the following:
(1) GBI/GDP per capita can be an effective supportive tool in identifying the state of gender balance improvement.
(2) Furthermore, gender balance improvement is subject not only to income level but also to cultural dimensions, particularly to "muscularity" and "individualism."
(3) The gender balance intensity level in 44 countries can be classified into EMCs, INCs, and CSCs.
(4) INCs demonstrate explicit performance in the trilateral coevolution between "ethnocultural development," gender balance improvement, and ICT advancement.
(5) EMCs remains at an extremely low level of this elasticity, resulting in the lowest performance in the trilateral coevolution. However, it is anticipated that once sufficient ICT advancement prevails, a virtuous cycle leading to income growth and gender balance improvement can be expected.

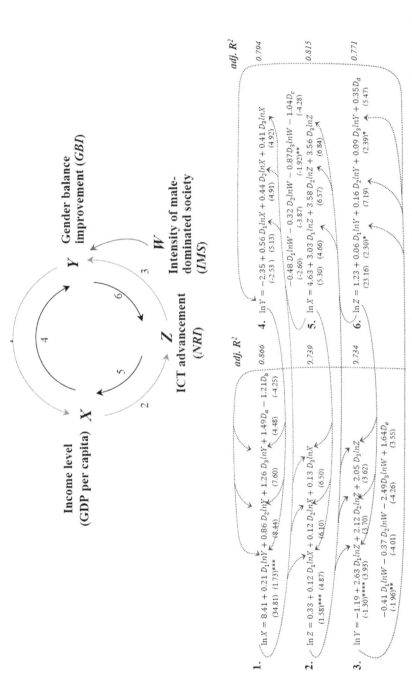

Figure 4.18 *Coevolutionary dynamism occurring among "econocultural" position, gender balance improvement, and information communication and technology advancement in 44 countries (2013). D: dummy variables—D_1, D_2, D_3 (EMC, INC, CSC = 1, others = 0, respectively), D_a (JPN, KOR = 1, others = 0), D_b (IND, PHL = 1, others = 0), D_c (JPN, CHL = 1, others = 0), D_d (CHE, JPN, KOR, SGP, TWN = 1, others = 0), D_e (SGP = 1, others = 0). Figures in parentheses are t-statistics; all are significant at the 1% level except* *2%, **5%, ***10%, and ****20%.

(6) Despite their high levels of income and ICT advancement, CSCs remain at the lowest level of gender balance intensity, which can be attributed to their traditional high-intensity male-dominated society.

These findings give rise to the following suggestions for respective countries about their successful trilateral coevolution:

(1) Every effort should focus on the construction of the trilateral coevolution between "ethnocultural development," gender balance improvement, and ICT advancement.

(2) The effective development and utilization of ICT should be of the highest priority for EMCs in constructing their trilateral coevolution.

(3) The construction of a coevolutionary acclimatization structure should be a significant endeavor for INCs and CSCs in this context.

(4) Address cultural dimensions that block gender balance improvement efforts in CSCs by constructing an ICT advancement system in male-dominated societies.

(5) To do this, the construction of a self-propagating function should be made the highest priority.

(6) This construction should lead the way to enable the emergence of uncaptured GDP, which in turn accelerates the harnessing of untapped resources.

This harnessing emerges a remarkable business model that transforms untapped resources and vision into a springboard for new innovation.

Further work should focus on complementing unexplored analyses as well as in-depth analysis of success and failure trajectories concerning gender balance improvement. Analyses of success and failure cases should be enriched.

4.3 Soft innovation resources

4.3.1 Harness the vigor of innovation resources in the four dimensions

The six remarkable disruptive business models reviewed in the preceding section can be considered products induced by the "great coevolution" due to the new stream of unique digital innovation created through spin-off dynamism, and the shift to new socioeconomic trends, as reviewed in Fig. 4.6 and illustrated in Fig. 4.19.

These businesses seek to harness the vigor of innovation resources in the four dimensions of space and time, as tabulated in Table 4.3.

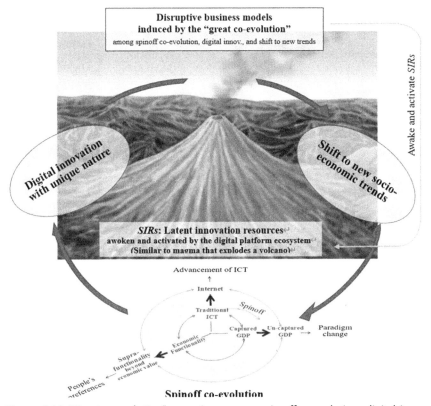

Figure 4.19 "Great coevolution" occurring among spin-off coevolution, digital inno-vation, and shifts to new trends that induce disruptive business models.

4.3.2 Emergence of soft innovation resources

While these innovation resources have not been efficiently utilized or have been unable to be utilized, advances in ICT and subsequent platforms that consolidate all stakeholders' challenges for social demands have turned such difficulties into a real deployment by awakening and activating latent re-sources. Thus, the foregoing remarkable disruptive business models can be perceived as typical IDBM with CCSD. They have awoken and activated latent innovation resources as follows:

(1) The driving force of coevolutionary dynamism among Internet advancement, dependence on uncaptured GDP, and a shift in people's preferences to suprafunctionality beyond economic value.

Table 4.3 Vigor of innovation resources in four dimensions.

Innovation resources / Time perspective	Past	Current	Future
Shift in people's preferences	Economic functionality	Suprafunctionality	Digital suprafunctionality
Uber's ridesharing revolution	Sleeping resources	Trust-based tripartism cooperation	Autonomous electronic transportation system
Trust-based digitally rich learning environments	Knowledge and experiences	Overdrawing past information	Brain computer interfaces
Commodification of past experiences	Utmost gratification ever experienced	Conceptualization of invisible voice of consumers	Commodification of experiences
Coevolution of streaming and live music	Past unforgettable memories and experiences	Invoking memories, synchronizing future dream	Virtual participation
Untapped resources of women's potential	Limited participation and opportunity	Harnessing the vigor of untapped resources	Ambitious vision for harnessing untapped resources

(2) **Sleeping resources** as nonoperational cars and drivers as well as idling time can be awoken and utilized effectively through the Internet and smartphones as observed by Uber's case.

(3) **Trust** by overdrawing past information that can be accelerated by the Internet.

(4) **The utmost gratification ever experienced** leading to consumption that effectively recalled by the Internet.

(5) **Memory and dreams** are recalled and drawn on actively by the Internet.

(6) **Untapped resources** are effectively utilized and envisioned by the Internet.

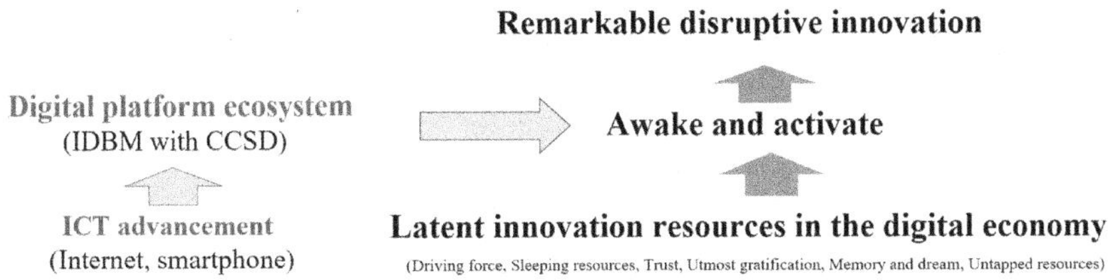

Remarkable disruptive innovation

Digital platform ecosystem
(IDBM with CCSD)

⇨   **Awake and activate**

ICT advancement
(Internet, smartphone)

Latent innovation resources in the digital economy
(Driving force, Sleeping resources, Trust, Utmost gratification, Memory and dream, Untapped resources)

Figure 4.20 Scheme of soft innovation resources in emerging disruptive innovation.

These latent innovation resources that are awoken and activated by the IDBM with CCSD can be called *SIRs*. *SIRs* can be defined as latent innovation resources to be awoken and activated by the digital platform ecosystem.[9] The emergence of *SIRs* depends on the advances in ICT, particularly the Internet as reviewed above. Thus, *SIRs* may produce disruptive innovation upon successfully utilized with this dynamism, as illustrated in Fig. 4.20.

4.3.3 Features and function of soft innovation resources

4.3.3.1 Specific features of soft innovation resources

SIRs are considered condensates and crystals of the advancement of the Internet (Tou et al., 2018a,b) and consist of the Internet-based resources that have either been sleeping, have been untapped or are the results of multisided interaction in the markets where consumers are looking for functionality beyond an economic value (Tou et al., 2018a). The magnitude of *SIRs* is proportional to the interactions with users according to Metcalfe's law.[10]

4.3.3.2 Role and function of soft innovation resources

The effective utilization of *SIRs* contributes to an increase in gross R&D (consisting of indigenous R&D investment and assimilated *SIRs*), which leads to growth and activates the latent self-propagating function indigenous to ICT (Watanabe and Hobo, 2004). This, in turn, induces functionality development, leading to suprafunctionality beyond economic value (Watanabe and Hobo, 2004). This corresponds to people's

---

[9] More precisely, *SIRs* are defined as latent innovation resources in the digital economy, which can be awoken and activated by deploying IDBM with CCSD. Their activation possibility can be attributed to ICT's indigenous self-propagating nature.

[10] The effect of a telecommunication network is proportional to the square of the number of connected users of the system.

preferences shift and induces further advancement of the Internet. Furthermore, this advancement accelerates the increasing dependence on uncaptured GDP, which leverages the harnessing of the vigor of *SIRs*. At the same time, the advancement of the Internet induces *SIRs*, as they are crystals of the Internet. Thus, a virtuous cycle exists between the emergence and utilization of *SIRs*, suprafunctionality beyond economic value, the advancement of the Internet, dependence on uncaptured GDP, and further leverage for *SIRs* emergence, as illustrated in Fig. 4.21 (Tou et al., 2019b).

4.3.4 Hybrid role of soft innovation resources

Moreover, it cannot be overlooked that *SIRs* also contribute to captured GDP increases by removing the structural impediments to its growth. An example of this can be observed in Finland's recent resurgence in GDP growth (Tou et al., 2018a,b).

It has been demonstrated that *SIRs* function in the removal of structural impediments of GDP growth (and subsequent growth of economic functionality), such as the conflict between the public, employers and labor

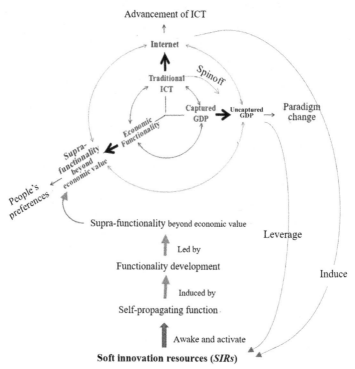

Figure 4.21 Scheme of soft innovation resources in emerging disruptive innovation.

unions, gender disparity, and the increasing discrepancies in an aging society. Thus, the spontaneous creation of uncaptured GDP through effective utilization of *SIRs* contributes to the resurgence of captured GDP growth by its hybrid function, which also activates a self-propagating function, as illustrated in the lower part of Fig. 4.21 (Watanabe et al., 2018c,d; Tou et al., 2018b). (See the mathematical details in A1.4.2 in Appendix I.)

4.3.5 Trigger of neo open innovation

The use of *SIRs* is a novel innovation applied to highly intensified R&D firms for their sustainable growth, thereby avoiding a decline in productivity. The authors in previous studies described this hypothetical view (Watanabe et al., 2016b, 2017a; Naveed et al., 2018) and identified that while such a transformative circumstance in the digital economy results in a decline in productivity, global ICT firms endeavor to survive by spontaneous creation of uncaptured GDP through harnessing the vigor of *SIRs* (Watanabe et al., 2018c,d).

Global R&D leader Amazon clearly demonstrates this in deploying its unique R&D-driven business model (see Chapter 6).

Based on its unique business model and ambitious attempt at customer-centric R&D-driven advancement, Amazon has developed its comprehensive empire chain, big data collection system, and the architecture for participation, harnessing the power of users, and leading to user-driven innovation. This innovation, in turn, accelerates the advancement of the Internet. The advanced Internet awakens and induces environmentally friendly *SIRs*.[11] Because *SIRs* are considered condensates and crystals of the advancement of the Internet (Tou et al., 2019b), in line with Metcalfe's law, the magnitude of *SIRs* is proportional to the interactions with users. Therefore, Amazon's user-driven innovation strongly awakens and induces broad areas of *SIRs* in a marketplace, as exemplified below, consisting of Internet-based resources that have been either sleeping or untapped, and it results in multisided interaction in the markets where the consumer is looking for functionality beyond economic value. For example, Amazon has been contributing to current global significant tasks to attain the sustainable development goals (*SDGs*), and its cloud service, Amazon Web Services (AWS), has helped 16 start-ups worldwide to achieve their *SDGs*.

---

[11] Amazon stressed that as Earth's most consumer-centric company, it works every day to offer the shopping experience with the lowest environmental impact on the planet (Phipps, 2018; Naveed et al., 2020).

(1) Shifts in preferences toward suprafunctionality beyond economic value, SDGs.(*The biggest river*—e.g., AWS, 2002)

(2) Sleeping resources(*All stakeholders working together*—e.g., Amazon Flex, 2015)

(3) Drawing upon past information and fostering trust(*Carrying every product from A to Z*—e.g., Amazon Prime, 2005)

(4) Providing the most gratification ever experienced(*Fusing physical and digital*—e.g., Amazon Go, 2016)

(5) Memory and future dreams(*Brick and mortar retailer*—e.g., Amazon Kindle, 2007)

(6) Untapped resources and vision(*Instilling dreams in customers*—e.g., Amazon Echo, 2014)

4.4 Assessment of soft innovation resources

With the understanding of the significant role of *SIRs* as a countermeasure for global ICT firms against productivity decline, their measurement and assessment were attempted in this section.

4.4.1 Innovation dynamism in the Internet of Things society activated by soft innovation resources

Fig. 4.22 illustrates innovation dynamism in the IoT society activated by *SIRs* (see details of mathematical development in A1.4.2 in Appendix I).

The dramatic advancement of the Internet and further progress of digitalized innovation over the last 2 decades have augmented permeation of the Internet into broad ICT as reviewed in A1,1 in Appendix I.

Based on this permeation trend, the above innovation dynamism in the IoT society that has been activated by *SIRs* can be described as follows:

(1) Because global ICT firms are at the forefront of the IoT society, *SIRs*, their critical resources against productivity decline in the digital economy, seem to be condensates or crystals of the Internet as reviewed earlier.

(2) *SIRs* activate a latent self-propagating function indigenous to ICT that can be attributed to the Internet permeating into *SIRs*.

(3) The activated self-propagating function induces functionality development that leads to suprafunctionality beyond economic value corresponding to a shift in people's preferences. This shift, in turn, induces further advancement of the Internet.

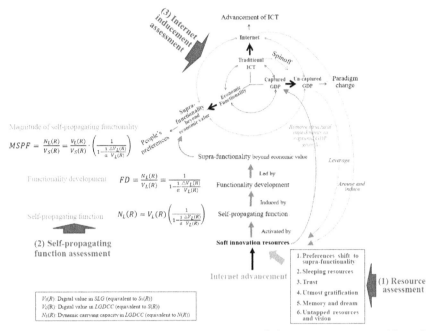

Figure 4.22 Innovation dynamism in the Internet of Things society activated by soft innovation resources.

4.4.2 Measurement of soft innovation resources as crystals of the internet

Based on the above understanding, the measurement of *SIRs* can be attempted by the following three approaches, which correspond to the above three postulates. In this case, the state of Internet dependence can serve as a proxy for the state of advancement of the Internet (see the details of the measurement of Internet dependence in Appendix I-5).

4.4.2.1 Correlation between advancement of the internet and soft innovation resources

First, taking typical *SIRs*, correlation with the advancement of the Internet was examined.

(1) Sleeping resources

Following the preceding analysis on "Uber's ridesharing revolution" in 4.2.2 (see also Watanabe et al., 2016b), the effect of the advancement of the Internet on Uber dependence was examined. Given the close relationship

Table 4.4 Correlation between smartphone and Uber in New York (Jun. 2013—Sep. 2015).

$\ln U_p = 12.07 - 2.17\,D_1\ln SP - 2.16\,D_2\ln SP - 0.16\,D$ *adj.* R^2 0.954
  (19.07) (-14.40)   (-14.72)   (-6.25)   *DW*   1.03

U_p: price of Uber (US$/trip); SP: smartphone share in the US telephone market (%). D: dummy variables—D_1: Jun. 2013—Oct. 2014 = 1, others = 0; D_2: Nov. 2014—Sep. 2015 = 1, others = 0; D: Jun. 2015—Sep. 2015 = 1. others = 0. Figures in parentheses are t-statistics; all are significant at the 1% level.

between the Internet and smartphone dependence (Fig. 4.4 and Table 4.1), the monthly trend in smartphone dependence was used. The result of the correlational analysis in New York over the period from June 2013 to September 2015 are summarized in Table 4.4 which is statistically significant and demonstrates that the advancement of the Internet (via smartphone) significantly contributed to the utilization of sleeping resources by reducing prices, typically observed in a trend observed in the rise of Uber.

(2) Trust

Following the preceding analysis on "coevolution between trust in teachers and higher education toward digital-rich learning environments" in 20 countries reviewed in 4.2.3 (see also Watanabe et al., 2016c), the effects of the advancement of the Internet on trust increase were examined. The result of the correlational analysis between them in 20 countries is summarized in Table 4.5 which is statistically significant and demonstrates that the advancement of the Internet contributed to the trust increase in 12 IACs.

Table 4.5 Correlation between internet dependence and trust in 20 countries (2013).

$\ln X = 2.59 + 0.32\,D_1\ln ID - 0.18\,D_2\ln ID - 2.14\,D_1 - 0.16\,D_\alpha + 0.10 D_\beta$ *adj.* R^2 0.734
  (4.94)   (1.96)* (-1.35)** (-2.20)* (-5.25)   (2.28)

X: level of trust in teachers to deliver a good education; ID: Internet dependence; D: dummy variables—D_1: Israel, Czech, Singapore, France, New Zealand, Germany, Korea, Switzerland, Japan, UK, Finland, Netherland = 1, others = 0; D_2: China, Turkey, Brazil, Italy, Greece, Portugal, USA, Spain = 1, others = 0; D_α: Korea, Japan = 1. others = 0; D_β: USA, Spain = 1, others = 0Figures in parentheses are t-statistics; all are significant at the 1% level except *5% and **10%.

Table 4.6 Correlation between smartphone and live music in the US (Jun. 2013–Sep. 2015).

$$\ln\!LM = 1.34 + 1.13 \ \ln\!SP - 0.02 \ D_1 + 0.02 \ D_2 \quad adj. \ R^2 \ 0.996$$
$$\quad\ \ (21.67) \ \ (77.85) \qquad (-2.46) \qquad (4.09) \qquad DW \quad 1.25$$

LM: revenue of live music (mil. US\$); SP: smartphone share of US telephone market (%); D: dummy variables—D_1: Feb. 2014 $=$ 1, others $=$ 0; D_2: Sep. 2014–Nov. 2014 $=$ 1, others $=$ 0. Figures in parentheses are t-statistics; all are significant at the 1% level.

(3) Memory and dreams

Following the preceding analysis on "coevolution between streaming and live music leads the way to the sustainable growth of the music industry" reviewed in 4.2.5 (see also Naveed et al., 2017), the effect of the advancement of the Internet on the reactivation of live music was examined. Similar to the case with Uber, the monthly trend in smartphone dependence was used. The result of the correlational analysis between smartphone share and revenue of live music in the US from June 2013 to September 2015 is summarized in Table 4.6, which is statistically significant and demonstrates that the advancement of the Internet (via smartphone) significantly contributed to reactivation of live music.

(4) Untapped resources

Similarly, following the preceding analysis on "ICT-driven disruptive innovation nurtures uncaptured GDP: Harnessing women's potential as untapped resources" in 44 countries reviewed in 4.2.6 (see also Watanabe et al., 2017b), the effects of the advancement of the Internet on the utilization of untapped resources were examined. The result of the correlational analysis between them in 44 countries is summarized in Table 4.7 which is

Table 4.7 Correlation between internet dependence, gender balance improvement, and male-dominated society in 44 countries (2013).

$$\ln Y = 0.99 + 0.30 D_1 \ln\!ID + 0.40 D_2 \ln\!ID + 0.36 D_3 \ln\!ID$$
$$\quad\ \ (1.46)^* \ \ (1.63)^* \qquad (2.63) \qquad\quad (2.16)$$
$$\qquad\quad - 0.31 D_2 \ln\!W - 2.93 D_3 \ln\!W - 0.98 D_a + 0.72 D_b \qquad adj. \ R^2 \quad 0.801$$
$$\qquad\quad (-2.60) \qquad\ \ (-5.58) \qquad\ \ (-7.57) \quad (3.12)$$

Y: Gender Balance Index; ID: Internet dependence; W: intensity of male-dominated society. D_1, D_2 and D_3: coefficient dummy variables corresponding to EMC (13 emerging countries), INC (27 industrialized countries) and CSC (4 countries with specific cultures), respectively. D: dummy variables—D_a: BEL, CHL, HUN, TWN, RUS, PRT, BRA, GRC, EGY $=$ 1, others $=$ 0; D_b: NOR, SAU $=$ 1, others $=$ 0. Figures in parentheses are t-statistics; all are significant at the 1% level except * 10%.

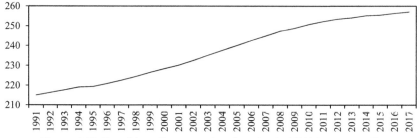

Figure 4.23 Trend in self-propagating function in UPM (1991−2017).

statistically significant and demonstrates that advancement of the Internet contributed to improving gender balance in the 44 countries examined.

All cases demonstrate that *SIRs* have been governed significantly by advancement of the Internet as condensates or crystals of the Internet.

4.4.2.2 Correlation between the self-propagating function and advancement of the internet

Next, the second postulate was examined: "*attributed to the advancement of the Internet SIRs activates a latent self-propagating function.*"

(1) Trend in self-propagating function

Fig. 4.23 illustrates the trend in self-propagating function in the world circular economy leader UPM (Watanabe et al., 2018f) over the last quarter-century.

(2) Internet inducement of self-propagating function

Fig. 4.24 demonstrates the correlation between Internet dependence and self-propagating function in UPM over the last quarter-century.

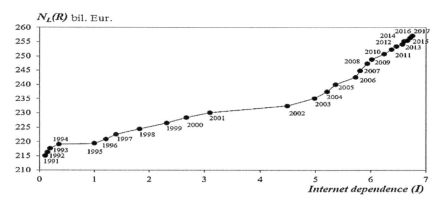

Figure 4.24 Correlation between internet dependence and self-propagating function in UPM (1991−2017).

Table 4.8 Correlation between internet dependence and the self-propagating function (1995—2017).

$\ln N_L(R) = 2.973 + 0.362\,D_1 \ln ID + 0.424\,D_2 \ln ID + 0.536\,D_3 \ln ID$ *adj.* R^2 *0.985*
    (109.79)   (11.30)   (21.51)   (32.91)   *DW*   1.20

$N_L(R)$: self-propagating function; ID: Internet dependence; D: dummy variables—D_1: 1995—2002 = 1, others = 0; D_2: 2003—7 = 1, others = 0. D_3: 2008—17 = 1, others = 0. Figures in parentheses are t-statistics; all are significant at the 1% level.

Based on Fig. 4.24, Table 4.8 summarizes the result of the correlation analysis between Internet dependence and self-propagating function in UPM between 1995 and 2017. The result is statistically significant and demonstrates that the advancement of the Internet contributed to increasing in self-propagating function significantly. Its contribution increased as Internet dependence increased.

4.4.2.3 Correlation between shifts in people's preferences and advancement of the internet

Third, inspired by the preceding two demonstrations, the third postulate was examined: "*activated self-propagating function induces functionality development leading to suprafunctionality beyond economic value corresponding to people's preferences shift and this shift, in turn, induces further advancement of the Internet.*"

Table 4.9 summarizes the correlation between suprafunctionality beyond economic value and advancement of the Internet in Japan (which is sensitive to institutional innovation against external shocks and crises) between 1994 and 2012.

Table 4.9 shows the result is statistically significant and demonstrates that people's preferences shift to suprafunctionality beyond economic value significantly induced the advancement of the Internet in Japan. This inducement increased as Internet dependence increased.

Table 4.9 Correlation between shifts in people's preferences advancement of the internet in Japan (1994—2012).

$\ln J = -34.77 + 8.81\,D_1 \ln Q + 9.34\,D_2 \ln Q + 9.50\,D_3 \ln Q - 1.11\,D$ *adj.* R^2 0.937
    (-2.97)   (3.05)   (3.24)   (3.33)   (-2.56)   *DW*   1.75

J: Internet dependence; Q: preference ratio of suprafunctionality beyond economic value; D: dummy variables—D_1: 1994—6 = 1, others = 0; D_2: 1997—2003 = 1, others = 0; D_3: 2004—12 = 1, others = 0; D: 1994 = 1, others = 0. Figures in parentheses are t-statistics; all are significant at the 1% level.

All three analyses demonstrate the significant correlation between advancement of the Internet and *SIRs* or development of their subsequent such as self-propagating function and people's preferences shift to suprafunctionality beyond economic value.

These results support the supposition that *SIRs* could be considered condensates or crystals of the advancement of the Internet.

4.5 Conclusion

The dramatic advancement of digital innovation initiated by the Internet incorporates the unique nature as simultaneous dissemination and digital solution to social demand.

This advancement has led us to the digital economy, which has changed how we conduct business and our daily lives.

Such changes induce further innovation, which in turn accelerates further changes in institutional systems, leading to emerging coevolution between digital innovation and institutional change.

While the further progression of digitized innovation has augmented the above change significantly and provided us with extraordinary, previously unanticipated services and welfare, such services and welfare could not be captured through the GDP data, which measures revenue, resulting in increasing dependence on uncaptured GDP.

Consequently, the dramatic advancement of the Internet induces spin-off from the coevolution of traditional ICT, captured GDP and economic functionality to new coevolution of Internet advancement, dependence on uncaptured GDP, and shift in people's preferences to suprafunctionality beyond economic value.

This spin-off coevolutionary dynamism rapidly advances coevolution with digital innovation (incorporating its unique nature) and notable new socioeconomic trends (such as the sharing economy and circular economy).

The previously discussed "great coevolution" due to the new stream of the digital economy under spin-off dynamism, digital innovation with its unique nature, and the shift to new socioeconomic trends induce remarkable disruptive business models that produce innovations in the digital economy.

Prompted by this hypothetical view, six remarkable disruptive business models that have emerged in the digital economy and are considered products induced by the "great coevolution" were analyzed in this chapter.

These business models seek to harness the vigor of innovation resources in the four dimensions of space and time.

While these innovation resources have not been efficiently utilized or have been unable to be utilized, advances in ICT and subsequent platform that consolidates all stakeholders' challenge for social demands have turned such difficulties into a real deployment by awakening and activating latent resources. Thus, these remarkable disruptive business models can be perceived as a typical IDBM with CCSD. They have awoken and activated latent innovation resources as follows:

(1) The driving force of coevolutionary dynamism among Internet advancement, dependence on uncaptured GDP, and a shift in people's preferences to suprafunctionality beyond economic value.

(2) Sleeping resources as nonoperational cars and drivers as well as idling time can be awoken and utilized effectively through the Internet and smartphones.

(3) Trust by overdrawing past information that can be accelerated by the Internet.

(4) The utmost gratification ever experienced leading to consumption, which is effectively recalled by the Internet.

(5) Memory and dreams are recalled and drawn on actively by the Internet.

(6) Untapped resources are effectively utilized and envisioned by the Internet.

These latent innovation resources that are awoken and activated by the IDBM with CCSD can be called *SIRs*, which can be defined as latent innovation resources to be awoken and activated by the digital platform ecosystem. The emergence of *SIRs* depends on the advances in ICT, particularly the Internet. Thus, *SIRs* may produce disruptive innovation when successful within this dynamism.

SIRs incorporate such specific features as condensates or crystals of the advancement of the Internet and consist of Internet-based resources that have either been sleeping, have been untapped, or are the results of multisided interaction in the markets where consumers are looking for functionality beyond economic value. The magnitude of *SIRs* is proportional to the interactions with users.

Effective utilization of *SIRs* contributes to an increase in gross R&D, which leads to growth and activates the latent self-propagating function indigenous to ICT, which induces functionality development, leading to suprafunctionality beyond economic value. This corresponds to shift in people's preferences and induces further advancement of the Internet.

Furthermore, this advancement accelerates the increasing dependence on uncaptured GDP, which leverages the harnessing of the vigor of *SIRs*. At the same time, advancement of the Internet induces *SIRs*, as they are crystals of the Internet. Thus, a virtuous cycle exists between the emergence and utilization of *SIRs*, suprafunctionality beyond economic value, advancement of the Internet, dependence on uncaptured GDP, and further leverage for *SIRs* emergence.

In addition, *SIRs* also contribute to captured GDP increases by removing the structural impediments to its growth, such as a conflict between public, employers and labor unions, a disparity of gender, and increasing the discrepancies toward an aging society. Thus, the spontaneous creation of uncaptured GDP through effective utilization of *SIRs* contributes to the resurgence of captured GDP growth by its hybrid function, which also activates a self-propagating function.

The use of *SIRs* is a novel innovation. When applied in highly intensified R&D firms for their sustainable growth, their use can avoid a decline in productivity. While a transformative circumstance in the digital economy results in a decline in productivity, global ICT firms attempt to survive by spontaneous creation of uncaptured GDP through harnessing the vigor of *SIRs*.

Therefore, an empirical analysis of a novel innovation that has been deployed by the global ICT leaders for their sustainable growth by pioneering and utilizing *SIRs* should be a priority.

References

Anderson, J., van Weert, T. (Eds.), 2002. Information and Communication Technology in Education: A Curriculum for Schools and Programme of Teacher Development. UNESCO, Paris.

Baudrilard, J., 1998. The Consumer Society: Myths and Structures. Sage Publications Ltd., London.

Belk, R., 2014. You are what you can access: sharing the collaborative consumption online. Journal of Business Research 67, 1595–1600.

Carrasco, A., Francoeur, C., Real, I., Laffarga, J., Ruiz-Barbadillo, E., 2012. Cultural Differences and Board Gender Diversity. HAL, pp. 2–28.

Catalyst, 2005. Corporate Performance and Women's Representation on Boards. http://www.catalyst.org/media/companies-more-women-board-directors-experience-higher-financial-performance-accoeding-latest/ (Retrieved 11 March 2017).

Chen, P.S.D., Lambert, A.D., Guidry, K.R., 2010. Engaging online learners: the impact of web-based learning technology on college student engagement. Computer and Education 54 (4), 1222–1232.

Choi, H., Burnes, B., 2013. The internet and value co-creation: the case of the popular music industry. Prometheus 31 (1), 35–53.

Cohen, B., Kietzmann, J., 2014. Ride on! mobility business models for the sharing economy. Organization & Environment 27 (3), 279–296.

Collaborative Research Center of Meisei University, 2010. Evaluation of Sensitive Information Based on Physiological and Psychological Activities Measured by Face Thermography. Collaborative Research Center of Meisei University, Tokyo, Japan.

Daechun, A., Kim, S., 2007. Relating hofstede's masculinity dimension to gender role portrayals in advertising. International Marketing Review 24 (2), 181–207.

Department of Broadband, Communications and the Digital Economy (DBCDE), 2009. Digital Economy Future Directions. DBCDE, Camberra.

Ehret, M., 2015. The zero marginal cost society: the Internet of things, the collaborative commons, and the eclipse of capitalism. The Journal of Sustainable Mobility 2 (2), 67–70.

FINNCHAM, 2016. The Sixth Women Directors and Executives Report 2016 - Women Directors on the Rise: Executive Positions Still Going to Men. HINNCHAM, Helsinki.

Fly, B., 2016. How Does Music Consumption Impact the Music Industry and Benefit Artists? Accounting Undergraduate Honors thesis University of Arkansas, p. 20.

Gibson, J.J., 1977. The theory of affordances. In: Shaw, R., Bransford, J. (Eds.), Perceiving, Acting and Knowing. Erlbaum, Hillsdale, NJ.

Gibson, J.J., 1979. The Ecological Approach to Visual Perception. Houghton Mifflin, Boston.

Hilgard, E.J., Atkinson, R.L., Atkinson, R.C., Smith, E.E., Ben, D.J., Nolen-Hoeksema, S., 1999. Hilgard's Introduction to Psychology. Wadsworth Publishing, London.

Hofstede, G., 1991. Cultures and Organizations. McGraw-Hill International, London.

Horpedahl, J., 2015. Ideology uber alles?: economics bloggers on uber, lyft, and other transportation network companies. Econ Journal Watch 12 (3), 360–374.

Ilmola, L., Casti, J., 2013. Seven shocks and Finland. Innovation and Supply Chain Management 7 (3), 112–124.

International Labour Organization (ILO), 2015. Women in Businesses and Management: Gaining Momentum. ILO, Geneva.

International Monetary Fund (IMF), 2018. Measuring the Digital Economy. IMF, Washington, D.C.

Isaac, E., Davis, U.C., 2014. Disruptive Innovation: Risk-Shifting and Precarity in the Age of Uber. BRIE Working Paper 2014-7.

Ishii, J., 2009. Business Insight — What's Creative Knowledge? Iwanami Shoten, Tokyo.

Japan Cabinet Office (JCO), 2010. White Paper on Japan's Economy and Public Finance 2010. JCO, Tokyo.

Japan Cabinet Office (JCO), 2012. National Survey of Lifestyle Preferences. JCO, Tokyo.

Japan Cabinet Office (JCO), 2018. National Survey of Lifestyle Preferences. JCO, Tokyo.

Jeffrey, L.M., Milne, J., Suddaby, G., 2014. Blended learning: how teachers balance the blend of online and classroom components. Journal of Information Technology Education 13, 121–140.

Katahira, H., 1987. Marketing Science. University of Tokyo Press, Tokyo.

Katahira, H., 2003. Brand Engineering. Nikkei Business Publications Inc., Tokyo.

King, S.P., 2015. Sharing economy: what challenges for competition law? Journal of European Law & Practice 6 (10), 729–734.

Kondo, R., Watanabe, C., Moriyama, K., 2007. A resonant development trajectory for IT development: lessons from Japan's i-mode. International Journal of Advances in Management Research 4 (2), 7–27.

Koopman, C., Mitchell, M., Thierer, A., 2014. The sharing economy and consumer protection regulation: the case for policy change. The Journal of Business, Entrepreneurshipand the Law 2014–2015 529–540.

Levenson, R.W., Ekman, P., Friesen, W.V., 1990. Voluntary facial action generates emotion-specific nervous system activity. Psychophysiology 27, 363–384.

Lovins, H., Cohen, B., 2011. Climate Capitalism in the Age of Climate Change. Hill & Wang, New York.

Luhmann, N., 1979. Trust and Power. John Wiley, Chchester.

Maslow, A., 1954. Motivation and Personality. Harper, New York.

Matsuda, H., 2010. Why Not Buy, How to Purchase. Asahi-shimbun, Tokyo.

Matsuda, H., 2012. Extricating from Stagnation as a Consequence of Consumption Hating. PHP Institute, Tokyo.

McDonagh, D., 2008. Satisfying needs beyond the functional: the changing needs of the silver market consumer. In: Presented at the International Symposium on the Silver Market Phenomenon – Business Opportunities and Responsibilities in the Aging Society, Tokyo, Japan.

McDonagh, D., Thomas, J., 2010. Disability + relevant design: empathic design strategies supporting more effective new product design outcomes. The Design Journal 13 (2), 180–198. https://doi.org/10.2752/175470710X12735884220899.

McDonough, W., 2020. Global change award celebrates a cradle to cradle circular economy. Global Change Award.

McKinsey & Company, 2019. Ten Trends for the Fashion Industry to Watch in 2019. McKinsey & Company, New York. https://www.mckinsey.com/industries/retail/our-insights/ten-trends-for-the-fashion-industry-to-watch-in-2019 (Retrieved 26.01.2020).

McKinsey Global Institute, 2015. The Internet of Things: Mapping the Value beyond the Hype. McKinsey & Company, San Francisco.

Ministry of Internal Affairs and Communication (MIC), 2011. White Paper on Japan's Information and Communication. MIC, Tokyo.

Modigliani, T., 1965. Life Cycle Hypothesis of Savings, the Demand for Wealth, and Supply of Capital. A Paper Presented to the Rome Congress of Economic Society.

Naveed, K., Watanabe, C., Neittaanmäki, P., 2017. Co-evolution between streaming and live music leads a way to the sustainable growth of music industry: lessons from the US experiences. Technology in Society 50, 1–19.

Naveed, K., Watanabe, C., Neittaanmäki, P., 2018. The transformative direction of innovation toward an IoT-based society: increasing dependency on uncaptured GDP in global ICT firms. Technology in Society 53, 23–46.

Naveed, N., Watanabe, C., Neittaanmäki, P., 2020. Co-evolutionary coupling leads a way to a novel concept of R&D: lessons from digitalized bioeconomy. Technology in Society 60, 101220.

OECD, 2014a. Trust: What it Is and Why it Matters for Governance and Education? OECD, Paris.

OECD, 2014b. Women, Government and Policy Making in OECD Countries: Fostering Diversity for Inclusive Growth. OECD, Paris.

OECD, 2016a. OECD Observer: The Digital Economy. OECD, Paris.

OECD, 2016b. Background Report: Conference on Improving Women's Access to Leadership. OECD, Paris.

Oreg, S., Goldenberg, J., 2015. Resistance to Innovation – its Sources and Manifestations. The University of Chicago Press, Chicago, and London.

Pew Research Center, 2016. Smartphone Ownership and Internet Usage Continues to Climb in Emerging Economies. Pew Research Center, Washington, D.C.

Phipps, L., September 12, 2018. How Amazon thinks inside and outside the box. Circular Weekly Newsletter. https://www.greenbiz.com/article/how-amazon-thinks-inside-and-outside-box (Retrieved 01.06.2019).

Polanyi, M., 1969. Knowing and Being. University of Chicago Press, Chicago.

Rutledge, L.L., Hupka, R.B., 1985. The facial feedback hypothesis: methodological concerns and new supporting evidence. Motivation and Emotion 9 (3), 219—240.

Sahlberg, P., 2010. The secret to Finland's success: educating teachers. Stanford Center for Opportunity Policy in Education 1—8.

Stead, J.G., Stead, W.E., 2013. The Co-evolution of sustainable strategic management in the global marketplace. Organization & Environment 26 (2), 162—183.

Stedham, Y.E., Yamamura, J.H., 2004. Measuring national culture: does gender matter? Women in Management Review 19 (2), 233—243.

Stehlik, T., 2016. Is "Pedagogical Love" the Secret to Finland's Educational Success? http://www.aare.edu.au/blog/?p=1578 (Retrieved 30 May 2016).

Tapscott, D., 1994. The Digital Economy: Promise and Peril in the Age of Networked Intelligence. McGraw-Hill, New York.

Toates, F., 1986. Motivational Systems. Cambridge University Press, Cambridge, England.

Tompkins, S.S., 1962. Affect, Imagery, Consciousness: Vol. 1. The Positive Affects. Springer, New York.

Tou, Y., Moriya, K., Watanabe, C., Ilmola, L., Neittaanmäki, P., 2018a. Soft innovation resources: enabler for reversal in GDP growth in the digital economy. International Journal of Managing Information Technology 10 (3), 21—39.

Tou, Y., Watanabe, C., Ilmola, L., Moriya, K., Neittaanmäki, P., 2018b. Hybrid role of soft innovation resources: Finland's notable resurgence in the digital economy. International Journal of Managing Information Technology 10 (4), 1—22.

Tou, Y., Watanabe, Moriya, K., Neittaanmäki, P., 2019a. Neo open innovation in the digital economy: harnessing soft innovation resources. International Journal of Managing Information Technology 10 (4), 53—75.

Tou, Y., Watanabe, C., Moriya, K., Neittaanmäki, P., 2019b. Harnessing soft innovation resources leads to neo open innovation. Technology in Society 58, 101114.

UNDP, 2010. Promoting an Economic and Legal Environment for Women's Empowerment. Speech by Helen Clark. http://www.undp.org/content/undp/en/home/presscenter/speeches/2010/03/25/promoting-an-economic-andlegal-environment-for-womens-empowerment-.html.

UNESCO, 2003. Towards Policies for Integrating Information and Communication Technologies into Education. UNESCO, Paris.

UNESCO, 2015. Countries of All Income Levels Nurturing a Digital Economy. UNESCO Science Report: towards 2030. UNESCO, Paris.

UNESCO, Institute of Statistics, 2014. Women in Science. UNESCO, Paris. http://www.uis.unesco.org/_LAYOUTS/UNESCO/women-in-science/index.html#!lang=en.

UNWomen, 2015. Collective Failure of Leadership on Progress for Women. Media Release. http//www.unwomen.org/en/news/stories (Retrieved 7 April 2017).

Varkey Gems Foundation (VGF), 2014. 2013 Global Teacher Status Index. VGF, London.

Watanabe, C., 2009. Co-evolutionary dynamism between innovation and institutional systems: the rise and fall of the Japanese system of management of technology. In: The Science of Institutional Management of Technology: Elucidation of Japan's Indigenous Co-evolutionary Dynamism and its Accrual to Global Assets. Tokyo Institute of Technology, Tokyo, pp. 21—34.

Watanabe, C., 2010. The resonance between signals emitted by innovation tempting consumption and signals emitted by consumers inducing innovation: Co-emergence of supra-functionality beyond economic value. In: Proceedings of the 25th Annual Meeting of the Japan Society for Science Policy and Research Management, Tokyo.

Watanabe, C., 2013. Innovation-consumption co-emergence leads a resilience business. Innovation and Supply Chain Management 7 (3), 92−104.

Watanabe, C., 2017. New Stream of Innovation toward IoT: Increasing Dependence on Uncaptured GDP. ICIS2017. Tsinghua University, Beijing.

Watanabe, C., Hobo, M., 2004. Creating a firm self-propagating function for advanced innovation-oriented projects: lessons from ERP. Technovation 24 (6), 467−481.

Watanabe, C., Zhu, B., Griffy-Brown, C., Asgari, B., 2001. Global technology spillover and its impact on industry's R&D strategies. Technovation 21 (5), 281−291.

Watanabe, C., Takayama, M., Nagamatsu, A., Tagami, T., Griffy-Brown, C., 2002. Technology spillover as a complement for high-level R&D intensity in the pharmaceutical industry. Technovation 22 (4), 245−258.

Watanabe, C., Kondo, R., Ouchi, N., Wei, H., Griffy-Brown, C., 2004. Institutional elasticity as a significant driver of IT functionality development. Technological Forecasting and Social Change 71 (7), 723−750.

Watanabe, Lei, S., Ouchi, N., 2009a. Fusing indigenous technology development and market learning for higher functionality development: an empirical analysis of the growth trajectory of canon printers. Technovation 29 (2), 265−283.

Watanabe, C., Moriyama, K., Shin, J.H., 2009b. Functionality development dynamism in a diffusion trajectory: a case of Japan's mobile phones development. Technological Forecasting and Social Change 76 (6), 737−753.

Watanabe, C., Nasuno, M., Shin, J.H., 2011. Utmost gratification of consumption by means of supra-functionality leads a way to overcoming global economic stagnation. Journal of Services Research 11 (2), 31−58.

Watanabe, C., Zhao, W., Nasuno, M., 2012a. The resonance between innovation and consumers: suggestions to emerging market customers. Journal of Technology Management for Growing Economies 3 (1), 7−31.

Watanabe, C., Kanno, G., Tou, Y., 2012b. Inside the learning dynamism inducing the resonance between innovation and high-demand consumption: a case of Japan's high-functional mobile phones. Technological Forecasting and Social Change 79 (7), 1292−1311.

Watanabe, C., Naveed, K., Zhao, W., 2015a. New paradigm of ICT productivity: increasing role of un-captured GDP and growing anger of consumers. Technology in Society 41, 21−44.

Watanabe, C., Naveed, K., Neittaanmäki, P., 2015b. Dependency on un-captured GDP as a source of resilience beyond economic value in countries with advanced ICT infrastructure: similarities and disparities between Finland and Singapore. Technology in Society 42, 104−122.

Watanabe, C., Naveed, K., Neittaanmäki, P., Tou, Y., 2016a. Operationalization of un-captured GDP: the innovation stream under new global mega-trends. Technology in Society 45, 58−77.

Watanabe, C., Naveed, K., Neittaanmäki, P., Tou, Y., 2016b. Co-evolution of three mega trends nature uncaptured GDP: Uber's ride-sharing revolution. Technology in Society 46, 164−185.

Watanabe, C., Naveed, K., Neittaanmäki, P., 2016c. Co-evolution between trust in teachers and higher education toward digitally-rich learning environments. Technology in Society 48, 70−96.

Watanabe, C., Naveed, K., Neittaanmäki, P., 2017a. Consolidated challenge to social demand for resilient platforms: lessons from Uber's global expansion. Technology in Society 48, 33−53.

Watanabe, C., Naveed, K., Neittaanmäki, P., 2017b. ICT-driven disruptive innovation nurtures uncaptured GDP: harnessing women's potential as untapped resources. Technology in Society 51, 81−101.

Watanabe, C., Moriya, K., Tou, Y., Neittaanmäki, P., 2018a. Structural sources of a productivity decline in the digital economy. International Journal of Managing Information Technology 10 (1), 1—20.

Watanabe, C., Moriya, K., Tou, Y., Neittaanmäki, P., 2018b. Consequences of the digital economy: transformation of the growth concept. International Journal of Managing Information Technology 10 (2), 21—39.

Watanabe, C., Naveed, N., Neittaanmäki, P., 2018c. Digital solutions transform the forest-based bioeconomy into a digital platform industry: a suggestion for a disruptive business model in the digital economy. Technology in Society 54, 168—188.

Watanabe, C., Tou, Y., Neittaanmäki, P., 2018d. A new paradox of the digital economy: structural sources of the limitation of GDP statistics. Technology in Society 55, 9—23.

Watanabe, C., Naveed, K., Tou, Y., Neittaanmäki, P., 2018e. Measuring GDP in the digital economy: increasing dependence on uncaptured GDP. Technological Forecasting and Social Change 137, 226—240.

Watanabe, C., Naveed, N., Neittaanmäki, P., 2018f. Digitalized bioeconomy: planned obsolescence-driven economy enabled by co-evolutionary coupling. Technology in Society 56, 8—30.

Weightman, D., McDonagh, D., 2004. Supra-functional factors in sustainable products. In: Bhamra, T., Hon, B. (Eds.), Design and Manufacture for Sustainable Development 2004. Wiley, pp. 91—101.

Wiles, J.A., Wiles, C., Tjernlund, A., 1995. A comparison of gender role portrayals in magazine advertising: The Netherlands, Sweden and the USA. European Journal of Marketing 29 (11), 35—49.

World Economic Forum (WEF), 2013a. The Global Competitiveness Report 2013—2014. WEF, Geneva.

World Economic Forum (WEF), 2013b. The Global Information Technology Report 2013. WEF, Geneva.

CHAPTER 5

Neo open innovation in the digital economy

Contents

5.1 R&D-driven growth in an Internet of Things society

R&D investment centered on information and communication technology (ICT) has played a decisive role in firm competitiveness in the digital economy (Watanabe, 2009; OECD, 2016; WEF, 2016; EU, 2017a). The advancement of the Internet of Things (IoT) has accelerated this trend (McKinsey Global Institute, 2015; Kahre et al., 2017; EU, 2017b). Consequently, global ICT firms have been striving for R&D-driven growth centered on sales increases[1] (Watanabe et al., 2014, 2015a; Naveed et al., 2018).

Fig. 5.1 demonstrates the development of the correlation between R&D and sales for the top 500 global ICT firms in 2016 (see the details of the definition and source in A1.2.2 of Appendix I).

---

[1] See the empirical evidence in A1.2.2 of the Appendix.

Transforming the Socio Economy with Digital Innovation
ISBN 978-0-323-88465-5
https://doi.org/10.1016/B978-0-323-88465-5.00007-6

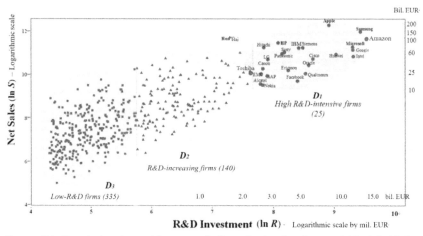

Figure 5.1 Correlational trend between R&D and sales for the top 500 global information and communication technology Firms (2016). *(Source: European Commission, Joint Research Center, 2017. The EU Industrial R&D Investment Scoreboard 2016. European Commission, Brussels; see Appendix A1.2.2.)*

Viewing Fig. 5.1, we note that global ICT firms have looked to increase their digital values by centering their efforts on sales (S). These firms can be divided into three clusters: 25 high-R&D-intensive firms, D_1 (including such gigantic firms as Google, Apple, Facebook, and Amazon (GAFA) and Samsung, Intel, Microsoft, and Huawei), 140 R&D-intensive firms, D_2, and 335 relatively low-R&D-intensive firms, D_3 (see Table A1-1 in the Appendix).

5.2 Bipolarization of information and communication technology—driven development

ICT in which network externalities function to alter the correlation between innovations and institutional systems creates new innovation features that lead to exponential growth (Watanabe et al., 2012). Schelling (1998) portrays an array of logistically developing and diffusing social mechanisms stimulated by these interactions. The advancement of the Internet further stimulates these interactions and accelerates ICT's logistically developing and diffusing features, which are typically traced by a sigmoid curve (Watanabe et al., 2001, 2004; Devezas et al., 2005).

The R&D-driven development trajectory of the top 500 global ICT firms, as illustrated in Fig. 5.1, is a typical example, and this trajectory exhibits logistic growth (see Table A1-1 in the Appendix). In this logistic growth trajectory, while R&D-driven productivity (which can be approximated as the marginal productivity of R&D in an IoT society) continues to increase before reaching an inflection point corresponding to the half the level of the carrying capacity (upper limit), it decreases once it exceeds the inflection point (see the detailed mathematical explanation in A1.3.2 of the Appendix).

Thus, ICT-driven logistic growth incorporates bipolarization fatality through an increase and a decrease in marginal R&D productivity before and after the inflection point, respectively (Watanabe, 2009).

For the top 500 global ICT firms in 2016, the R&D level of *EUR* 2.1 billion identifies the inflection point where the 25 high-R&D-intensive firms (D_1) are bifurcated from the remaining 475 firms $(D_2$ and $D_3)$, as illustrated in Fig. 5.2 (see details in A1.3.2 of the Appendix).

This bipolarization can be attributed to the two-faced nature of ICT, as illustrated in Fig. 5.3.

As reviewed earlier, while ICT advancement generally contributes to enhanced ICT prices via improvements and expansions in functionality, the dramatic advancement of the Internet has led to reduced ICT prices resulting from ICT's unique nature, which is characterized by being

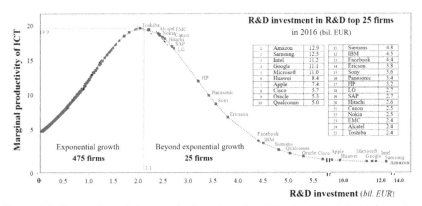

Figure 5.2 Comparison of the marginal productivity of the top 500 global information and communication technology Firms (2016). *(Source: European Commission, Joint Research Center, 2017. The EU Industrial R&D Investment Scoreboard 2016. European Commission, Brussels; see Appendix A1.2.2.)*

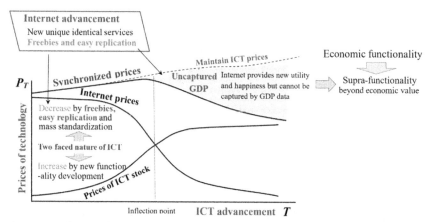

Figure 5.3 The two-faced nature of information and communication technology. *(Authors' elaboration based on Watanabe, C., Naveed, K., Zhao, W., 2015a. New paradigm of ICT productivity: increasing role of un-captured GDP and growing anger of consumers. Technology in Society 41, 21–44.)*

centered on the Internet with its freebies, easy replication, and mass standardization (Watanabe et al., 2015b).

The continued drop in ICT prices has resulted in declining marginal ICT productivity at leading ICT firms, as this productivity corresponds to relative price when firms pursue profit maximization in competitive markets.

The fundamental nature and fatal consequences of digital innovation are highlighted in Fig. 5.4.

Consequently, the above bipolarization has become inevitable in the competitive game engaged in by global ICT firms. High R&D-intensive

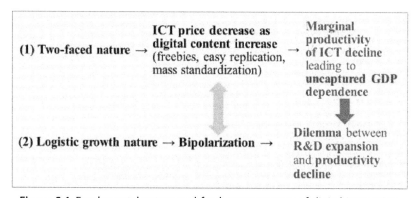

Figure 5.4 Fundamental nature and fatal consequences of digital innovation.

firms are closing in on a zero marginal cost state (Rifkin, 2011). Provided that these firms pursue maximum profit in the competitive market, prices will decrease as a consequence of the excessive ICT advancement and result in a decline in marginal ICT productivity. Fig. 5.2 demonstrates such phenomena concerning the top 500 global ICT firms in 2016. This figure demonstrates the explicit bipolarization of high-R&D-intensive firms (*HRIFs*: D_1 in Fig. 5.1) from the remaining neutral- and low-R&D-intensive firms (*LRIFs*: D_2 and D_3). *HRIFs* have fallen into a vicious cycle of R&D expenditures centered on ICT and its marginal productivity as increases in the former lead to declines in the latter. Conversely, *LRIFs* have maintained a virtuous cycle, as R&D increases have led to increases in marginal productivity.

The tendency toward industry bipolarization stemming from the two-faced nature of ICT is another unique feature of ICT firms. In addition, productivity in the digital economy has likewise declined in ICT-advanced countries (OECD, 2016; The US Council on Competitiveness, 2016; The World Bank, 2016; IMF, 2017; Watanabe et al., 2018a,b), and recent fears of stagnating trends for ICT giants (The Economist, 2018) can be attributed to this feature (Cowen, 2011; Brynjolfsson and McAfee et al., 2014).

5.3 R&D expansion versus declining productivity

Contrary to the decisive role in the digital economy of R&D centered on ICT, the dilemma of expansions in R&D and associated declines in productivity has become a worldwide concern that most digital economies are now confronting (Tou et al., 2018b, 2019b).

Sales (S) represents the R&D-driven digital value creation behavior of the top 500 global ICT firms in an IoT society and is depicted by the product of the marginal productivity of ICT ($\frac{\partial S}{\partial R}$: *MP*) and R&D ($R$) as follows (see the mathematical details in A1.2 and A1.3 of the Appendix):

$$S = F(R) = \frac{\partial S}{\partial R} \cdot R$$

where R is R&D investment and $\frac{\partial S}{\partial R}$ is marginal productivity of ICT in terms of R&D to sales (*MP*).[2]

---

[2] This is equivalent to marginal productivity of ICT to sales for the global ICT firms in an IoT society (see A 1.2 of Appendix I).

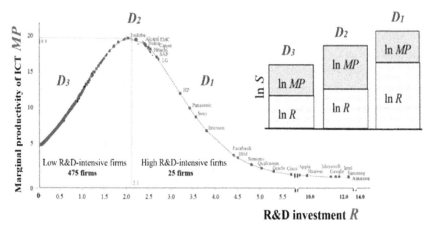

Figure 5.5 Dilemma of R&D expansion and declining productivity.

Taking logarithm
$\ln S = \ln MP + \ln R$.

Fig. 5.5 compares the magnitudes of the factors contributing to sales among low-R&D-intensive firms (D_3), R&D-intensive firms (D_2), and high-R&D-intensive firms (D_1).

As reviewed in Fig. 5.1, global ICT firms are attempting to achieve sales growth by leveraging ICT's contribution to sales growth, consisting of increases in marginal ICT productivity (MP) and ICT as represented by R&D (R). The product of both factors $(MP \times R)$ represents the contribution of ICT to sales.

Fig. 5.5 illustrates this strategy through the stages of global position by level of R&D (R).

This strategy can be attained by constructing a virtuous cycle between MP and R (an increase in R leads to an increase in MP, which in turn induces further increases in R). While this virtuous cycle can be maintained as long as a global ICT firm remains a $LRIF$ (stage D_3 or D_2 in Fig. 5.5), once it moves up to become an $HRIF$ (stage D_1), it will fall into a vicious cycle (an increase in R results in declining MP).

To address this pitfall, MP recovery can be attained by reducing R (moving back to a D_3 level of R&D), which will result in a diminished sales growth target.

Thus, $HRIFs$ have been suffering through the dilemma of R&D expansion centered on ICT that results in declining productivity.

This dilemma is the case not only for R&D-intensive firms but also for ICT-advanced countries.

As reviewed in Fig. 1.8 in Chapter 1, ICT-advanced countries suffer from marginal productivity declines as ICT advances.

Consequently, productivity in the ICT-advanced countries of the digital economy has shown an apparent decline, as illustrated in Fig. 1.7 in Chapter 1.

5.4 Neo open innovation

5.4.1 Self-propagating function

Under such circumstances, to attain the target sales growth essential for the survival of global ICT firms, *HRIFs* should find a solution to overcome this dilemma. Thus, global ICT leaders have endeavored to transform from traditional to new business models in their quest to find an effective solution (Watanabe et al., 2018a,b). Given that this dilemma stems from the unique feature of the logistic growth of ICT, this feature will likely need to be transformed in some manner.

As long as the development trajectory depends on the foregoing logistic growth trajectory (simple logistic growth: *SLG*), its digital value saturates with the fixed carrying capacity (upper limit of growth *N*), which inevitably results in the above dilemma. However, innovation that incorporates dynamic carrying capacity ($N_L(R)$), which creates new carrying capacity

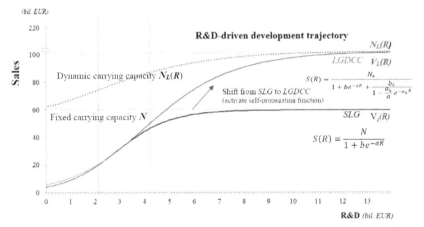

Figure 5.6 Dynamism in activating the self-propagating function in the R&D-driven development trajectory of the top 500 global information and communication technology Firms (2016).

during the diffusion process (logistic growth within a dynamic carrying capacity: *LGDCC*), enables digital value to increase because it successively creates new carrying capacity during the process of development, as illustrated in Fig. 5.6. This dynamism corresponds to activating the self-propagating function indigenous to ICT (Watanabe et al., 2004; Watanabe and Hobo, 2004).

Increases in digital value as well as its growth rate enhance dynamic carrying capacity,[3] which enables the sustainable growth of digital value and leads to a virtuous cycle between growth and carrying capacity (see the detailed mathematics in A1.4.2 of the Appendix).

Therefore, the key to the sustainable growth of the ICT-driven development trajectory of global ICT leaders is in identifying how to construct a virtuous cycle by incorporating a self-propagating function. Since ICT incorporates an indigenous self-propagating function utilizing network externalities (Watanabe et al., 2004), the point for sustainable growth corresponds to awakening and activating the latent self-propagating function indigenous to ICT.

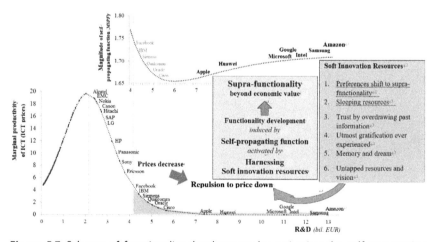

Figure 5.7 Scheme of functionality development by activating the self-propagating function—high-R&D-intensive global information and communication technology Firms (2016).

---

[3] Dynamic carrying capacity $N_L(R) = V_L(R) \left(\dfrac{1}{1-\dfrac{1}{a}\cdot\dfrac{\Delta V_L(R)}{V_L(R)}} \right)$ where $V_L(R)$: digital value.

5.4.2 Repulsive power against declining productivity

Efforts to awaken and activate this latent self-propagating function are reflections of the repulsive power of price (marginal productivity) reductions as a consequence of the bipolarization fatality resulting from excessive R&D. Fig. 5.7 illustrates this dynamism.

This repulsive power forces ICT leaders to absorb resources for innovation through (1) incorporation of the vigor of *LRIFs* that enjoy a virtuous cycle between *R* and *MP* and/or (2) harnessing the vigor of external innovation resources that do not experience declines in their own *MPs*.

The former option can be expected by harnessing the vigor of *LRIFs* that also enjoy the benefit of digital innovation. Some authors have postulated the significance of coevolutionary acclimatization strategies for this option that may provide the possibility for further ICT advancement in *HRIFs*[4] (e.g., Watanabe et al., 2015a, 2017a). However, since *HRIFs* confront a rising capital intensity, this option is no longer realistic, as this subsequently increases the burden of such investments (The Economist, 2018). Consequently, the latter option has become a more promising option to be expected with the new disruptive business model that corresponds to the digital economy.

5.4.3 Spin-off to uncaptured GDP

The above analyses demonstrate the significance of new disruptive business models that utilize external innovation resources to awaken and activate the latent self-propagating function indigenous to ICT. The activated self-propagating function induces functionality development leading to supra-functionality beyond economic value that encompasses social, cultural, emotional, and aspirational value (McDonagh, 2008; McDonagh and Thomas, 2010; Watanabe et al., 2011, 2015a). This, in turn, corresponds to the shift in people's preferences (Watanabe, 2013; Japan Cabinet Office, 2019). This shift then induces further advancement of the Internet (Watanabe et al., 2012, 2015b) and leverages the coevolutionary advancement of innovation in the digital economy (Tou et al., 2019a).

---

[4] While *HRIFs* enable further advancement of ICT, this results in a decline in *MP* due to a vicious cycle between them. Thus, such advancement capability should be addressed to the advancement of *LRIFs* that, given the ICT advancement capability, can enjoy a virtuous cycle between their *MP* increases that leads to sustainable growth. *HRIFs* can harness the fruit of growth in *LRIFs* and thereby coevolutionary acclimatization between two clusters of firms can be expected.

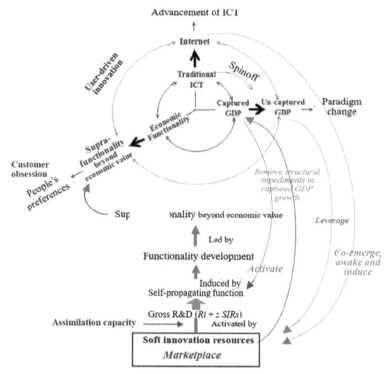

Figure 5.8 The dynamism of spin-off to uncaptured GDP and subsequent R&D transformation. *(Authors' elaboration based on Watanabe, C., Naveed, N., Neittaanmäki, P., 2018c. Digitalized bioeconomy: planned obsolescence-driven economy enabled by co-evolutionary coupling. Technology in Society 56, 8–30; Tou, Y., Watanabe, C., Moriya, K., Naveed, N., Vurpillat, V., Neittaanmäki, P., 2019b. The transformation of R&D into neo open innovation: a new concept of R&D endeavor triggered by Amazon. Technology in Society 58, 101141.)*

Using this dynamism, which is identical to the digital economy triggered by the dramatic advancement of the Internet, and by postulating that the Internet promotes a free culture that provides utility and happiness to people that cannot be captured through GDP (Lowrey, 2011), the authors have previously emphasized the significance of the digital economy's increasing dependence on uncaptured GDP (e.g., Watanabe et al., 2015a,b).

Shifts in people's preferences induce further advancement of the Internet (Watanabe et al., 2015b) that intensifies the digital economy's increasing dependence on uncaptured GDP.

Thus, a spin-off transformation of the coevolution among traditional ICT, captured GDP, and economic functionality to a new coevolution comprising the advancement of the Internet, the increasing dependence on uncaptured GDP, and people's shifting preferences to beyond economic value have been accelerated as illustrated in the upper double circle in Fig. 5.8 (Watanabe et al., 2015a,b, 2016) as reviewed earlier in Fig. 1.9 in Chapter 1.

5.4.4 Soft innovation resources of global ICT leaders

With this dynamism, global ICT leaders have attempted to transform their traditional business models into new ones.

The key direction is toward a new disruptive business model utilizing external innovation resources that awaken and activate the latent self-propagating function indigenous to ICT without causing a decline in productivity.

Table 5.1 reviews the transformative direction of seven leading global ICT firms in harnessing such innovation resources over the period from 1970 to 2020. Seven leaders were top seven R&D firms in 2016: Amazon, Samsung, Intel, Google, Microsoft, Huawei, and Apple.

Table 5.2 summarizes the key transformative directions of the top seven ICT leaders.

Tables 5.1 and 5.2 demonstrate that the top seven ICT leaders have been seeking to transform themselves with a new business model that creates suprafunctionality by harnessing the vigor of external innovation resources to awaken and activate the latent self-propagating function as demonstrated in Fig. 5.9. These external resources can be considered the typical *SIRs* deployed by the top seven R&D global ICT leaders.

As the top seven ICT leaders transformed their firms using new business models, *SIRs* have emerged as part of the remarkable disruptive business models that are seen as the solution to the productivity dilemma. As reviewed in Chapter 4, these business models were induced by the "great coevolution" due to the new stream of the digital economy under spin-off dynamism, digital innovation with its unique nature, and the shift to new socioeconomic trends. Fig. 5.8 demonstrates this "great-coevolution" dynamism.

As reviewed in Chapter 4, such *SIRs* consist of Internet-based resources permeating into broad ICT in the digital platform economy. These have been sleeping or untapped, or are the results of multisided markets interactions where the consumer is looking for suprafunctionality beyond

Table 5.1 Transformation direction of the seven leading global information and communication technology firms (1970–2020).

	1970–80	1981–90	1991–2000	2001–10	2011–20
			Book store	*Top online retail store*	*Fusing net and real*
1. Amazon			**1994: Amazon launched** **1997:** IPO (NYSE, Nasdaq) Buys bookpages.co.uk Launches Amazon UK **1998:** CDs and DVDs **1999:** Toys and electronics	**2000:** Marketplace, Amazon's third-party business **A to the Z** in Amazon launches **2001:** Takeover Borders.com Borders collapse 10 years later Amazon makes its first profit **2002:** Amazon web services cloud computing platform **2003:** Selling jewelry **2004:** Selling shoes **2005:** Prime membership **2006:** Fresh (food online)	**2011:** Kindle fire tablet **2012:** Buys Kiva, a robotics company, for US$775 million to obtain the technology for itself **2013:** Big cloud systems contract of US$600 million for 17 US intelligence agencies Prime air drone delivery plans **2014:** Echo voice device 8th generation fulfillment centers **2015:** Brick-and-mortar store Flex a-piece-rate delivery (Uber mode.) Exceeds Walmart in market capitalization **2016:** Captures 50% of online spending in the US Doubles its distribution facilities

Continued

	Mechatronics	Computers	Mobile phones, digital TVs	Smartphones, smart TVs	Tablets, wearables, VR, IoT		
						2007: Kindle e-reader 2008: Games 2009: Buys Zappos 2010: Logistics infrastructure scaling Amazon studios to create original television content	Amazon Go store 2017: Acquires whole foods 2018 **R&D**: **28.8** US$ bil. 2019: Acquires dispatch 2019: Acquires health navigator 2020: World top prospecting company in the pandemic (June)
2. Samsung	**1938: Samsung founded** as a grocery trading store **1969:** Samsung–Sanyo electronics established 1970: Black-and-white TV 1972: Washing machine Refrigerator	1980: Air conditioner 1983: Personal computers (PCs) 1984: Export of VCRs 1986: Smallest videotape recorder 1987: **SAIT established**	1992: Mobile phones HDD, DRAMs Industrial robots **China expansion** 1993: Digital video recorder (DVD-R) 1994: Electric car (SEV-III) 1995: MPEG-3 technology	2004: World largest LCD TV (46″) Smartphones 2008: World's first dual-color bezel TV 2009: World's slimmest LED TV 2010: **World's first TV app store** World's first FHD 3D TV	2011: Galaxy tablets Hard disk biz sold to seagate 2012: Samsung and Apple patent infringement controversy Samsung shares on the KOSPI the index fell 7.7% 2013: World's first curved TV 2014: Gear VR devices Galaxy Note 4 World's first bendable UHD TV Stopped music streaming business, Music Hub app		

Table 5.1 Transformation direction of the seven leading global information and communication technology firms (1970–2020).—cont'd

1970–80	1981–90	1991–2000	2001–10	2011–20
1977: Color television **1979**: Microwave ovens		**1996**: Fastest CPU (alpha chip) 33″ double-screen TV **1997**: World lightest TVs 30″ TFT-LCD display **1998**: Digital TV, flat-screen TV **1999**: Smartphone, wireless Internet phone, multifunction phone **2000**: 50-millionth mobile phone		**2015**: Granted world's most patents World's largest curved UHD TV **2016**: IoT, partnership with microsoft Smartwatch (gear fit 2, etc.) Icon-X, Galaxy Note 7 **2018**: Launches the world's largest mobile manufacturing facility in Noida, India **2018 R&D: 16.5** US$ bil **2020**: Group chairman Lee Kun-hee died

3. Intel	Integrated electronics	Computer boards, chips	Processors	Cell phone microchips	Supporting technologies for IoT and wearables
	1968: **Cofounded** by Gordon Moore and Robert Noyce 1969: Worlds first MOS 1970: First property, the first board 1971: New era in integrated electronics 1972: First international factory in Malaysia 1975: Computers get personal 1979: 486th position in fortune 500	1982: PC industry takes off 1983: US$1 billion annual revenue 1984: One of the 100 best companies to work for in America 1985: Supercomputer Intel 386 processor 1987: Second-generation supercomputer 1988: Intel foundation established 1990: Robert Noyce died	1992: Largest semiconductor supplier in the world 1993: Intel pentium processor 1995: Became a chipset leader 1998: Intel strong ARM processor 1999: Intel pentium III, xeon Processor 2000: Intel pentium 4 processor	2002: Hyperthreading technology, more power at lower cost 2003: Cellular phone microchips 2004: 46th in fortune 100 best Companies to work for 2005: 40th anniversary of Moore's law 2006: World's first quad-core processor 2008: 45-nm transistor 2009: Intel atom processor Going green Paid US$1.25 billion to AMD in lawsuit settlement 2010: Buys McAfee i7 processor, intel app-up store	2011: Intel ultrabook 2012: 450-nm manufacturing technology 2013: **New generation of processors** i3, i5, i7 2014: Intel quark chip powering IoT and wearable devices 2016: Announces withdrawal from smartphone market Acquires Movidus 2017: Announces R&D center in Bangalore 2018: Acquires eASIC 2018 **R&D: 13.5** US$ bil 2019: Acquires Omnitek 2019: Acquires Habana labs 2020: Acquires rivet networks

Continued

Table 5.1 Transformation direction of the seven leading global information and communication technology firms (1970–2020).—cont'd

	1970–80	1981–90	1991–2000	2001–10	2011–20
			Information search	*Gmail, earth, YouTube, smartphones, OS, apps*	*Google (play store, glass, balloons), cloud, IoT*
4. Google			**1998: Google founded** 2000: World's largest search engine	2001: Image search 2002: Google news 2004: Gmail 2005: Google earth, maps, talk, video, Books, mobile search, scholar 2006: Android, google trends 2007: YouTube 2008: Google chrome, street view 2009: Google translate 2010: Google nexus phone	2011: Google Panda, acquired Motorola, google + 2012: Google play store 2013: Google Nexus 7 tablet Google Hangouts, google balloons 2014: Acquires DeepMind 2015: Restructures as alphabet 2016: Launches smart home speakers 2018 **R&D: 21.4** US$ bil. 2019: Acquires CloudSimple 2020: Acquires stratozone

5. Microsoft		Software	Software, play stations	Cloud, platforms, analytics, IoT
1975: **Microsoft founded** 1979: Shifted from new Mexico to Washington	**1981:** Microsoft incorporates IBM first PC with MS–DOS 1.0 **1986:** Moves to Redmond, Washington **1989:** The earliest version of office suite **1990:** Microsoft launches windows 3.0	**1995:** Microsoft launches windows 95 Bill gates outlines Microsoft's commitment to the internet **1998:** Microsoft launches windows 98 **2000:** Steve ballmer named president and CEO for windows 2000	**2001:** Windows XP, office XP Xbox play station **2002:** Tablet PC **2003:** Windows Server 2003 MS office system **2004:** Xbox 360 next generation **2006:** Zune music player **2007:** Windows vista MS Office 2007 **2008:** Windows server, SQL server Visual studio **2010:** Windows phone OS MS Office 2010	**2011:** Windows phone, Xbox Kinect Office 365 **2012:** Surface tablets Windows 8, windows phone 8 Windows server **2013:** Surface 2, pro 2, Xbox one Office 2013 **2014:** Buys Nokia devices & services Buys minecraft, office iPad Android, surface pro 3 **2015:** Windows 10, Office 2016, Lumia 950, Lumia 95 XL Surface 3, pro 4 **2016:** LinkedIn, surface studio, dial Book, visual Studio 2017 **2018 R&D: 14.7 US$ bil** **2019:** Trillion company

Continued

Table 5.1 Transformation direction of the seven leading global information and communication technology firms (1970–2020).—cont'd

	1970–80	1981–90 *Distributor*	1991–2000 *Fixed-line and digital network products*	2001–10 *Mobile networks*	2011–20 *Smartphones, cloud, IoT*
6. Huawei		**1988: Huawei founded** as a distributor of imported PBX products	**1993**: Digital telephone switch with capacity over 10,000 circuits **1996**: Wins first big overseas contract for fixed-line network products From Hong Kong's Hutchison–Whampoa	**2003**: Joint venture with 3Com Cisco systems sues for copyright violations **2004**: Overseas sales surpass domestic sales for the first time **2008**: Contract orders rose 46% to US$23.3 billion World's 3rd largest mobile network gear maker **2009**: World's top patent seeker Head the UN WIPO list	**2011**: Announces its enterprise business **2012**: Deploys business in 170 countries **2014**: World's largest telecom equipment **2015**: Smartphones, Huawei P8 Huawei P8 max **2017**: Narrowband IoT city-aware network **2018**: Sold 200 mil. Smartphones **2018 R&D: 15.3 US$ bil** **2019**: Establishes Malaysia training center **2019**: Revenue of US$ 122 bil **2020**: The world's top smartphones seller

	Computers, printers	Computers	Laptop computers	iPod, iTunes, smartphones, tablets	Smart devices, platforms, IoT
7. Apple	**1976: Apple founded** 1976: Apple I 1977: Apple II 1978: Apple (writer, file type) 1979: 1980: Apple III	1981: Apple ProFile 1982: Apple printers (dot matrix, letter quality)	2000: PowerBook prismo Cinema display 22″	2001: iPod 1st gen 2002: iPod 2nd gen, iBook 14″, iMac 2003: iPod 3rd gen, PowerBook G4 2004: iPod mini (1st gen) iPod (4th gen) 2005: iPod mini (2nd gen) iPod nano (1st gen) iPod (4th gen) iPod shuffle 2006: MacBook pro (15″, 17″) iPod Hi-Fi, iPod nano (2nd gen) iPod shuffle (2nd gen)	2011: iPad 2 (16, 32, 64 GB) iPhone 4S 2012: iPad, iPad mini, iPhone 5 2013: iPhone 6, iPhone 6 plus iPad air 2, iPad mini 3 2014: Apple watch, iPhone 6S iPad mini 4, iPad pro **2015:** iPhone 7, iPhone 7 plus iPad pro **2016:** iPhone 7, iPhone 7 plus with camera 2017: iPhone 8, iPhone 8 plus 2018: iPhone XS, iPhone XS max 2018 **R&D: 14.2** US$ bil 2019: iPhone 11, iPhone 11 pro, iPhone 11 pro max 2019: Acquires Intel's smartphone business 2020: Acquires mobeewave 2020: Acquires next VR 2020: 2 trillion company

Continued

Table 5.1 Transformation direction of the seven leading global information and communication technology firms (1970–2020).—cont'd

1970–80	1981–90	1991–2000	2001–10	2011–20
			2007: Apple TV (1st gen) iPhone (4, 8 GB) **2008**: iPhone 3G (8, 16 GB) iPhone (16 GB) **2009**: iPhone 3 GS **2010**: iPad (WiFi + 3G), iPhone 4	

Authors' elaboration based on Naveed, K., Watanabe, C., Neittaanmäki, P., 2018. The transformative direction of innovation toward an IoT-based society – increasing dependency on uncaptured GDP in global ICT firms. Technology in Society 53, 23–46.

Table 5.2 Key transformative direction of the top seven information and communication technology leaders.

Amazon	"Fusing net and real" Merging physical and digital and real bricks and mortar
Samsung	"User experiences **through** smart design **and technology**" Inspire the world, create future design and technology innovation. (smartphones, art-frame TVs, smart appliances)
Intel	"Empowering **the technologies of the** future dream" makes possible the most amazing experiences of the future. (Intel technologies transforming businesses and accelerating the use of artificial intelligence)
Google	"**Enabling overdrawing of information through search**" "One-click" access to the world's information. (Internet search, advertising, OS and platforms, Google apps)
Microsoft	"**Harnessing the utmost gratification of** consumer delight" productivity and platform company for mobile-first and cloud-first world.
Huawei	"**Building a better** connected world" Driving ICT transformation through innovation and transformation
Apple	"Personalized user experiences **through top-quality products**" Face of the earth to make great products Simple, user-friendly and better design: Focus on innovation, collaboration, and excellence

economic value. Therefore, *SIRs* are considered condensates and crystals of the Internet.[5] A common feature of *SIRs* is that contrary to the value they contribute to suprafunctionality, the value they create is not accountable in traditional GDP terms[6] (Watanabe et al., 2018a,b).

---

[5] Based on the augmented permeation of the Internet into broad ICT and the subsequent creation of a new social ecosystem, particularly with smartphones (see Fig. A1 in the Appendix), authors in their previous analyses (Tou et al., 2019a) have demonstrated the significant correlations between six typical *SIRs* utilized by seven global ICT leaders (Naveed et al., 2018) and the advancement of the Internet/smartphone as follows: suprafunctionality beyond economic value with *a self-propagating function of the circular economy leader UPM* as a proxy; sleeping resources with *the price of Uber*; trust with *the level of trust in teachers to deliver a good education*; utmost gratification with *people's preferences ratio*; memory and dream with *revenue of live music*; untapped resources with *gender balance index* (see 4.4 in Chapter 4).

[6] The authors have pointed out the structural change in the concept of output in the digital economy and revealed the limitation of GDP in measuring the output of the digital economy by demonstrating the economy's increasing dependence on uncaptured GDP (Watanabe et al., 2015b; Ahmad and Schreyer, 2016; Byrne and Corrado, 2016; Dervis and Qureshi, 2016; Feldstein, 2017).

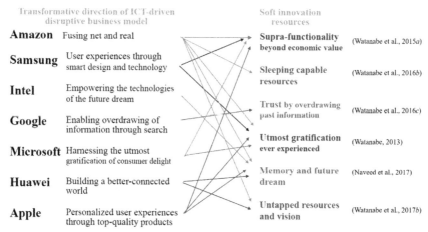

Figure 5.9 Soft innovation resources of global information and communication technology leaders. *(Authors' elaboration based on Naveed, K., Watanabe, C., Neittaanmäki, P., 2018. The transformative direction of innovation toward an IoT-based society — increasing dependency on uncaptured GDP in global ICT firms. Technology in Society 53, 23—46.)*

By assimilating *SIRs*, *HRIFs* can increase their gross R&D by not depending on excessive R&D that causes productivity declines, as illustrated at the bottom of Fig. 5.8. Gross R&D growth activates a latent self-propagating function, which induces functionality development that leads to suprafunctionality beyond economic value, corresponding to the shift in consumer preferences. This shift further induces the advancement of the Internet, which awakens and induces further *SIRs* as its condensates and crystals. Thus, a virtuous cycle among them can be constructed, as illustrated in Fig. 5.8.

5.4.5 The hybrid role of soft innovation resources

The use of *SIRs* is a novel innovation applied by *HRIFs* to encourage sustainable growth and avoid a decline in productivity. In previous studies, the authors have described this hypothetical view (Watanabe et al., 2018a,b) and identified that while such a transformative circumstance in the digital economy results in a decline in productivity, global ICT firms attempt to survive by spontaneous creation of uncaptured GDP through harnessing the vigor of *SIRs* (Tou et al., 2018a, 2019a,b).

It has been demonstrated that *SIRs* help remove the structural impediments of GDP growth (and subsequent growth of economic functionality) such as the conflict between public, employers and labor union, gender disparities, and the increasing discrepancies of an aging society. The spontaneous creation of uncaptured GDP through effective utilization of *SIRs* contributes to the resurgence of captured GDP growth by its hybrid function. Finland's recent resurgence can be attributed to this hybrid role as demonstrated in Fig. 3.13 in Chapter 3 (OECD, 2017; Tou et al., 2018b).

This resurgence also activates a self-propagating function, as illustrated in the lower part of Fig. 5.8, and reinforces the abovementioned virtuous cycle (Watanabe et al., 2018c; Tou et al., 2018b). Amazon's acquisition of Whole Foods in 2017 functioned as this reinforcement (Watanabe et al., 2020; Tou et al., 2020).

5.4.6 Neo open innovation

Neo open innovation that harnesses the vigor of *SIRs* corresponding to the digital economy has thus become a promising solution to the critical dilemma.

Fig. 5.10 illustrates the concept of neo open innovation in the digital economy. Similar to traditional open innovation (Chesbrough, 2003; Chesbrough et al., 2008; West et al., 2014), *SIRs* (which are identical to the digital economy and play functions similar to R&D investment) maintained growth without depending on R&D investment increases[7] that decrease *MP*.

Increased gross R&D consisting of indigenous R&D and assimilated *SIRs* contributes to increased sales without a resulting decline in *MP*. This increases the activation of the self-propagating function by enhancing dynamic carrying capacity, as illustrated in Fig. 5.6, which enables sustainable sales growth and leads to a virtuous cycle between R&D and sales (see the mathematical details in A1.4.2 of the Appendix). Thus, the assimilation of *SIRs* into their businesses can be considered substantial contributors to growth rather than only additional expenditures that result in a decline in productivity, as suggested in Fig. 5.8.

As discussed in Chapter 4, the magnitude of *SIRs* is proportional to user interactions according to Metcalfe's law. The assimilation capacity depends on the level of R&D stock and its growth rate (Watanabe et al., 2002).

---

[7] *SIRs* substitute for additional R&D investment that may cause declines in marginal productivity and induce production factors contributing to growth in production (Tou et al., 2018b).

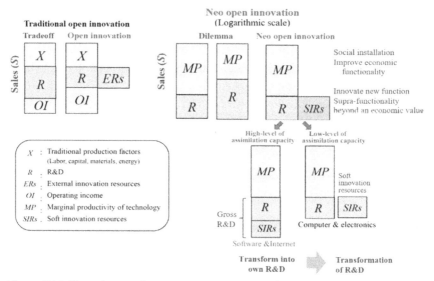

Figure 5.10 The scheme of neo open innovation. *(Authors' elaboration based on Tou, Y., Watanabe, C., Moriya, K., Neittaanmäki, P., 2019a. Harnessing soft innovation resources leads to neo open innovation. Technology in Society 58, 101114.)*

Since Amazon, the global ICT leader in R&D, demonstrates notable user interactions for user-driven innovation based on the architecture of participation[8] and a high level of assimilation capacity based on rapidly increasing R&D investment (Tou et al., 2019b), these systems may be a source enabling it to demonstrate noteworthy accomplishments in both R&D and sales growth by overcoming the dilemma between them, as demonstrated in Fig. 5.11.

In line with these observations, the next chapter attempts to demonstrate this hypothetical view by investigating the transformative direction of innovation for the sustainability of global ICT leaders. The new concept triggered by Amazon for the transformation of R&D into neo open innovation is analyzed.

5.5 Conclusion

Advanced digital economies have recently been confronting the dilemma increases in inputs that result in decreased output (i.e., decreased

---

[8] "Architecture of participation" was postulated by O'Reilly (2003) and implies that users help extend the platform.

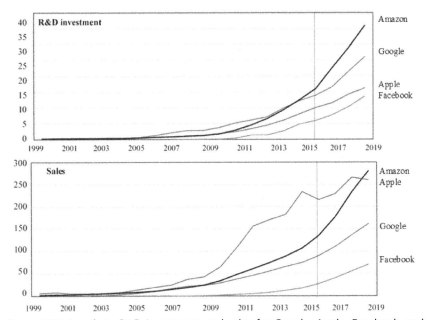

Figure 5.11 Trends in R&D Investment and sales for Google, Apple, Facebook, and Amazon (GAFA) (1999–2019), USD billion. *(Financial statements of GAFA US Security and Exchange Commission (SEC), 2020a. Annual Report Pursuant to Section 13 or 15(d) of the Security Exchange Act of 1934 for the Fiscal Year 2019, Alphabets Inc. SEC, Washington, D.C; US Security and Exchange Commission (SEC), 2020b. Annual Report Pursuant to Section 13 or 15(d) of the Security Exchange Act of 1934 for the Fiscal Year 2019, Amazon.com, Inc. SEC, Washington, D.C; US Security and Exchange Commission (SEC), 2020c. Annual Report Pursuant to Section 13 or 15(d) of the Security Exchange Act of 1934 for the Fiscal Year 2019, Apple Inc. SEC, Washington, D.C; US Security and Exchange Commission (SEC), 2020d. Annual Report Pursuant to Section 13 or 15(d) of the Security Exchange Act of 1934 for the Fiscal Year 2019, Facebook, Inc. SEC, Washington, D.C. See Table A4 in the Appendix.)*

productivity). Contrary to traditional expectations, an excessive increase in input results in a decline in productivity.

This chapter attempted to identify the transformative direction of R&D-intensive firms that encourages sustainable growth while avoiding the dilemma.

An empirical analysis of the development trajectory of the top 500 global ICT firms was used to investigate a structural source of the dilemma, dynamism, and pioneering endeavors made by global ICT leaders to maintain sustainable growth while avoiding the dilemma.

Noteworthy findings include the following:

(1) Amid the advancement of the digital economy and subsequent IoT society, contrasting trends between highly R&D-intensive firms and less-R&D-intensive firms concerning productivity have been observed at the forefront for global ICT firms.

(2) This can be attributed to the consequence of the two-faced logistic growth nature of ICT, which leads to bipolarized global ICT firms.

(3) Contrary to the virtuous cycle that less-R&D-intensive global ICT firms enjoy between R&D investment and increased marginal ICT productivity, highly R&D-intensive firms fall into a vicious cycle between increased R&D and declining productivity.

(4) Against such circumstances, the only way for highly R&D-intensive firms to achieve sustainable growth is to harness the vigor of *SIRs*.

(5) *SIRs* activate the latent self-propagating function indigenous to ICT.

(6) The activated self-propagating function induces functionality development leading to suprafunctionality beyond economic value that corresponds to a shift in people's preferences.

(7) This shift induces further advancement of the Internet, which in turn activates *SIRs*. Thus, a virtuous cycle can be constructed.

(8) Under such circumstances, leading global ICT firms have attempted to explore and harness the vigor of *SIRs,* such as the locomotive power of a preference shift to suprafunctionality, sleeping resources, trust by overdrawing past information, utmost gratification ever experienced, memory and dream, and untapped resources.

(9) These *SIRs* have emerged within the remarkable disruptive business models initiated by ICT leaders during their transformation into new business models in seeking a solution to the dilemma.

(10) These business models were induced by the "great coevolution" due to the new stream of the digital economy under spin-off dynamism, digital innovation with its unique nature, and the shift to new socioeconomic trends.

(11) Assimilated *SIRs* increase gross R&D, consisting of indigenous R&D and assimilated *SIRs,* and contribute to sales increases without decreasing productivity, which enables sustainable sales growth and leads to a virtuous cycle between R&D and sales.

(12) Thus, the assimilation of *SIRs* into a business can be considered a substantial contributor to growth but not an additional expenditure that results in a decline in productivity.

(13) This analysis suggests that gross R&D that encompasses assimilated *SIRs* contributes to growth without effecting a decline in productivity. This growth activates a self-propagating function leading to

construction of the above virtuous cycle that enables sustainable growth while avoiding the dilemma.

(14) This dynamism can be enabled by harnessing the vigor of *SIRs* that lead to neo open innovation in the digital economy.

(15) Neo open innovation that harnesses the vigor of *SIRs* that correspond to the digital economy has become a promising solution to the critical dilemma.

These findings give rise to the following suggestions for optimal trajectory management in the digital economy at both national and firm levels:

(1) The exploration and utilization of new *SIRs* should be continued.

(2) Given the recent resurgence of GDP growth by world ICT leader Finland, the hybrid role of *SIRs* in both activating the coevolution comprising a shift in people's preferences, the advancement of the Internet, and increasing dependence on uncaptured GDP and leveraging captured GDP growth by removing structural impediments in captured GDP growth should be sought.

(3) The noteworthy inducement of *SIRs* initiated by a bioeconomy-based circular economy should be further accelerated.

(4) The new concept of open innovation that accounts for *SIRs* should be developed.

Future work should focus on comparative assessment of the success and failure of effective utilization of *SIRs* that depend on institutional systems as reviewed in 4.2.2.4 (Uber's case) as well as among global ICT leaders (e.g., among the GAFA). A new concept of R&D that can transform into neo open innovation should be envisioned thereon.

References

Ahmad, N., Schreyer, P., 2016. Are GDP and productivity measures up to the challenges of the digital economy? International Productivity Monitor 30, 4–27.

Brynjolfsson, E., McAfee, A., 2014. The Second Machine Age. W.W. Norton & Company, New York.

Byrne, D., Corrado, C., 2016. ICT Prices and ICT Services: What Do They Tell About Productivity and Technology? Economic Program Working Paper Series, EPWP #16-05 The Conference Board, New York.

Chesbrough, H.W., Vanhaverbeke, W., West, J., 2008. Open Innovation: Researching a New Paradigm. Oxford University Press, Oxford.

Chesbrough, H.W., 2003. Open Innovation: The New Imperative for Creating and Profiting From Technology. Harvard Business School Press, Boston.

Cowen, T., 2011. The Great Stagnation: How America Ate All the Low-Hanging Fruit of Modern History, Got Sick, and Will (Eventually) Feel Better. A Penguin eSpecial from Dutton, Penguin, New York.

Dervis, K., Qureshi, Z., 2016. The Productivity Slump — Fact or Fiction: The Measurement Debate. Global Economy and Development at Brookings, Washington, D.C.

Devezas, T.C., Linstone, H.A., Santos, H.J.S., 2005. The growth dynamics of the internet and the long wave theory. Technological Forecasting and Social Change 72, 913–935.

EU, 2017a. Economics of Industrial Research and Innovation. EU, Brussels.

EU, 2017b. The Internet of Things: Digital Single Market. EU, Brussels.

European Commission, Joint Research Center, 2017. The EU Industrial R&D Investment Scoreboard 2016. European Commission, Brussels.

Feldstein, M., 2017. Understanding the real growth of GDP, personal income, and productivity. The Journal of Economic Perspectives 31 (2), 145–164.

International Monetary Fund (IMF), 2017. Measuring the Digital Economy: IMF Statistical Forum. IMF, Washington D.C.

Japan Cabinet Office, 2019. National Survey of Lifestyle Preferences. Japan Cabinet Office, Tokyo.

Kahre, C., Hoffmann, D., Ahlemann, F., 2017. Beyond business-IT alignment-digital business strategies as a paradigmatic shift: a review and research agenda. In: Proceedings of the 50th Hawaii International Conference on System Sciences, Hawaii, pp. 4706–4715.

Lowrey, A., 2011. Freaks, Geeks, and GDP. Slate. http://www.slate.com/articles/business/moneybox/2011/03/freaks_geeks_and_gdp.html (retrieved 20.06.2017).

McDonagh, D., 2008. Satisfying needs beyond the functional: the changing needs of the silver market consumer. In: Proceedings of the International Symposium on the Silver Market Phenomenon — Business Opportunities and Responsibilities in the Aging Society, Tokyo.

McDonagh, D., Thomas, J., 2010. Disability + relevant design: empathic design strategies supporting more effective new product design outcomes. The Design Journal 13 (2), 180–198. https://doi.org/10.2752/175470710X12735884220899.

McKinsey Global Institute, 2015. The Internet of Things: Mapping the Value beyond the Hype. McKinsey & Company, New York.

Naveed, K., Watanabe, C., Neittaanmäki, P., 2017. Co-evolution between streaming and live music leads a way to the sustainable growth of music industry: lessons from the US experiences. Technology in Society 50, 1–19.

Naveed, K., Watanabe, C., Neittaanmäki, P., 2018. The transformative direction of innovation toward an IoT-based society — increasing dependency on uncaptured GDP in global ICT firms. Technology in Society 53, 23–46.

OECD, 2016. OECD Observer: The Digital Economy. OECD, Paris.

OECD, 2017. OECD Review of Innovation Policy: Finland Assessment and Recommendation. OECD, Paris.

O'Reilly, T., 2003. The Open Source Paradigm Shift. O'Reilly & Associates, Inc., Sebastopol. https://www.oreilly.com/tim/archives/ParadigmShift.pdf (retrieved 10.01.2019).

Rifkin, J., 2011. The Third Industrial Revolution: How Lateral Power is Transforming Energy, the Economy, and the World. Macmillan, New York.

Schelling, T.C., 1998. Social mechanisms and social dynamics. In: Hedstrom, P., Swedberg, R. (Eds.), Social Mechanisms: An Analytical Approach to Social Theory. Cambridge Univ. Press, Cambridge, pp. 32–43.

The Economist, November 3, 2018. Schumpeter: The Tech Sell-Off. The Economist.

The US Council on Competitiveness (USCC), 2016. No Recovery: An Analysis on Long-Term U.S. Productivity Decline. USCC, Washington, D.C.

The World Bank, 2016. Digital Dividends. The World Bank, Washington D.C.

Tou, Y., Moriya, K., Watanabe, C., Ilmola, L., Neittaanmäki, P., 2018a. Soft innovation resources: enabler for reversal in GDP growth in the digital economy. International Journal of Managing Information Technology 10 (3), 9–29.

Tou, Y., Watanabe, C., Ilmola, L., Moriya, K., Neittaanmäki, P., 2018b. Hybrid role of soft innovation resources: Finland's notable resurgence in the digital economy. International Journal of Managing Information Technology 10 (4), 1—22.

Tou, Y., Watanabe, C., Moriya, K., Neittaanmäki, P., 2019a. Harnessing soft innovation resources leads to neo open innovation. Technology in Society 58, 101114.

Tou, Y., Watanabe, C., Moriya, K., Naveed, N., Vurpillat, V., Neittaanmäki, P., 2019b. The transformation of R&D into neo open innovation: a new concept of R&D endeavor triggered by Amazon. Technology in Society 58, 101141.

Tou, Y., Watanabe, C., Neittaanmäki, P., 2020. Fusion of technology management and financing management: amazon's transformative endeavor by orchestrating techno-financing systems. Technology in Society 60, 101219.

US Security and Exchange Commission (SEC), 2020a. Annual Report Pursuant to Section 13 or 15(d) of the Security Exchange Act of 1934 for the Fiscal Year 2019. Alphabets Inc. SEC, Washington, D.C.

US Security and Exchange Commission (SEC), 2020b. Annual Report Pursuant to Section 13 or 15(d) of the Security Exchange Act of 1934 for the Fiscal Year 2019. Amazon.com, Inc. SEC, Washington, D.C.

US Security and Exchange Commission (SEC), 2020c. Annual Report Pursuant to Section 13 or 15(d) of the Security Exchange Act of 1934 for the Fiscal Year 2019. Apple Inc. SEC, Washington, D.C.

US Security and Exchange Commission (SEC), 2020d. Annual Report Pursuant to Section 13 or 15(d) of the Security Exchange Act of 1934 for the Fiscal Year 2019. Facebook, Inc. SEC, Washington, D.C.

Watanabe, C., 2009. Managing Innovation in Japan: The Role Institutions Play in Helping or Hindering How Companies Develop Technology. Springer Science & Business Media, Berlin.

Watanabe, C., 2013. Innovation-consumption co-emergence leads a resilience business. Innovation and Supply Chain Management 7 (3), 92—104.

Watanabe, C., Hobo, M., 2004. Creating a firm self-propagating function for advanced innovation-oriented projects: lessons from ERP. Technovation 24 (6), 467—481.

Watanabe, C., Zhu, B., Miyazawa, T., 2001. Hierarchical impacts of the length of technology waves: an analysis of technolabor homeostasis. Technological Forecasting and Social Change 68 (1), 81—104.

Watanabe, C., Takayama, M., Nagamatsu, A., Tagami, T., Griffy-Brown, C., 2002. Technology spillover as a complement for high level R&D intensity in the pharmaceutical industry. Technovation 22 (4), 245—258.

Watanabe, C., Kondo, R., Ouchi, N., Wei, H., Griffy-Brown, C., 2004. Institutional elasticity as a significant driver of IT functionality development. Technological Forecasting and Social Change 71 (7), 723—750.

Watanabe, C., Nasuno, M., Shin, J.H., 2011. Utmost gratification of consumption by means of supra-functionality leads a way to overcoming global economic stagnation. Journal of Services Research 11 (2), 31—58.

Watanabe, C., Kanno, G., Tou, Y., 2012. Inside the learning dynamism inducing the resonance between innovation and high-demand consumption: a case of Japan's high-functional mobile phones. Technological Forecasting and Social Change 79 (7), 1292—1311.

Watanabe, C., Naveed, K., Zhao, W., 2014. Institutional sources of resilience in global ICT leaders — harness the vigor of emerging power. Journal of Technology Management in Growing Economies 5 (1), 7—34.

Watanabe, C., Naveed, K., Zhao, W., 2015a. New paradigm of ICT productivity: increasing role of un-captured GDP and growing anger of consumers. Technology in Society 41, 21—44.

Watanabe, C., Naveed, K., Neittaanmäki, P., 2015b. Dependency on un-captured GDP as a source of resilience beyond economic value in countries with advanced ICT infrastructure: similarities and disparities between Finland and Singapore. Technology in Society 42, 104—122.

Watanabe, C., Naveed, K., Neittaanmäki, P., Tou, Y., 2016a. Operationalization of uncaptured GDP: the innovation stream under new global mega-trends. Technology in Society 45, 58—77.

Watanabe, C., Naveed, K., Neittaanmäki, P., Tou, Y., 2016b. Co-evolution of three mega trends nature uncaptured GDP: uber's ride-sharing revolution. Technology in Society 46, 164—185.

Watanabe, C., Naveed, K., Neittaanmäki, P., 2016c. Co-evolution between trust in teachers and higher education toward digitally-rich learning environments. Technology in Society 48, 70—96.

Watanabe, C., Naveed, K., Neittaanmäki, P., 2017a. Consolidated challenge to social demand for resilient platforms: lessons from uber's global expansion. Technology in Society 48, 33—53.

Watanabe, C., Naveed, K., Neittaanmäki, P., 2017b. ICT-driven disruptive innovation nurtures uncaptured GDP: harnessing woemen's potential as untapped resources. Technology in Society 51, 81—101.

Watanabe, C., Tou, Y., Neittaanmäki, P., 2018a. A new paradox of the digital economy: structural sources of the limitation of GDP statistics. Technology in Society 55, 9—23.

Watanabe, C., Naveed, K., Tou, Y., Neittaanmäki, P., 2018b. Measuring GDP in the digital economy: increasing dependence on uncaptured GDP. Technological Forecasting and Social Change 137, 226—240.

Watanabe, C., Naveed, N., Neittaanmäki, P., 2018c. Digitalized bioeconomy: planned obsolescence-driven economy enabled by co-evolutionary coupling. Technology in Society 56, 8—30.

Watanabe, C., Tou, Y., Neittaanmäki, P., 2020. Institutional systems inducing R&D in Amazon: the role of an investor surplus toward stakeholder capitalization. Technology in Society 63, 101290.

West, J., Salter, A., Vanhaverbeke, W., Chesbrough, H.W., 2014. Open innovation: the next decade. Research Policy 43 (5), 805—811.

World Economic Forum (WEF), 2016. The Global Competitiveness Report, 2016. WEF, Geneva.

CHAPTER 6

The transformation of R&D into neo open innovation

Contents

6.1 A new concept of R&D in neo open innovation

6.1.1 R&D as a culture

Contrary to the dilemma of R&D expansion coupled with declining productivity that most digital economies now confront (Tou et al., 2019a), Amazon has accomplished notable performance (Galloway, 2017) by conspicuously increasing its R&D to become the world's top R&D firm in 2017 while it also experienced a skyrocketing increase in its market capitalization that has nearly made it the world's most valuable company, as demonstrated in Figs. 6.1 and 6.2.

Transforming the Socio Economy with Digital Innovation
ISBN 978-0-323-88465-5
https://doi.org/10.1016/B978-0-323-88465-5.00008-8

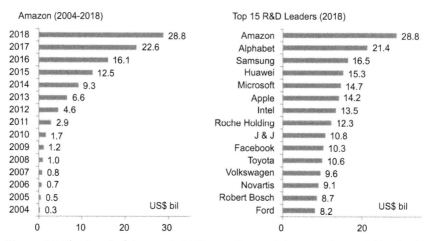

Figure 6.1 The trend of Amazon's R&D spending as it became the world leader in R&D. *(Sources: Same as those of Fig. 1.4 (see Table A1).)*

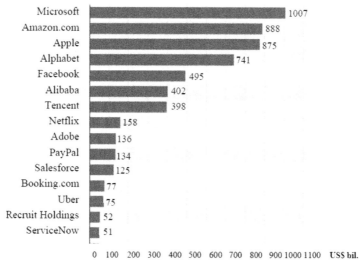

Figure 6.2 Market capitalization of the top 15 internet companies (June 2019). *(Sources: Statista, 2019. Top Internet Companies: Global Market Value 2018. Statista, Hamburg. https://www.statista.com/statistics/277483/market-value-of-the-largest-internet-companies-worldwide/ (retrieved 10.01.2019). See Table AII-2.)*

Amazon's rapid growth can be attributed to an R&D-driven disruptive business model that attempts a new concept of transforming R&D into neo open innovation to harness the vigor of soft innovation resources (*SIRs*) (Tou et al., 2019a, 2019b; Watanabe and Tou, 2020).

Table 6.1 Brief chronology of Amazon's major steps to becoming an innovation giant.

1994	Founded
1997	IPO
2002	AWS envisioned
2005	Amazon Prime
2006	AWS opened up to outside customers
	Amazon Elastic Compute Cloud (Amazon EC2)
2007	Amazon Kindle
2010	Migrated retail web services to AWS
2011	Kindle Fire
2014	Amazon Echo (Alexa Voice Service)
2016	Amazon Go store
2017	Acquisition of Whole Foods

AWS, Amazon Web Services; *IPO*, initial public offering.

Amazon has sought to be an R&D-driven company since its inception in 1994, as demonstrated in Table 6.1.

Amazon's fundamental strategy is R&D as a culture, something emphasized by its founder and CEO, Jeffrey Bezos, in his 2010 Letter to Shareholders (Bezos, 2010).[1] The company has promoted company-wide experimentation (Bezos, 2013)[2] to create customers obsessed with making purchase decisions, as highlighted at the top of its 14 leadership principles (Amazon, 2018):

(1) customer obsession
(2) ownership
(3) invent and simplify
(4) be right often
(5) learn and be curious
(6) hire and develop the best
(7) insist on the highest standards
(8) think big
(9) have a bias for action
(10) practice frugality

---

[1] Bezos explained the importance of R&D activities while also highlighting aspects of Amazon's culture: innovation and growth are built into every segment of the company, not just R&D.

[2] In his 2013 letter to shareholders (Bezos, 2013), Bezos stressed the following: *"Innovation comes from distributed decision-making. Top-down teams are effective at optimizing existing processes and enforcing the completion of work, but only decentralized, bottom-up teams can consistently generate new ideas."*

Figure 6.3 Illustration of Amazon's R&D. *(Source: Authors' elaboration based on the work of Tou, Y., Watanabe, C., Moriya, K., Naveed, N., Vurpillat, V., Neittaanmäki, P., 2019b. The transformation of R&D into neo open innovation: a new concept of R&D endeavor triggered by Amazon. Technology in Society 58, 101141.)*

(11) earn trust

(12) dive deep

(13) have backbone, disagree, and commit

(14) deliver results

Such a sophisticated system can be attributed to strong inertia induced by the customer-centric, visionary leadership of Bezos, with motivated, brilliant, and consistently innovative employees who are equipped with species survival and a system of evolution that watches for the necessity of disruptive business change (University of Toronto, 2013), as illustrated in Fig. 6.3.

This system has led to Amazon's unique resource allocation strategy. Most of Amazon's profits come from its high-tech division, which includes its cloud computing operation and Amazon Web Services (AWS). These profits have been reinvested in its business and its employees, not in dividends and buybacks. Amazon has not paid a dividend since its initial public offering (IPO) in 1997, nor has it bought back any shares since 2012. That strategy is reflected in its R&D spending on activities to increase customer obsession, leading to Amazon becoming the world's top R&D firm over a short period.

6.1.2 User-driven innovation

Its business model has enabled Amazon to extensively absorb external resources and assimilate them into its indigenous business through a high-level assimilation capacity developed by rapid and notable increases in R&D, as demonstrated in Fig. 6.4 (Watanabe et al., 2002; Tou et al., 2019b).

This model has enabled Amazon to deploy an architecture for participation (Colin, 2016) that leads to the emergence of new digital

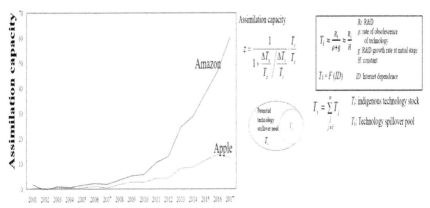

Figure 6.4 Trends in the assimilation capacities of Amazon and Apple (2001–17). *(Source: Authors' elaboration based on the work of Tou, Y., Watanabe, C., Moriya, K., Naveed, N., Vurpillat, V., Neittaanmäki, P., 2019b. The transformation of R&D into neo open innovation: a new concept of R&D endeavor triggered by Amazon. Technology in Society 58, 101141.)*

technologies by harnessing the power of users (Ritala et al., 2014), as illustrated in Fig. 6.5.

This dynamism can be attributed to the significant effect of coopetition (cooperation and competition) (Brandenburger and Nalebuff, 1996). Ritala

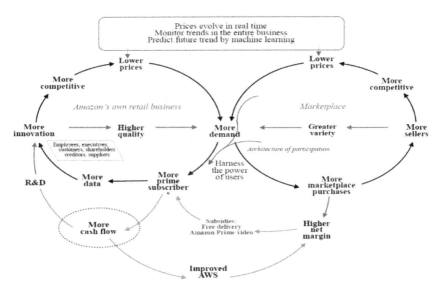

Figure 6.5 The dynamism of user-driven innovation at Amazon. *(Source: Authors' elaboration based on the work of Tou, Y., Watanabe, C., Moriya, K., Naveed, N., Vurpillat, V., Neittaanmäki, P., 2019b. The transformation of R&D into neo open innovation: a new concept of R&D endeavor triggered by Amazon. Technology in Society 58, 101141.)*

et al. (2014) demonstrated that by collaborating with its competitors, Amazon has built new capabilities, gained better leverage, and boosted its brand and technologies. Evans and Forth (2015) investigated Amazon's strategic competitive actions. They stressed that Amazon seized strategic opportunities presented by successive waves of disruption, ruthlessly cannibalizing its own business where necessary.

Thus, Amazon has constructed a unique user-driven innovation system by making itself indispensable to e-commerce and enjoying sustained growth in business from its users and its rivals as both cooperators and competitors (Khan, 2017).

6.1.3 The virtuous cycle of neo open innovation that transforms R&D

6.1.3.1 New concept of R&D

User-driven innovation based on the architecture of participation accelerates the dramatic advancement of the Internet (O'Reilly, 2003), which in turn accelerates coemergence and the awakening and inducement of *SIRs* in the marketplace, as illustrated in Fig. 5.8 in the preceding chapter. Thus, the coevolutionary coemergence of user-driven innovation and the emergence of *SIRs* can be expected (Tou et al., 2018a, 2018b, 2019b).

Because Amazon has developed high-level assimilation capacity, as reviewed in Fig. 6.4, it fully assimilates these emerging *SIRs*, leading to increased gross R&D spending, as illustrated in Fig. 5.8. This increased investment in R&D leads to growth that in turn activates the latent self-propagating function indigenous to information and communication technology (ICT).[3] The activated self-propagating function induces the development of functionalities that lead to suprafunctionality beyond economic value that corresponds to a shift in people's preferences. This shift induces the further advancement of the Internet and leverages the coevolutionary advancement of innovation in the digital economy (Watanabe et al., 2018b, 2018c) as illustrated in Fig. 5.8. Also, *SIRs* function in the removal of structural impediments to GDP growth (i.e., the growth of traditional economic functionality), such as conflicts between the public,

---

[3] With network externalities (Ruttan, 2001), ICT construct a self-propagating virtuous cycle between the expanding number of users and the rising value of networks (Watanabe and Hobo, 2004; Watanabe et al., 2004. See mathematical details in A1.4 in Appendix I).

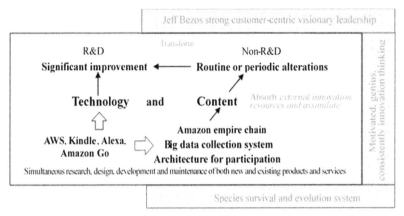

Figure 6.6 The scheme of Amazon's unique R&D model. *(Source: Watanabe, C., Tou, Y., 2020. Transformative direction of R&D: lessons from Amazon's endeavor. Technovation 88, 102081.)*

employers, and labor unions; gender disparities; and the increasing discrepancies of an aging society (Tou et al., 2018b), as reviewed in Chapter 4.

These successive efforts have functioned as a virtuous cycle, leading to the transformation of "routine or periodic alterations" (classified as non-R&D by traditional accounting standards and sought in traditionally captured GDP as shown in Fig. 5.8) into "significant improvement" (similarly classified as R&D, and sought primarily in uncaptured GDP) (FASB, ASC, 2018; National Science Foundation, 2018) during R&D process, as illustrated in Fig. 6.6.

Notwithstanding such an increase in expenses for business activities generally categorized as R&D spending, Amazon insists on describing these as "technology and content" expenditures, as detailed in Table 6.2. While

Table 6.2 Comparison of the R&D investment descriptions used by Amazon and Apple (2017).

	Category	Description
Amazon	Technology and content	Technology and content costs include payroll and related expenses for employees involved in the research and development of new and existing products and services, development, design, and maintenance of our websites, curation and display of products and services made available on our online stores [web pages], and infrastructure costs. Infrastructure costs

Continued

Table 6.2 Comparison of the R&D investment descriptions used by Amazon and Apple (2017).—cont'd

	Category	Description
		include servers, networking equipment, and data center-related depreciation, rent, utilities, and other expenses necessary to support Amazon Web Services and other business efforts. Collectively, these costs reflect the investments we make to offer a wide variety of products and services to our customers.
Apple	Research and development	Because the industries in which the company competes are characterized by rapid technological advances, the company's ability to compete successfully depends heavily upon its ability to ensure a continual and timely flow of competitive products, services, and technologies to the marketplace. The company continues to develop new technologies to enhance existing products and services and to expand the range of its offerings through R&D, licensing of intellectual property, and acquisition of third-party businesses and technology.

Sources: Amazon.com, Inc. 2018 annual report (2019a). Apple Inc. 2017 annual report (2018).

the former focuses on business activities for "significant improvement," the latter encompasses those for "routine or periodic alterations."

Generally accepted accounting principles in the United states are provided by FASB-ASC[4] and specify the activities typically included in and excluded from research & development (FASB-ASC, 2018) as an accounting category.[5] The former activities (i.e., R&D) contribute to

---

[4] The Accounting Standards Codification (ASC) of the Financial Accounting Standards Board (FASB).

[5] *Research* is a planned search or critical investigation aimed at discovery of new knowledge with the hope that such knowledge will be useful in developing a new product or service (hereinafter "product") or a new process or technique (hereinafter "process") or in bringing about a significant improvement to an existing product or process.

Development is the translation of research findings or other knowledge into a plan or design for a new product or process or for a significant improvement to an existing product or process, whether intended for sale or use. It includes the conceptual formulation, design, and testing of product alternatives, construction of prototypes, and operation of pilot plants.

significant improvement, whereas the latter activities (i.e., non-R&D) contribute only to routine or periodic alterations. Amazon claims that the boundary between the two types of activities has become blurred in the digital economy and that its R&D and non-R&D activities are difficult to separate, as its R&D activities are implemented such that simultaneous research, design, development, and maintenance of both new and existing products and services occur in a holistic business operation. Moreover, Amazon conducts R&D activities to transform routine or periodic alterations into significant improvement during the R&D process when it absorbs *SIRs* from external environments and assimilates them into its routine or periodic alteration activities, thus transforming these activities so they lead to significant improvement (see the details of Amazon's principle in research by Tou et al., 2019b).

6.1.3.2 Transformation of R&D

Amazon has invested considerable resources in extremely innovative business areas such as AWS, Kindle, Alexa, and Amazon Go for the improvement of the former (significant improvement). In parallel with such leading-edge innovations, Amazon endeavors to absorb external innovation resources, particularly *SIRs* from external markets (Tou et al., 2019b), and assimilate them into its business model, which transforms the latter business activities (routine or periodic alterations) into the former during the R&D process.[6]

This transformation corresponds to creating suprafunctionality beyond economic value that stimulates customer obsession by awakening and activating the latent self-propagating function through effective assimilation of *SIRs* in the marketplace.

Unlike Apple, Google, and Microsoft, Amazon is not fixated on a tightly designed ecosystem of interlocking apps and services, as demonstrated by Table 6.2. Bezos instead emphasizes platforms, each of which serves its customers in the best and fastest way possible. *"Our customers are loyal to us right up until the second somebody offers them a better service,"* he says. *"And I love that. It's super-motivating for us."* That impulse has spawned an awesome stream of creative firsts (Robischon, 2017), as if being fired from

---

[6] See the details of Amazon's profound implications on its unique R&D model in a series of letters between the US Securities and Exchange Commission (SEC) and Amazon during the fall and winter of 2017–18 (Fox, 2018; Tou et al., 2019b).

the right side of Fig. 6.3 (members with motivated, bright, and consistently innovative thinking who actively assimilate *SIRs*).

Given this impulse, Amazon seems to have explored a newer R&D model that also transforms "routine or periodic alterations" into "significant improvement" by deploying the full-fledged function of its sophisticated management system to extensively absorb external resources and assimilate them into its business.

Noteworthy is that "technology" leverages "content," which in turn induces further advancement of "technology," leading to a coevolutionary complementary system.

Thus, we could conclude that Amazon has constructed an R&D-driven disruptive business model, one that generates a new concept of R&D that overcomes the dilemma of R&D expansion that results in declining productivity.

This success can be attributed to a virtuous cycle among user-driven innovation, advancement of the Internet, coemergence of *SIRs*, and activation of a self-propagating function that induces functionality development, leading to suprafunctionality beyond economic value that satisfies shifts in consumer preferences. This virtuous cycle is based on Amazon's unique R&D model, which transforms "routine or periodic alterations" into "significant improvement" during the R&D process. This unique transformation-seeking R&D model harnesses the locomotive power of spin-off coevolution, as illustrated in Fig. 6. 7, to create the "great coevolution" of digital innovation with shifts to new trends, as well as inducing disruptive business models, as reviewed in Fig. 4.19 in Chapter 4.

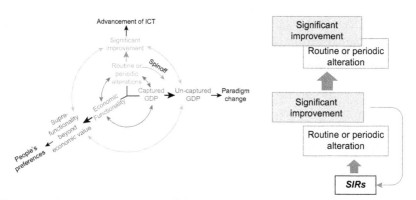

Figure 6.7 Amazon's unique spin-off from coevolution based on routine or periodic alterations to one that seeks significant improvement.

6.2 The fusion of technology management and financial management

6.2.1 Using the cash conversion cycle to drive cash flow generation for aggressive R&D

Amazon's unique R&D-inducing system gives rise to proposals for a new concept of R&D in neo open innovation that overcomes the dilemma of R&D expansion that is associated with a decline in productivity. It does so by transforming routine or periodic alteration activities into significant improvement activities during its R&D process. This occurs through the assimilation of external innovation resources based on an empire chain, a big data collection system, and a participation architecture.

Consequently, elucidation of the black box of its technomanagement system that has enabled it to secure such extraordinary levels of R&D investment has become a critically important subject.[7]

Amazon has constructed a sophisticated marketplace cash conversion cycle (CCC) (Price, 2013; Fox, 2014; Naruge, 2018) that creates affluent cash flow (CF) that enables aggressive R&D. This in turn incorporates characteristics of uncertainty, long lead times, and successive inflows of large amounts of funding without interruption (Watanabe, 2009).

To address its target of being an R&D-driven company, Bezos put Amazon's financial focus on long-term growth in free cash flow (FCF) per share, as he reminded stakeholders in his 2004 letter (Bezos, 2005).

Based on these strategies, Amazon succeeded in fusing its unique R&D transformation system (as reviewed in the preceding section) and a sophisticated financing system centered on CCC-driven CF management, as illustrated in Fig. 6.8, to induce the following dynamism (Tou et al., 2020):

(1) With strong user-driven innovation, Amazon constructed overwhelming power for both customers and vendors in its marketplace (Naruge, 2018).

(2) This power enabled the construction of an extremely advanced CCC of -30 to -20 days (Fig. 6.9) (Panigrahi, 2013; Oral and Akkaya, 2015; Zakari and Saidu, 2016; Zeidan and Shapir, 2017).

(3) Amazon's advanced CCC reduced the average interest rate on its operating funds, leading to decreases in the prices of goods and services

---

[7] For example, in light of the vast amounts of money coming and going from particular segments of ICT giants like Amazon, the SEC paid special attention to Amazon's allocation of R&D spending, and conducted investigation in 2017 (see Tou et al., 2019b).

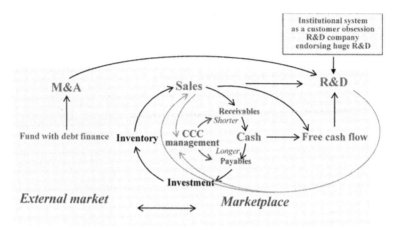

Figure 6.8 Amazon's cash flow management scheme.

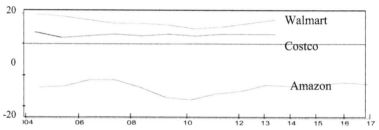

Figure 6.9 Cash conversion cycles (in days) of Walmart, Costco, and Amazon (2004–13). *(Sources: Fox, J., 20 Oct. 2014. At Amazon, It's All about Cash Flow. Finance & Accounting. https://hbr.org/resources/images/article_assets/2014/10/inadifferentleague. png. (retrieved 26.06.2019); Uenlue, M., Aug. 22, 2018. Amazon Business Model: Three Customer Value Propositions. Innovation Tactics. https://www.innovationtactics.com/ amazon-business-model-part-2/. (retrieved 10.06.2019).)*

(Tou et al., 2020) and enabled Amazon to deploy dynamic pricing, which induced customer interactions while improving FCF (Fig. 6.10) (Uenlue, 2018; Tou et al., 2020).

(4) The induced interactions in turn further advanced CCC, leading to the *first virtuous cycle.*

(5) Endorsed and supported by increased FCF, induced interactions accelerated the transformation of R&D, leading to an increase in Amazon's qualified technology stock (Tou et al., 2020).

Figure 6.10 Amazon's virtuous cycle of pricing leading to data network externalities. *(Original source: Uenlue, M., Aug. 22, 2018. Amazon Business Model: Three Customer Value Propositions. Innovation Tactics. https://www.innovationtactics.com/ amazon-business-model-part-2/. (retrieved 10.06.2019).)*

(6) Increased stock contributed to sales growth and the construction of a lean cost structure.[8]

(7) Both of the factors in (6) contributed to an increase in operating profits and a subsequent increase in FCF, thus constructing the *second virtuous cycle* (the statistical details can be found in Tables AII-5 and AII-6 in the Appendix).

(8) Increased sales contributed to further advances in CCC management, leading to the *third virtuous cycle*.

Thus, three virtuous cycles were constructed from Amazon's CCC management, enabling the notable CF management illustrated in Fig. 6.11 (Tou et al., 2020).

6.2.2 The optimal combination of acquisitions and R&D

In addition to this CF-based financing, Amazon uses a different method for financing its business acquisitions and investments. It considers capital market conditions and then deploys an exquisite combination of its own cash and debt financing (Hong et al., 2013).

It aims to make acquisitions that reinforce its business model by capturing a growth engine and assimilating external resources for innovation.

Acquiring Whole Foods Market in 2017 for USD 13,700 million has been Amazon's largest and most impressive acquisition (Amazon, 2019a). It was not merely quantitatively impressive but also significantly reinforced

---

[8] Bezos repeatedly stressed to work to increase operating profit by focusing on improving all aspects of the customer experience to grow sales and by maintaining a lean cost structure (e.g., Amazon 2019b,c).

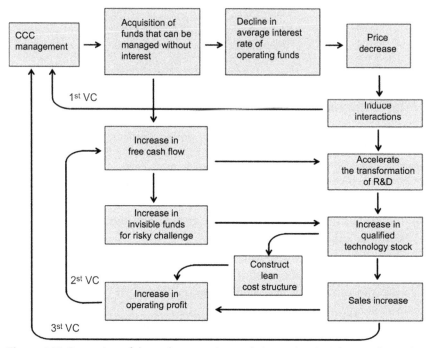

Figure 6.11 Dynamism of the cash conversion cycle in accelerating the transformation of R&D. *(Source: Authors' elaboration based on Tou, Y., Watanabe, C., Neittaanmäki, P., 2020. Fusion of technology management and financing management: Amazon's transformative endeavor by orchestrating techno-financing systems. Technology in Society 60, 101219.)*

Amazon's R&D model (Berthene, 2019), helping to construct a virtuous cycle in neo open innovation, as illustrated in Fig. 5.8 (Tou et al., 2020).

Whole Foods is a high-end supermarket with 450 stores in the US that focuses on organic foods. It has maintained sustainable growth with a strong brand and popularity as an eco-friendly firm. For 20 consecutive years, Whole Foods was included in *Fortune's* illustrious list of 100 Best Companies to Work For. However, Whole Foods was not necessarily digitally advanced and was thus running short on the online transition capability and fulfillment power essential for success in the digital economy. Peaking in 2013, it lost market share and online transition capability.

Acquiring Whole Foods was expected to be a way for Amazon to develop its coopetition strategy with real stores that were not online. While Whole Foods provided Amazon with know-how about delivery management and quality control for fresh foods and paved the way for Amazon's entry into real stores and sales, it also contributed to developing

Whole Foods' online transition capabilities. Capturing the growth engine that Whole Foods had been constructing for many years reinforced Amazon's development trajectory by activating the latent self-propagating function that leads to the creation of suprafunctionality. Moreover, this acquisition corresponded to consumers' increasing concern with the firm's eco-consciousness (Ferdousi and Qiang, 2016), to which Amazon is sensitive (Phipps, 2018; Watanabe et al., 2018a, 2018d; Naveed et al., 2020).

6.2.3 Sophisticated consolidated machine

All of Amazon's financing and R&D-driven business development strategies have been deployed as part of a sophisticated consolidated machine constructed through three phases of development following its 1997 IPO, as illustrated in Fig. 6.12.

These strategies are as follows:

(1) Phase I (1997—2001)

Focal efforts were devoted to establishing financial and R&D bases beyond books and the US market through active mergers and amalgamations (M&A) largely dependent on long-term debt.

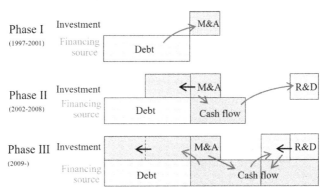

Figure 6.12 Amazon's scheme for the development trajectory of R&D financing. —➤ : Business/R&D emergence; ➤ : Cash flow creation; ➤ : Expansion. *(Source: Authors' elaboration based on Tou, Y., Watanabe, C., Neittaanmäki, P., 2020. Fusion of technology management and financing management: Amazon's transformative endeavor by orchestrating techno-financing systems. Technology in Society 60, 101219.)*

(2) Phase II (2002–08)

Amazon developed business activities by fully utilizing the fruits of the advancement of M&A, leading to a gain in operating income that enabled CCC-oriented CF creation; thereby, R&D was promoted, which accelerated R&D substitution for M&A, leading to strengthening of the indigenous R&D base and decreasing dependence on long-term debt.

(3) Phase III (2009–18)

Amazon increased its CF, particularly FCF, through advancement of the business and the construction of a lean cost structure, which induced R&D significantly and led to further advancement of the business and subsequent CCC management. Thus, a virtuous cycle was constructed that reactivated M&A, including that of Whole Foods, the company's largest acquisition to date. This functioned as the capture of a growth engine and reinforced the fragility of the virtuous cycle.

Fig. 6.13 demonstrates this sophisticated consolidated machine by illustrating trends in R&D, operating CF, long-term debt, and the number of Amazon acquisitions (bar graph) from 1998 to 2018.

It is noteworthy that all of these functions are well-orchestrated as a consolidated, sophisticated machine—marketplace dynamism that induces CCC advancement, CCC-driven CF management, and R&D investment that transforms routine or periodic alterations into significant improvement during the R&D process.

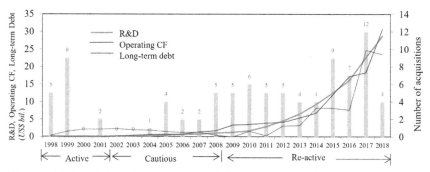

Figure 6.13 Trends in R&D, operating cash flow, long-term debt, and number of acquisitions for Amazon (1998–2018). *(Source: Author's elaboration based on Tou, Y., Watanabe, C., Neittaanmäki, P., 2020. Fusion of technology management and financing management: Amazon's transformative endeavor by orchestrating techno-financing systems. Technology in Society 60, 101219.)*

Table 6.3 Financial sources inducing Amazon's R&D investment (1997–2018).

$\ln R = 1.12 + 0.33 D_2 \ln OCF + 0.72 D_3 \ln OCF + 0.89 D_1 \ln LTD - 1.04 D_2 \ln LTD + 1.04 D_3 \ln LTD$
(1.79**) (2.90*)   (7.71)   (20.42)   (-5.63)   (3.80)

$-2.46 D_1 + 10.42 D_2 - 0.79 D_{31}$ $adj. R^2$ 0.996 DW 1.86
(-3.55)   (5.53)   (-6.42)

D, dummy variables (D_1: 1997–2001 = 1, others = 0; D_2: 2002–8 = 1, others = 0; D_3: 2009–18 = 1, others = 0; D_{31}: 2009, 2010 = 1, others = 0); LTD, long-term debt; OCF, operating cash flow; R, R&D investment.
The figures in parentheses are t-statistics; all are significant at the 1% level except *(5%) and **(15%).

Based on these observations, Table 6.3 demonstrates the financial sources that have induced Amazon's conspicuous R&D investment since its IPO in 1997.

Table 6.3 demonstrates that Amazon has accomplished a notable R&D transformation that has made it a top-R&D-driven company using the above orchestration.

Thus, we could conclude that Amazon has succeeded in creating a unique R&D transformation system. This transformation was endorsed by its institutional system as an R&D-driven company and a sophisticated financing system centered on CCC-driven CF management. The company combined this with debt financing that aimed to acquire the fruits of growth. Furthermore, Amazon depended on capital market conditions and maximized the effects of external resource assimilation through coopetition with broad stakeholders.

6.3 Investor surplus to leverage stakeholder capitalization

6.3.1 The value of institutional system endorsement for risky investments in R&D

As the digital economy has developed, securing R&D funding has determined competitiveness. As reviewed earlier, Amazon, a company with a 2018 market capitalization of USD 1,000 billion, has been a world leader in R&D investment since 2017. In 2018, it invested USD 28,800 million in R&D, 35% more than the second-biggest investor, Google. The rapid increase in this investment showed no sign of slowing down in 2019, amounting to USD 35,900 million, as reviewed in Fig. 1.11 in Chapter 1 (US SEC, 2020b).

Such a remarkable accomplishment can be attributed to its institutional systems. These technofinancing systems fuse a unique R&D transformation system and a sophisticated financing system centered on the CCC, as demonstrated in the preceding section. These institutional systems also incorporate a special function that supports and endorses aggressive investment in risky ventures such as R&D. R&D embeds characteristics such as uncertainty, long lead-times, and successive large, uninterrupted funding inflows, as a lack of funds turns the return of all previous efforts to ashes.

While some of this investment can be endorsed by Amazon's positive business results, such as sustained increases in sales and FCF (see the detailed statistics in Table AII-5 in the Appendix), such a large amount of aggressive investment is beyond endorsement. In addition to actual economic performance, investors have been betting on a high level of risky investment with an expectation of Amazon's future success and trusting its R&D-inducing institutional systems.

While the former case of investing based on actual accomplishments can be considered a general reaction to a producer surplus, the latter case of investing on high expecations for future success can be postulated as an investor surplus in which investors bet on overly optimistic prospects. This is similar to a consumer surplus in which consumers pay more than the actual market price for attractive goods and services (Hausman, 1997; Greenwood and Kopecky, 2013; Fouquet, 2018).

In light of Amazon's notable success in rapidly increasing its investment in R&D while simultaneously accomplishing remarkable increases in productivity and subsequent production despite the R&D—productivity dilemma, elucidation of the special function incorporated in Amazon's institutional systems that support and endorse commitments of large amounts of financing to aggressive R&D has become a global concern. The particular concern goes to its unique function of leveraging the expectations of a wide range of stakeholders who bet on Amazon's future prospects through the risky investment vehicle of aggressive R&D.

To elucidate this unique function, Amazon's R&D-driven market capitalization (MC) formation process was analyzed.

MC represents gross market value (Bae and Kim, 2003), which reflects the value of the company's institutional systems that support and endorse the large, high-risk (European Central Bank ECB, 2008) investments that Amazon continues to make in aggressive R&D projects.

MC can be decomposed into the following equation consisting of objectively reflecting economic performance and subjectively reflecting the notion of a "dream," i.e., an expectation related to the company's future success:

$$MC = N \times \frac{E}{N} \times \frac{S_p}{E/N}$$

where N: number of shares outstanding; E: earning (net income); S_p: stock prices.

While E/N depicts earnings per share (*EPS*), and with N, it represents actual economic performance in reaction to a producer surplus, $S_p/(E/N)$ depicts the price-to-earnings ratio (*PER*), which is highly subjective and represents a similar reaction to a consumer surplus.

Thus, the gross market value depicted by this equation can be decomposed into the actual economic value (in terms of N and *EPS*) with the producer surplus function and the value of the "dream" of future success (*PER*) with the consumer surplus function.

Amazon's financial focus is on its target of being an R&D-driven company focused on long-term growth in FCF per share rather than on earnings, as Bezos reminded readers in his 2004 letter to stakeholders (Bezos, 2005), as reviewed earlier.

Given this identical focus, the next equation, substituting FCF per share (*FCF/N*) for *EPS* in the above equation, replicates the financial focus of a world-leading R&D-driven company:

$$MC = N \times \frac{FCF}{N} \times \frac{S_p}{FCF/N}$$

While the product of the first two factors ($N \times FCF/N$) in this equation represents a producer surplus by demonstrating actual objective economic performance, the third factor (the price-to-FCF ratio, or $\frac{S_p}{FCF/N}$) represents an investor surplus in which investors bet on the company's future prospects based on utilizing FCF to enable risky investments such as R&D. This ratio is highly subjective and reflects largely uncaptured GDP in the digital economy, where customer preferences have been shifting to suprafunctionality beyond economic value, a trend to which Amazon has been devoted, striving for customer obsession with purchase decisions as analyzed earlier.

6.3.2 Inducing role of investor surplus

Aiming at identifying Amazon's unique performance in constructing an investor surplus, Fig. 6.14 compares the price-to-FCF ratio of the big four online service companies, Google, Apple, Facebook, and Amazon (GAFA), which reveals a noteworthy contrast explaining the performance in constructing an investor surplus that induces R&D.

Looking at Fig. 6.14, we note that among GAFA companies, Amazon demonstrates the highest dependence on investor surplus, as represented by the price-to-FCF ratio, $\left(\dfrac{S_p}{FCF/N}\right)$, which suggests that investors are betting on continuation of Amazon's solid growth with its aggressive investment in R&D, supported and endorsed by its institutional systems.

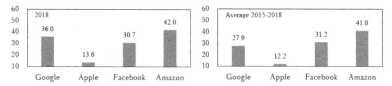

Figure 6.14 *A Comparison of the price-to-free-cash-flow ratios of Google, Apple, Facebook, and Amazon (2018; 2015—8 average).* Market capitalization uses the quarterly average for each respective year. *(Sources: US Security and Exchange Commission (SEC), 2020a. Annual Report Pursuant to Section 13 or 15(d) of the Security Exchange Act of 1934 for the Fiscal Year 2019. Alphabets Inc. SEC, Washington, D.C; US Security and Exchange Commission (SEC), 2020b. Annual Report Pursuant to Section 13 or 15(d) of the Security Exchange Act of 1934 for the Fiscal Year 2019. Amazon.com, Inc. SEC, Washington, D.C; US Security and Exchange Commission (SEC), 2020c. Annual Report Pursuant to Section 13 or 15(d) of the Security Exchange Act of 1934 for the Fiscal Year 2019. Apple Inc. SEC, Washington, D.C; US Security and Exchange Commission (SEC), 2020d. Annual Report Pursuant to Section 13 or 15(d) of the Security Exchange Act of 1934 for the Fiscal Year 2019. Facebook, Inc. SEC, Washington, D.C; Macrotrends, 2020. The Premier Research Platform for GAFA Financial Statements 2005—2020. Zacks Investment Research Inc., Chicago.   www.macrotrends.net/stocks/charts/GOOG/alphabet/financial-statements   https:// www.macrotrends.net/stocks/charts/AMZN/amazon/financial-statements   https://www. macrotrends.net/stocks/charts/AAPL/apple/financial-statements   https://www.macrotrends. net/stocks/charts/FB/facebook/financial-statements. (retrieved 30.01.2020).)*

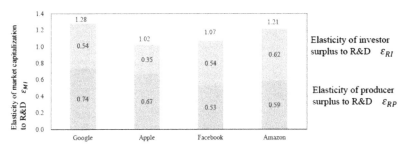

Figure 6.15 Comparison of the elasticity of market capitalization to R&D investment of Google, Apple, Facebook, and Amazon (2005–18).

Amazon's high investor surplus significantly induces R&D investment. Fig. 6.15 compares the elasticity of MC to R&D investment by decomposing it to that of a producer surplus and an investor surplus.[9]

Fig. 6.15 demonstrates that Amazon has the highest elasticity of investor surplus to R&D among the GAFA companies.

These analyses demonstrate that Amazon has constructed a high level of investor surplus, and this surplus significantly induces R&D investment. This unique function incorporates the way that Amazon's institutional systems leverage the expectation that investors will bet on Amazon's future prospects through risky investments such as aggressive R&D.

Amazon has tried to provide investors with convincing evidence of the promising returns that can be expected from such R&D practices.

The number of patent applications can be considered a notable and objective outcome that convinces investors of promising returns from investments in R&D. Amazon has made intensive effort to convince investors in this way, as illustrated in Fig. 6.16.[10]

---

[9] Elasticity of MC to R (MC elasticity to R) ε_{RM} implies 1% increase in MC increases ε_{RM} % increase in R and represents the efficiency of MC in inducing R.
Because M is a product of a producer surplus (P) and an investor surplus (I) as

$$M = P \cdot I, \frac{\partial R}{\partial M} = \frac{\partial R}{\partial PI} = \frac{\partial P}{\partial PI} \cdot \frac{\partial R}{\partial P} + \frac{\partial I}{\partial PI} \cdot \frac{\partial R}{\partial I} = \frac{1}{\frac{\partial PI}{\partial P}} \cdot \frac{\partial R}{\partial P} + \frac{1}{\frac{\partial PI}{\partial I}} \cdot \frac{\partial R}{\partial I} = \frac{1}{I} \cdot \frac{\partial R}{\partial P} + \frac{1}{P} \cdot \frac{\partial R}{\partial I}$$

$$\varepsilon_{RM} = \frac{\partial R}{\partial M} \cdot \frac{M}{R} = \frac{M}{R} \left(\frac{1}{I} \cdot \frac{\partial R}{\partial P} + \frac{1}{P} \cdot \frac{\partial R}{\partial I} \right) = \frac{1}{I} \cdot \frac{\partial R}{\partial P} \cdot \frac{PI}{R} + \frac{1}{P} \cdot \frac{\partial R}{\partial I} \cdot \frac{PI}{R} = \frac{\partial R}{\partial P} \cdot \frac{P}{R}$$
$$+ \frac{\partial R}{\partial I} \cdot \frac{I}{R} = \varepsilon_{RP} + \varepsilon_{RI}$$

Respective elasticities were measured by correlations between ln R and ln X ($X = M$, P, I) as $\varepsilon_{RX} = \frac{\partial \ln R}{\partial \ln X}$.

[10] Similar to the method of Fig. 6.20, R&D elasticity to patent application (Pa). $\varepsilon_{PaR} = \frac{\partial \ln Pa}{\partial \ln R}$

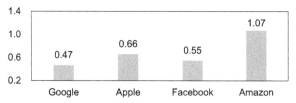

Figure 6.16 R&D elasticity to patent applications of Google, Apple, Facebook, and Amazon (2014–18). *(Sources: LexisNexis, 2019. Total Patent One. Ken Hattori of WHDA LLP, Washington, D.C; Macrotrends, 2020. The Premier Research Platform for GAFA Financial Statements 2005–2020. Zacks Investment Research Inc., Chicago. www.macrotrends.net/ stocks/charts/GOOG/alphabet/financial-statements   https://www.macrotrends.net/stocks/ charts/AMZN/amazon/financial-statements   https://www.macrotrends.net/stocks/charts/ AAPL/apple/financial-statements   https://www.macrotrends.net/stocks/charts/FB/facebook/ financial-statements. (retrieved 30.01.2020).)*

6.3.3 Implications of investor surplus

The foregoing contrast highlights the significant role of investor surplus for Amazon and supports the supposition that investors bet on the continuation of Amazon's solid growth with its aggressive investment in large amounts of R&D.

Amazon has not paid a dividend since its IPO in 1997, nor has it bought back any of its shares since 2012, as reviewed in 6.1.1.

Therefore, it is natural to ask the question of what investors expect from Amazon's enormous investment risk (Watanabe et al., 2020a, 2020b).

Its user-driven innovation that addresses changes in customer preferences in the digital economy to achieve customer obsession as reviewed in 6.1 provides a reasonable answer to this question, with significant implications for Amazon's investor surplus. First, investors incorporate not only shareholders but also broad stakeholders who are centered on users. Second, these stakeholders expect economic value as well as suprafunctionality beyond such value, encompassing social, cultural, emotional, and ecological values, as reviewed in 5.1.2.

Thus, Amazon has taken the initiative in terms of stakeholder capitalism, leading it to realize an outstanding CCC and secure abundant FCF as well as enabling aggressive R&D that excites investors and broad stakeholders. This corresponds to a new corporate governance doctrine encouraging the company to shift from shareholder capitalism to stakeholder capitalism (Business Roundtable, 2019).

As analyzed in 6.1, based on its unique business model and ambitious attempts at customer-centric R&D-driven advancement, Amazon has developed a comprehensive empire chain, big data collection system, and architecture for participation. It has also discerned how to harness the power of its users, which leads to user-driven innovation. This innovation accelerates further advancement of the Internet. An advanced Internet awakens and successively induces environmentally friendly *SIRs* by making full utilization of digital technologies such as AI, IoT, VR/AR, and mobile services.[11]

Consequently, the following virtuous cycle is constructed—*user-driven innovation → advancement of the Internet → awakening and inducement of SIRs in the marketplace → increase in gross R&D → sustainable growth → activation of self-propagating function → emergence of suprafunctionality beyond economic value → acceleration of user-driven innovation* (Watanabe and Tou, 2020)—as illustrated in Fig. 6.17.

6.4 Orchestrating technofinancing systems

The secret of Amazon's success in constructing such a sophisticated virtuous cycle dynamism can be attributed to securing gross R&D that enabled customer-centric R&D-driven advancement while avoiding the dilemma of R&D expansion with a productivity decline. Gross R&D consists of indigenous R&D investment and assimilated *SIRs*. While the increase in the former results in a productivity decline, this increase and its speed enhances assimilation capacity, leading to neo open innovation by effectively utilizing the assimilated *SIRs*. In case the latter effect exceeds the former harmful effect due to productivity declines, sustainable growth can be enabled, which activates the latent self-propagating function and induces

---

[11] Typical *SIRs* can be exemplified as follows by synchronizing its business mission and core technologies: (1) Shifts in preferences toward suprafunctionality beyond economic value, *SDGs (the biggest river*—e.g., Amazon Web Services: AWS (2002)), (2) Sleeping resources (*all stakeholders working together*—e.g., Amazon Flex (2015)), (3) Drawing upon past information and fostering trust (*carrying every product from A to Z*—e.g., Amazon Prime (2005)), (4) Providing the most gratification ever experienced (*fusing net and real*—e.g., Amazon Go (2016)), (5) Memory and future dreams (*brick-and-mortar retailer*—e.g., Amazon Kindle (2007)), and (6) Untapped resources and vision (*instilling dreams in customers*—e.g., Amazon Echo (2014)).
Also, the successive introduction of new innovative fashion models with coevolutionary nature between sociocultural change and innovation (Nagurney and Yu, 2011; Kaiser, 2012; Runfola and Guercini, 2013; Ciarniene and Vienazindiene, 2014) in 2018 as *Prime Wardrobe, Personal Shopper by Prime Wardrobe, Echo Look, the Drop, AI algorithm for designing clothes,* and *AR mirror* have accelerated coevolutional advancement of these *SIRs* (Danziger, 2020; Nakano, 2020; Watanabe et al., 2020a).

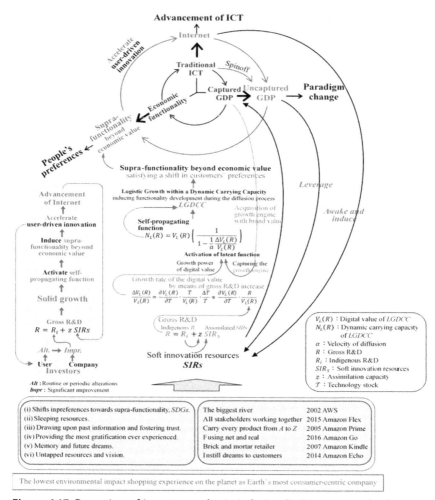

Figure 6.17 Dynamism of investor surplus in inducing R&D investment by Amazon.

suprafunctionality beyond economic value corresponding to customer preferences. This in turn accelerates the virtuous cycle dynamism.

Therefore, the key to constructing such virtuous cycle dynamism depends on timely R&D investment with optimal volume and speed that exceeds the harmful effect of declines in productivity.

As reviewed in 6.1, Amazon has deployed its comprehensive technology management system by consolidating its R&D transformation and technopreneurial strategies, as illustrated in Fig. 6.18. The R&D transformation strategy has been equipped with species survival and an evolution system that watches for the necessity of disruptive business change as

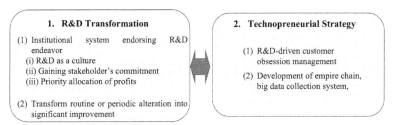

1. R&D Transformation

(1) Institutional system endorsing R&D endeavor
(i) R&D as a culture
(ii) Gaining stakeholder's commitment
(iii) Priority allocation of profits

(2) Transform routine or periodic alteration into significant improvement

2. Technopreneurial Strategy

(1) R&D-driven customer obsession management
(2) Development of empire chain, big data collection system,

Figure 6.18 Amazon's technology management system—consolidation of its R&D transformation and technopreneurial strategies.

illustrated in Fig. 6.3 (University of Toronto, 2013). This system manages the abovementioned optimal volume and speed of R&D investment.[12]

As reviewed in Section 6.1, this well-functioning consolidation can be attributed to a virtuous cycle among user-driven innovation, the advancement of the Internet, coemergence of *SIRs*, and activation of a self-propagating function that induces functionality development, leading to suprafunctionality beyond economic value that satisfies shifts in customer preferences.

The key enabler of this virtuous cycle is Amazon's unique R&D model that transforms "routine or periodic alterations" into "significant improvement" during its R&D process. This unique transformation-seeking R&D model plays a locomotive role, generating spin-off coevolution that creates a "great coevolution" with digital innovation and a shift to new socioeconomic trends. This "great coevolution" induces disruptive business models that cause the emergence of disruptive innovation by harnessing the vigor of activated *SIRs,* as illustrated in Fig. 6.19.

The six remarkable disruptive business models reviewed in Chapter 4 can be considered products induced by the "great coevolution" due to the new stream of the digital economy under spin-off dynamism, digital innovation with its unique nature, and the shift to new socioeconomic trends. Amazon's transformation-seeking R&D model leverages spin-off dynamism and drives the emergence of the "great coevolution" with digital innovation and new socioeconomic trends.

When there is sufficient assimilation capacity due to sufficient volume and the speed of timely R&D investment, the disruptive innovation that

---

[12] This system plays a compass role for consistent innovation with disruptive performance (Tou et al., 2019b).

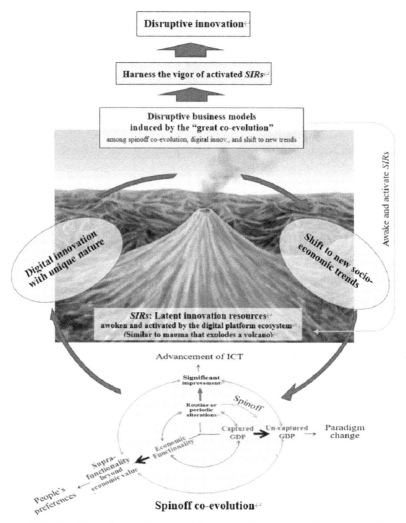

Figure 6.19 The disruptive business models induced by Amazon's "great coevolution."

emerges is incorporated into gross R&D, which makes a significant contribution to growth and activates a self-propagating function, as illustrated in Fig. 6.20.

Amazon has succeeded in activating this high-level self-propagating function, as demonstrated in Fig. 6.21.[13]

---

[13] See Eqs. A1-15 in Appendix A1.4 in Appendix I for computation of self-propagating function. A coefficient is based on Tou et al. (2019b).

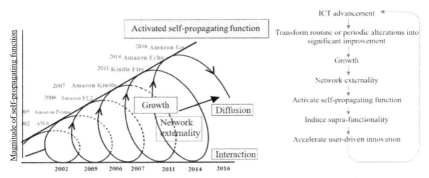

Figure 6.20 Dynamism in activating Amazon's self-propagating function.

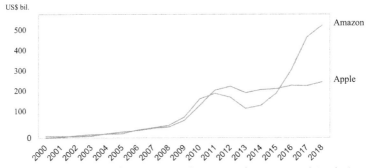

Figure 6.21 Trends in the self-propagating functions of Amazon and Apple (2000—18 and 3-year moving average).

Successful activation of the high-level self-propagating function depends on sufficient assimilation capacity to enable the incorporation of activated *SIRs* into gross R&D whereby the growth essential for activation of the self-propagating function can be ensured.

As noted, sufficient volume and timely R&D investment is required for the building of assimilation capacity, as reviewed earlier (Fig. 6.4). Amazon has created a system for this requirement because it has also deployed a sophisticated financial management system by consolidating market development and CCC-driven CF generation, as illustrated in Fig. 6.22.

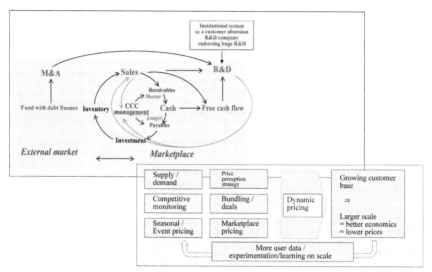

Figure 6.22 Amazon's financial management system—consolidation of market development and cash conversion cycle—driven cash flow generation.

An essential part of this transformative endeavor has been Amazon's orchestration of technofinancing systems, fusing the systems for both technology management and financing management as illustrated in Fig. 6.23.

This orchestration creates a threefold virtuous cycle (CCC advancement vs. interaction intensity; transformation of R&D vs. increases in FCF; and sales increases vs. CCC advancement) leading to a high level of investor surplus that induces R&D bets from a broad array of stakeholders.

This system enables Amazon to secure extraordinary amounts of R&D funding in a timely manner that are sufficient for building assimilation capacity that leads to the comprehensive virtuous cycle.

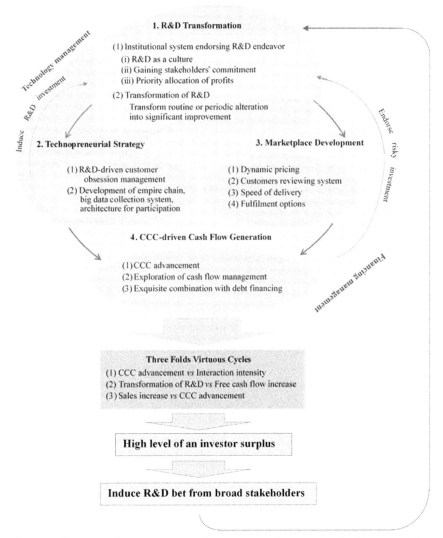

Figure 6.23 Amazon's orchestration of technofinancing systems that lead to stakeholder capitalization.

6.5 Conclusion

There is clear significance to the operationalization of neo open innovation that transforms R&D by utilizing external resources and avoiding the dilemma of R&D expansion coupled with declining productivity. This chapter has attempted to provide a new insight into firms' coevolutionary trajectories between solid growth and gross R&D that optimize indigenous R&D and external resource dependency.

This chapter has examined Amazon's significant increases in R&D, as it overcame the aforementioned dilemma through user-driven innovation that assimilates external resources. This chapter has used the preceding analyses as well as a techno-economics analysis focusing on the R&D-driven development trajectory of global ICT firms, particularly the trajectories of firms that are leaders in terms of their high R&D intensities. The goal was to elucidate the black box of the institutional systems governing Amazon's technofinancial development trajectory.

Noteworthy findings include the following:

(1) Amazon attempts to make customer-centric R&D-driven advancement the basis of its business model.

(2) With this business model, it has strove for pioneering innovation and company-wide experimentation to achieve empire growth and a subsequent big data collection system.

(3) This leads to notable interaction with users for user-driven innovation based on an architecture of participation as well as high-level assimilation capacity based on rapidly increasing R&D investment.

(4) This enables Amazon to harness the power of users who seek *SIRs,* which functions as a virtuous cycle leading to the transformation of "routine or periodic alterations" into "significant improvement" during the R&D process.

(5) These systems are considered a source that enables Amazon to deploy successful neo open innovation, which leads to its outstanding accomplishments in both R&D and sales increases by overcoming the dilemma between them.

(6) This deployment has been enabled by fusing a unique R&D system and a sophisticated financing system centered on CCC-driven FCF management.

(7) With this orchestration of R&D and financing, Amazon leverages the expectations of a wide range of stakeholders by providing suprafunctionality beyond economic value and takes the initiative of stakeholder capitalism in which stakeholders bet on its future prospects driven by aggressive R&D.

(8) Consequently, a notable virtuous cycle is constructed: *user-driven innovation → advancement of the Internet → awakening, and inducement of SIRs in a marketplace → increase in gross R&D → solid growth → activation of self-propagating function → emergence of suprafunctionality beyond economic value → acceleration of user-driven innovation.*

These findings lead to the following proposals for leveraging a new concept of R&D and subsequent neo open innovation in the digital economy:

(1) The coevolutional development between Amazon's user-driven innovation and the disruptive advancement of *SIRs* should be applied to any disruptive business model aiming to overcome the dilemma between R&D expansion and a decline in productivity.

(2) The dynamism enabling this coevolution should be elucidated and conceptualized.

(3) The function incorporated in Amazon's institutional systems that tempt broad stakeholders to invest in it should be further elucidated, conceptualized, and then applied to broad stakeholder capitalization.

(4) The dynamism of the advancement of *SIRs* through orchestrating shifts in the digital economy, the sharing economy, the circular economy, and a post-COVID-19 contactless society should be applied for further advancement of neo open innovation.

The responses to these proposals will transform the following lessons from Amazon's success into a practical road map that supports neo open innovation for operationalization of uncaptured GDP by *SIRs*:

(1) The virtuous cycle among user-driven innovation, the advancement of the Internet, coemergence of *SIRs*, and activation of a self-propagating function that induces functionality development, leading to suprafunctionality beyond economic value that satisfies shifts in customer preferences

(2) The unique R&D model that transforms "routine or periodic alterations" into "significant improvement" during its R&D process, which creates a locomotive power of spin-off coevolution that in turn creates a "great coevolution" with digital innovation and a shift to new trends

(3) "The great coevolution," which induces disruptive business models that explore disruptive innovation by harnessing the vigor of activated *SIRs*

(4) Orchestrating technofinancing systems that fuse technology management and financing management systems to create a threefold virtuous cycle (CCC advancement vs. interaction intensity; transformation of R&D vs. increases in FCF; and sales increase vs. CCC advancement) and enable timely R&D investment with optimal volume and a speed that exceeds the harmful effect of productivity decline

(5) **A high level of investor surplus** that induces R&D bets from a broad group of stakeholders, resulting in a system that enables Amazon to secure extraordinary amounts of R&D funding in a timely manner that are sufficient to build assimilation capacity for the comprehensive virtuous cycle

A broadly applicable and practical approach for assessing R&D investment in neo open innovation for operationalization of uncaptured GDP through *SIRs* can thus be provided.

Amazon's catchphrase, "Fusing the net and real," provides an insightful compass for society after COVID-19. Further elucidation, conceptualization, and operationalization of the functions of the above orchestration and how it may transform the concept of growth will pave the way to a post-COVID-19 society.

References

Amazon, 2018. Amazon Leadership Principles. Amazon.Com, Inc., Seattle.
Amazon, 2019a. Annual Report 2018. Amazon.com, Inc., Seattle. https://ir.aboutamazon.com/static-files/0f9e36b1-7e1e-4b52-be17-145dc9d8b5ec (retrieved 02.07.2019).
Amazon, 2019b. Income Statement. Amazon.com. Inc., Seattle. https://fairlyvalued.com/company/AMZN. (Accessed 2 July 2019). retrieved.
Amazon, 2019c. Cash Flow Statement. Amazon,com, Inc. Annual Financials for Amazon.com, Inc., Seattle. https://www.marketwatch.com/investing/stock/amzn/financials/cash-flow (retrieved 05.08.2019).
Apple, 2018. Annual Report 2017. Apple Inc., Cupertino. https://investor.apple.com/investor-relations/financial-information/ (retrieved 06.01.2019).
Bae, S.C., Kim, D., 2003. The effect of R&D investments on market value of firms: evidence from the U.S., Germany, and Japan. The Multinational Business Review 11 (3), 51—77.
Berthene, A., 2019. How Amazon's Whole foods acquisition changed the grocery industry. Digital Commerce 360. https://www.digitalcommerce360.com/2019/06/21/how-amazons-whole-foods-acquisition-changed-the-grocery-industry/ (retrieved 05.08.2019).
Bezos, J.P., 2005. 2004 Letter to Shareholders. Amazon.com, Inc., Seattle.
Bezos, J.P., 2010. 2010 Letter to Shareholders. Amazon.com, Inc., Seattle.
Bezos, J.P., 2013. 2013 Letter to Shareholders. Amazon.com, Inc., Seattle.
Brandenburger, A.M., Nalebuff, B.J., 1996. Co-Opetition. Currency Doubleday, New York.
Business Roundtable, Aug. 19, 2019. Statement on the Purpose of a Corporation. https://www.businessroundtable.org/business-roundtable-redefines-the-purpose-of-a-corporation-to-promote-an-economy-that-serves-all-americans (retrieved 20.01.2020).
Colin, N., Jan. 18, 2016. 11 Notes on Amazon. The Family Papers #010. https://salon.thefamily.co/11-notes-on-amazon-part-1-cf49d610f195 (retrieved 06.01.2019).
Ciarniene, R., Vienazindiene, M., 2014. Management of contemporary fashion industry: characteristics and challenges. Procedia — Social and Behavioral Sciences 156, 63—68.
Danziger, P.N., Jan. 28, 2020. Amazon, Already the Nation's Top Fashion Retailer, Is Positioned to Grab Even More Market Share. Forbes. https://www.forbes.com/sites/

pamdanziger/2020/01/28/amazon-is-readying-major-disruption-for-the-fashion-in-dustry/#2114545767f3 (retrieved 11.04.2020).

Evans, P., Forth, P., Apr. 22, 2015. Borges' Map: Navigating a World of Digital Disruption. BCG. Com. Publications. https://www.bcg.com/publications/2015/borges-map-navigating-world-digital-disruption.aspx (retrieved 06.01.2019).

Ferdousi, F., Qiang, D., 2016. Implementing circular economy and its impact on consumer ecological behavior. Journal on Innovation and Sustainability 7 (1), 3–10.

Financial Accounting Standards Board (FASB) Accounting Standards Codification (ASC), 2018. Generally Accepted Accounting Principles (GAAP) for Business. FASB, ASC, Washington, D.C.

Fox, J., Oct. 20, 2014. At Amazon, It's All about Cash Flow. Finance & Accounting. https://hbr.org/resources/images/article_assets/2014/10/inadifferentleague.png (retrieved 26.06.2019).

Fox, J., Apr. 13, 2018. Amazon, the Biggest R&D Spender, Does Not Believe in R&D. Bloomberg Opinion. https://www.bloomberg.com/view/articles/2018-04-12/amazon-doesn-t-believe-in-research-and-development-spending (retrieved 22.09.2018).

Fouquet, R., 2018. Consumer surplus from energy transitions. The Energy Journal 39 (3), 167–188.

European Central Bank (ECB), 2008. Risk-taking and risk compensation as elements in the monetary policy transmission process. Monthly Bulletin, ECB, August 2008.

Galloway, S., 2017. The Hidden DNA of Amazon, Apple, Facebook, and Google. Penguin Random House LLC, New York.

Greenwood, J., Kopecky, K.A., 2013. Measuring the welfare gain from personal computers. Economic Inquiry 51, 336–347.

Hausman, J., 1997. Valuation of new goods under perfect and unperfect competition. In: Bresnahan, T., Gorden, R. (Eds.), The Economics of New Products. University of Chicago Press, Chicago.

Hong, A., Bhattacharyya, D., Geis, G.T., 2013. The role of M&A in market convergence: Amazon, Apple, Google and and Microsoft. Global Economy and Finance Journal 6 (1), 53–73.

Kaiser, S.B., 2012. Fashion and Cultural Studies. Berg Publishers, Oxford.

Khan, L.L., 2017. Amazon's antitrust paradox. The Yale Law Journal 126, 710–805.

LexisNexis, 2019. Total Patent One. Ken Hattori of WHDA LLP, Washington, D.C.

Macrotrends, 2020. The Premier Research Platform for GAFA Financial Statements 2005–2020. Zacks Investment Research Inc., Chicago. www.macrotrends.net/stocks/charts/GOOG/alphabet/financial-statements https://www.macrotrends.net/stocks/charts/AMZN/amazon/financial-statements https://www.macrotrends.net/stocks/charts/AAPL/apple/financial-statements https://www.macrotrends.net/stocks/charts/FB/facebook/financial-statements (retrieved 30.01.2020).

Nakano, K., 2020. Apparel Innovators. Nihon Jitsugyou Syuppansha, Tokyo.

Nagurney, A., Yu, M., 2011. Fashion supply chain management through cost and time minimization from a network perspective. Fashion Supply Chain Management: Industry and Business Analysis 1–20.

Naruge, M., 2018. Amazon, The World Top Strategy. Diamond Co., Tokyo.

National Science Foundation (NSF), 2018. Definitions of R&D: An Annotated Compila-tion of Official Sources. NSF, Alexandria, Virginia, USA. https://www.nsf.gov/statistics/randdef/#chp3 (retrieved 10.01.2019).

Naveed, N., Watanabe, C., Neittaanmäki, P., 2020. Co-evolutionary coupling leads a way to a novel concept of R&D: lessons from digitalized bioeconomy. Technology in Society 60, 101220.

Oral, C., Akkaya, G.C., 2015. Cash flow at risk: a tool for financial planning. Procedia Economics and Finance 23, 262–266.

O'Reilly, T., 2003. The Open Source Paradigm Shift. O'Reilly & Associates, Inc., Sebastopol. https://www.oreilly.com/tim/archives/ParadigmShift.pdf (retrieved 10.01.2019).

Panigrahi, A.K., 2013. Cash conversion cycle and firms' profitability. International Journal of Current Research 6, 1484−1488.

Phipps, L., Sept. 12, 2018. How Amazon thinks inside and outside the box. Circular Weekly Newsletter. https://www.greenbiz.com/article/how-amazon-thinks-inside-and-outside-box (retrieved 01.06.2019).

Price, R., 2013. Cash flow at Amazon.com. Accounting Education 28 (2), 353−374.

Ritala, P., Golnam, A., Wegmann, A., 2014. Coopetition-based business models: the case of Amazon.com. Industrial Marketing Management 43, 236−249.

Robischon, N., May 2, 2017. Why Amazon is the world's most innovative company of 2017? Fast Company Magazine. https://www.fastcompany.com/3067455/why-amazon-is-the-worlds-most-innovative-company-of-2017 (retrieved 10.01.2019).

Runfola, A., Guercini, S., 2013. Fast fashion companies coping with internationalization: driving the change or changing the model? Journal of Fashion Marketing and Management 17, 190−205.

Ruttan, V.W., 2001. Technology, Growth, and Development: An Induced Innovation Perspective. Oxford University Press, New York.

Statista, 2019. Top Internet Companies: Global Market Value 2018. Statista, Hamburg. https://www.statista.com/statistics/277483/market-value-of-the-largest-internet-companies-worldwide/ (retrieved 10.01.2019).

Tou, Y., Moriya, K., Watanabe, C., Ilmola, L., Neittaanmäki, P., 2018a. Soft innovation resources: enabler for reversal in GDP growth in the digital economy. International Journal of Managing Information Technology 10 (3), 9−29.

Tou, Y., Watanabe, C., Ilmola, L., Moriya, K., Neittaanmäki, P., 2018b. Hybrid role of soft innovation resources: Finland's notable resurgence in the digital economy. International Journal of Managing Information Technology 10 (4), 1−22.

Tou, Y., Watanabe, C., Moriya, K., Neittaanmäki, P., 2019a. Harnessing soft innovation resources leads to neo open innovation. Technology in Society 58, 101114.

Tou, Y., Watanabe, C., Moriya, K., Naveed, K., Vurpillat, V., Neittaanmäki, P., 2019b. The transformation of R&D into neo open innovation: a new concept of R&D endeavor triggered by Amazon. Technology in Society 58, 101141.

Tou, Y., Watanabe, C., Neittaanmäki, P., 2020. Fusion of technology management and financing management: Amazon's transformative endeavor by orchestrating techno-financing systems. Technology in Society 60, 101219.

Uenlue, M., Aug. 22, 2018. Amazon Business Model: Three Customer Value Propositions. Innovation Tactics. https://www.innovationtactics.com/amazon-business-model-part-2/ (retrieved 10.06.2019).

University of Toronto, 2013. Amazon Business Model Case Study. APS1012 Management of Innovation − Final Team Projects, Spring 2013. University of Toronto, Faculty of Applied Science and Engineering, Toronto. http://www.amgimanagement.com/founder/ProjectSummaries/APS1012_2013_spring_03_Amazon%20business%20model%20case%20study.pdf (retrieved 10.01.2019).

US Security and Exchange Commission (SEC), 2020a. Annual Report Pursuant to Section 13 or 15(d) of the Security Exchange Act of 1934 for the Fiscal Year 2019. Alphabets Inc. SEC, Washington, D.C.

US Security and Exchange Commission (SEC), 2020b. Annual Report Pursuant to Section 13 or 15(d) of the Security Exchange Act of 1934 for the Fiscal Year 2019. Amazon.com, Inc. SEC, Washington, D.C.

US Security and Exchange Commission (SEC), 2020c. Annual Report Pursuant to Section 13 or 15(d) of the Security Exchange Act of 1934 for the Fiscal Year 2019. Apple Inc. SEC, Washington, D.C.

US Security and Exchange Commission (SEC), 2020d. Annual Report Pursuant to Section 13 or 15(d) of the Security Exchange Act of 1934 for the Fiscal Year 2019. Facebook, Inc. SEC, Washington, D.C.

Watanabe, C., 2009. Managing Innovation in Japan: The Role Institutions Play in Helping or Hindering How Companies Develop Technology. Springer Science & Business Media, Berlin.

Watanabe, C., Hobo, M., 2004. Creating a firm self-propagating function for advanced innovation-oriented projects: lessons from ERP. Technovation 24 (6), 467−481.

Watanabe, C., Tou, Y., 2020. Transformative direction of R&D: lessons from Amazon's endeavor. Technovation 88, 102081.

Watanabe, C., Takayama, M., Nagamatsu, A., Tagami, T., Griffy-Brown, C., 2002. Technology spillover as a complement for high level R&D intensity in the pharmaceutical industry. Technovation 22 (4), 245−258.

Watanabe, C., Kondo, R., Ouchi, N., Wei, H., Griffy-Brown, C., 2004. Institutional elasticity as a significant driver of IT functionality development. Technological Forecasting and Social Change 71 (7), 723−750.

Watanabe, C., Naveed, N., Neittaanmäki, P., 2018a. Digital solutions transform the forest-based bioeconomy into a digital platform industry: a suggestion for a disruptive business model in the digital economy. Technology in Society 54, 168−188.

Watanabe, C., Tou, Y., Neittaanmäki, P., 2018b. A new paradox of the digital economy: structural sources of the limitation of GDP statistics. Technology in Society 55, 9−23.

Watanabe, C., Naveed, K., Tou, Y., Neittaanmäki, P., 2018c. Measuring GDP in the digital economy: increasing dependence on uncaptured GDP. Technological Forecasting and Social Change 137, 226−240.

Watanabe, C., Naveed, N., Neittaanmäki, P., 2018d. Digitalized bioeconomy: planned obsolescence-driven economy enabled by Co-evolutionary coupling. Technology in Society 56, 8−30.

Watanabe, C., Akthar, W., Tou, Y., Neittaanmäki, P., 2020a. Fashion-driven textiles as a crystal of new stream for stakeholder capitalism: Amazon's endeavor. International Journal of Managing Information Technology 12 (2), 19−42.

Watanabe, C., Tou, Y., Neittaanmäki, P., 2020b. Institutional systems inducing R&D in Amazon: the role of an investor surplus toward stakeholder capitalization. Technology in Society 63, 101290.

Zakari, M., Saidu, S., 2016. The impact of cash conversion cycle on firm profitability: evidence from Nigerian listed telecommunication companies. Journal of Finance and Accounting 4 (6), 342−350.

Zeidan, R., Shapir, O.M., 2017. Cash conversion cycle and value-enhancing operations: theory and evidence for a free lunch. Journal of Corporate Finance 45, 203−219.

Further reading

Byrne, D., Corrado, C., 2016. ICT Prices and ICT Services: What Do They Tell about Productivity and Technology? Economic Program Working Paper Series, EPWP #16-05 The Conference Board, New York.

Knott, A.M., 2017. How Innovation Really Works: Using the Trillion-Dollar R&D Fix to Drive Growth. McGraw Hill, New York.

McDonagh, D., 2008. Satisfying needs beyond the functional: the changing needs of the silver market consumer. In: Proceedings of the International Symposium on the Silver Market Phenomenon. Business Opportunities and Responsibilities in the Aging Society, Tokyo.

McKinsey Global Institute, 2015. The Internet of Things: Mapping the Value beyond the Hype. McKinsey & Company, New York.

Rifkin, J., 2015. The Zero Marginal Cost Society. St. Martin's Press, New York.

CHAPTER 7

Operationalizing uncaptured GDP with neo open innovation

Contents

7.1 New research directions for future neo open innovation

The research in the preceding chapters used five-dimensional empirical analyses to gather new insights into the coevolutional trajectory between solid growth and gross increases in R&D that optimizes indigenous R&D and external resource dependency by overcoming the critical dilemma of R&D expansion coupled with declining productivity. This approach has shown that the concept of innovation should not be limited to the technical and mechanical aspects of goods and services but that biological, esthetic, qualitative, and suprafunctional aspects should be considered as well.

An enlightening discovery is that the rules and regulations that coordinate producers and users are changed in the transformation from a nondigital to digitalizing state.

A pioneering result at the strategic forefront of global information and communication technology (ICT) leaders, as observed in endeavors by Amazon, is the following remarkable, virtuous cycle as a potential solution to the aforementioned critical issue:

Transforming the Socio Economy with Digital Innovation
ISBN 978-0-323-88465-5
https://doi.org/10.1016/B978-0-323-88465-5.00009-X

User-driven innovation → advancement of the Internet → awakening and inducement of soft innovation resources (SIRs) in a marketplace → increase in gross R&D → solid growth → activation of self-propagating function → emergence of suprafunctionality beyond economic value → acceleration of user-driven innovation.

This business model corresponds to the prior insight concerning transformation of the traditional R&D model (University of Toronto, 2013; Tou et al., 2019, 2020; Watanabe et al., 2020). In light of this, further conceptualization and operationalization of this notable cycle could pave the way for a general solution to the current worldwide dilemma of R&D expansion coupled with declining productivity that most digital economies are now facing.

With these concerns in mind, if we look at this cycle (Fig. 6.17) carefully, the following important postulates emerge:

(1) The virtuous cycle consists of transforming processes between the non-digital and digitalizing state. Spin-off coevolution from the coevolution of traditional GDP captured by ICT and economic functionality to a new coevolution of Internet advancement, uncaptured GDP dependence, and people's shift in preference to suprafunctionality represents a transformation from a nondigital to digitalizing state (Watanabe et al., 2015a, 2015b, 2016). The activation process of the self-propagating function leveraged by gross R&D-driven growth for the inducement of suprafunctionality also corresponds to transformation from a nondigital to digitalizing state.

(2) A virtuous cycle can thus be constructed that bridges the nondigital and digitalizing states (bridging physical and virtual spaces). Amazon's success in orchestrating the management of technology and financing can be attributed to this virtual bridge. While R&D inputs are generally managed according to rules and regulations governed by the pricing mechanism initiated by the "invisible hand of GOD," their outputs are valued by results measured in the digitalizing world, which in turn reflect R&D input management in the nondigitalizing world. However, regulatory adjustments nearly always lag digital entrepreneurial activities (Read, 2016).

(3) Capturing the engine of growth plays an important role in reinforcing this virtuous cycle as observed in Amazon's acquisition of Whole Foods in 2017 (Berthene, 2019). This strategy inspired a new concept of growth beyond on that is purely mechanical (Marshall, 1898, reprinted 1966), and reminds us of the significance of a novel R&D concepts that embed growth characteristics during R&D processes (Naveed et al., 2020).

While it is generally understood in physics that two objects are coupled when they interact with each other, biological organisms can achieve a variety of functions efficiently by using the coupling effects of multiple factors and demonstrate optimal environmental adaptations (Ren and Liang, 2010). Since a growth characteristic is one of the core functions of biological coupling, this provides insightful suggestions for the management of R&D growth in the digital economy by avoiding the dilemma of R&D expansion coupled with declining productivity and by minimizing the financial burdens and risks that have become critical problems.

Thus, harnessing a growth characteristic via biological coupling involves such functions as leveraging the awakening and activating of the latent self-propagating functions indigenous to ICT (Watanabe and Hobo, 2004; Henfridsson and Bygstad, 2013) and essential for sustainable innovation in the digital economy (Naveed et al., 2020).

These postulates highlight the significance of further innovative research on the following subjects. The move toward stable neo open innovation in the future could enable a general solution to operationalizing uncaptured GDP:

(1) Conceptualizing and operationalizing the transformation process and identifying the rules and regulations that govern the post transformed world

(2) Tracking the input return journey as an outcome via digital transformation

(3) Embracing the novel concept of R&D that embeds a growth characteristic during an R&D process

7.2 Conceptualizing and operationalizing the transformation process

Neo open innovation dynamics that operationalize uncaptured GDP that are initiated by pioneering endeavors at the forefront of strategies being used by global ICT leaders are illustrated in Fig. 7.1.

This virtuous cycle consists of transforming processes between the nondigital and digitalizing states. The spin-off from traditional to new coevolution is illustrated by the dual cycles shown in the upper part of Fig. 7.1, which represent the transformation from a nondigital to digitalizing state.

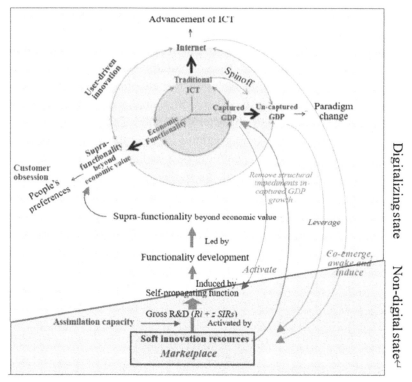

Figure 7.1 Neo open innovation dynamics that operationalize uncaptured GDP. The nondigitalized state is illustrated in the central circle and lower trapezoid.

Similarly, the activation process of the self-propagating function leveraged by gross R&D-driven growth for the inducement of supra-functionality corresponds to the transformation from a nondigital to digitalizing state.

The nondigitalized state is highlighted in orange, while the digitalizing state is in purple in Fig. 7.1.

Table 7.1 compares the structural system constituting the nondigital and digitalizing states by identifying the respective domain, target, function, and governor.

While an increasing number of studies have attempted to analyze the dynamism emerging in the digitalized world with a view to measuring its impacts (e.g., Brynjolfsson and McAfee, 2014; Ahmad and Schreyer, 2016), none has elucidated the black box of this transformation dynamism from the standpoint of the dynamic consequences of development trajectory

Table 7.1 Comparison of structural system between nondigital and digitalizing states.

State	Nondigital state	Digitalizing state
Domain	Market (producers vs. users)	Platform (all stakeholders collaborate)
Target	Profit maximum (producer), utility maximum, cost minimum (user)	Satisfaction of social demand
		Maximum suprafunctionality beyond economic value
		Improved performance of the economy (Stam, 2015)
Function	Price mechanism	Neo price mechanism
Governor	Invisible hand of GOD	Invisible eye for information (sensor)
		Invisible brain for time (artificial intelligence)
		Invisible hand for resources (price mechanism)

options. Existing studies tend to analyze emerging dynamism in the digitalized world using a lens made for analyzing dynamism of the traditional nondigital state.[1]

The works of Sussan and Acs (2017) and Gestrin and Staudt (2018) are invaluable exceptions. These researchers attempted to identify the transformation from a nondigital to digitalizing state by analyzing the process of an economy as it becomes increasingly digital.

While the former worker proposed to integrate well-established concepts of the digital and entrepreneurial ecosystems, the latter worker suggested the integration of digital data and technologies into operations and business models, learning from the preceding efforts initiated by digital policy and broadening the adoption of digital technologies across different sectors. Their attempts provide inspiring suggestions for the practical analysis of this transformation dynamism.

Sussan and Acs (2017) focused on the ecosystem function as a purposeful collaborating network of dynamic interacting systems with an ever-

---

[1] For further advancement of the practical application of such a virtualization server that enables the display of physical data differently, virtual data views in business fields are still expected (Oracle, 2011).

changing set of dependencies within a given context. They then postulated the conceptual framework of a digital entrepreneurship ecosystem that explains firms' behavior in the digitalizing state by integrating two ecosystems, as illustrated in Fig. 7.2. The two ecosystems are (1) digital ecosystems with a focus on digital infrastructure and users and (2) entrepreneurial ecosystems with a focus on agency (coordination and execution activities) and the role of institutions. The performance of the digital leaders with multisided platforms at the forefront of the digitalizing world can be traced by such frameworks (Evans and Schmalensce, 2016).

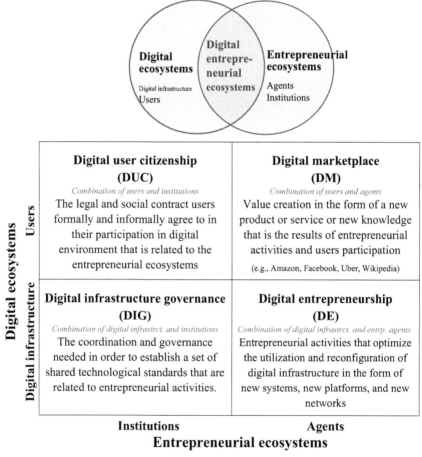

Figure 7.2 Conceptual framework of the digital entrepreneurship ecosystem. *(Authors' elaboration based on work of Sussan, F., Acs, Z.J., 2017. The digital entrepreneurial ecosystem. Small Business Economics 49 (1), 55–73.)*

Amazon's technology management system—consolidation of R&D transformation and technopreneurial strategy as demonstrated in Fig. 6.18 in Chapter 6—can be explained to some extent by this digital ecosystem. Similarly, its financial management system—the consolidation of market development and CCC-driven cash flow generation in Fig. 6.19—can be explained by entrepreneurial ecosystems. Thus, entrepreneurial ecosystems can support tracing of Amazon's endeavors to orchestrate technofinancing systems (Fig. 6.20) that operate by cross-transforming between nondigital and the digitalizing states.

Therefore, further empirical experimentation with Amazon's sophisticated virtuous cycle, which is based on orchestrating the technofinancing system, from the viewpoint of integrating digital and entrepreneurial ecosystems may provide significant insights into operationalization of the transformation process and identification of the rules and regulations that govern the post transformed world.

7.3 Tracking input return journeys as outcomes via digital transformation

Fig. 7.3 illustrates Amazon's R&D-inducing dynamism. As reviewed in Chapter 6, the company's R&D represents crystallization of the orchestrating of both technology and financial management, a process that leads to a virtuous cycle bridging the nondigital and the digitalizing states.

While R&D inputs are generally managed according to economic rules and regulations that are governed by price mechanism initiated by the "invisible hand of GOD" that ideally optimizes profit maximization and the cost minimum trajectory, the outputs of R&D in the digital economy are valued by the results as assessed by a digitalizing world that seeks noneconomic values as uncaptured GDP and suprafunctionality beyond economic value. Such noneconomic values in turn reflect the management of R&D inputs in the nondigitalizing world.

Thus, Amazon's sophisticated virtuous cycle to induce R&D is based on virtual bridges that link the nondigital and digitalizing states and then again the nondigital state.

Current R&D management focuses on how to maximize R&D-driven outputs such as sales, operating incomes, number of patents, and market capitalization relative to inputs by managing the timing R&D implementation, the pace of increases in investment, and the volume of investment (Watanabe et al., 2002)(Watanabe, 2009)(Watanabe et al., 2009). This management is based on economic terms without accounting for the intermediate process when R&D is functioning in the digital domain.

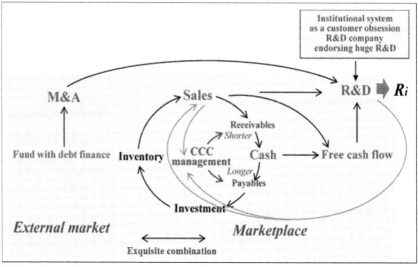

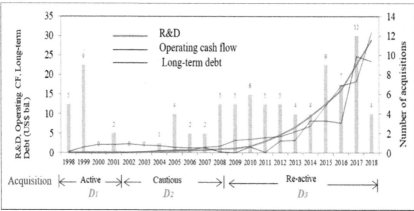

Figure 7.3 Amazon's R&D-inducing dynamism. *(Sources: Figs. 6.7 and 6.12 and Table 6.2.)*

However, this missing process plays a critical role in digital innovation because it governs the core function by activating the latent self-propagating function (Watanabe et al., 2004; Watanabe and Hobo, 2004; Tilson et al., 2010; Henfridsson and Bygstad, 2013).

Tracking R&D journeys across the nondigital to digitalizing state has become important because of the increasing significance of R&D management in the digital economy. In this view of R&D growth, the goal is to avoid the dilemma of R&D expansion coupled with declining productivity while minimizing financial burdens and risks.

This journey can be compared with the salmon's tour from the Sea of Okhotsk to the Bering Sea near Alaska before returning to the Sea of Okhotsk where it is fished in Japan. See Fig. 7.4.

Although salmon is a popular meal, its travel route has remained a mystery.

While its tour through the Sea of Okhotsk can be tracked, its tour farther in the journey to the Bering Sea is beyond tracking, similar to the abovementioned intermediate process of the R&D journey.

However, a recent Japanese study has found that the salmon's travel record is contained in its bones. The study identified that most Japanese river salmon wander far, to the continental shelf of the Bering Sea, and it had been estimated that the salmon's growth and fertility depend on this tour (Nihon Keizai Shimbun (NKS), 2020).

Nihon Keizai Shimbun (NKS) reported that in March 2020, research by the Japan Agency for Marine-Earth Science and Technology was published that detailed the salmon's migration route for the first time. At the end of a long journey, salmon arrive on the continental shelf of the Bering Sea where they feed before returning to Japan via the Sea of Okhotsk.

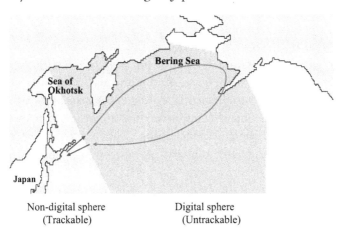

Figure 7.4 The salmon's tour from the Sea of Okhotsk to the Bering Sea and back.

The research team searching for the salmon's migratory route failed to track the path by observing the swimming route or by using a global positioning system. Surprisingly, it was salmon's spines that retained a record of its trip.

NKS stressed that some fish bones grow like carving rings, and when the bones are cut into slices, the effects of its environment at younger ages can be seen as one moves closer to the center of the cross-section.

The research team analyzed the elements in collagen that make up salmon vertebrae. The proportion of nitrogen was different in the parts that grew during the fry, juvenile, and adult stages.

As siblings, the elements have isotopes of the same type but with slightly different weights. The ratio of nitrogen isotopes varies from sea to sea due to the function of plankton in the sea. In the sea where living things are active, excrements and carcasses accumulate on the seabed. Of the nitrogen content of the sediments, light nitrogen easily leaves the atmosphere and heavy nitrogen remains on the seabed. At shallow ports, blanket nitrogen is likely to be taken up by heavy nitrogen on the seafloor.

Differences in proportions also appear in the vertebrae of salmon that eat plankton. By comparing the age-based ratio of the spine and the ratio of the sea area, the researchers were able to narrow down which sea the salmon had been swimming in previously. This was how they identified the migration route from Japan to the continental shelf of the Bering Sea (NKS, 2020).

This research serves as a metaphor for how to track R&D journeys across the nondigital state (the Sea of Okhotsk where the journey can be tracked) to the digitalizing state (the Bering Sea where the journey cannot be tracked).

In tracking Amazon's R&D journey by its virtuous cycle as illustrated in Fig. 6.17, trends in its assimilation capacity (Fig. 6.4) and self-propagating function (Fig. 6.21) serve as evidence in the same way that the nitrogen content in salmon bones does. By comparing these trends with the elasticity of investor surplus to R&D (Fig. 6.14), the prospect of tracking Amazon's R&D journey across the nondigital to the digitalizing state may be obtained as this elasticity represents the improvement of the performance of the economy toward stakeholder capitalization. This improvement is considered the goal of the digital entrepreneurial ecosystem (Stam, 2015).

7.4 A novel R&D concept that embeds a growth characteristic during an R&D process

Given the increasing role of R&D in competitive markets of the digital economy while confronting the dilemma of R&D expansion coupled with declining productivity, transformation of the R&D model has become a crucial subject for global digital leaders.

As demonstrated in Chapter 6, Amazon has deployed neo open innovation and harnessed the vigor of external innovation resources. These are then developed into a new concept of R&D that self-transforms during an R&D process initiated by user coupling.

The authors further develop these postulates by proposing the embedding of a growth characteristic identical to biological coupling through an empirical analysis focusing on the pioneering endeavors of global bioeconomy firms as well as by Amazon (Naveed et al., 2020).

A notable attempt in the circular economy initiated by global leader UPM- Kymmene Corporation (UPM) of Finland demonstrated the significance of the coupling effect with downstream digital commerce leader Amazon (Watanabe et al., 2018c). This effect can be attributed to harnessing the function of a growth characteristic that is identical to biological coupling through the coevolution of the dual coupling of the bioeconomy and digitalization and of upstream and downstream operations as illustrated in Fig. 7.5.

This coevolutionary coupling is expected to provide a novel R&D concept whose function grows in a self-propagating way during the R&D process.

Amazon is sensitive to consumers' ecological behaviors and keen to construct a win—win strategy with upstream leaders toward the circular economy. It has been stressed that as Earth's most customer-centric company, Amazon works every day to achieve a shopping experience with the lowest environmental impact on the planet.

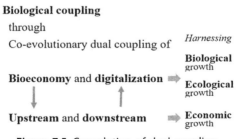

Figure 7.5 Coevolution of dual coupling.

Thus, upstream and downstream coupling is indispensable for achieving the goal of transition from a fossil to circular economy.

UPM and Amazon are members of the Sustainable Packaging Coalition, and they are dedicated to collaborating on an eco-friendly sustainable packaging system as demonstrated in Fig. 7.6.

Thus, UPM has deployed coevolutionary coupling (the coevolution of the dual couplings of bioeconomy and digitalization and upstream and downstream operations) as demonstrated in Fig. 7.7.

Figure 7.6 Coevolutional coupling of Amazon and UPM- Kymmene Corporation.

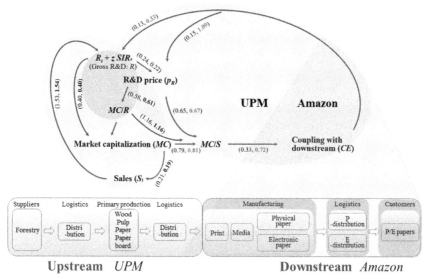

Upstream *UPM*   Downstream *Amazon*

Figure 7.7 *Coevolutionary coupling of UPM- Kymmene Corporation (1990–2017).* Numerical values indicate elasticity (1990–2010 and 2011–17, respectively). *(Source: Naveed, N., Watanabe, C., Neittaanmäki, P., 2020. Co-evolutionary coupling leads a way to a novel concept of R&D: lessons from digitalized bioeconomy. Technology in Society 60, 101220.)*

It was identified that with natures identical to those of growth characteristics, biological organisms can achieve a variety of biological functions efficiently using the coupling effects of multiple factors. In this way, they can demonstrate optimal environmental adaptations.

These findings support the significance of incorporating coevolutionary coupling with bioeconomy to embed growth characteristics, as illustrated in Fig. 7.8.

Therefore, further investigation of the resonance between upstream and downstream leaders, as illustrated in Fig. 7.9, may provide constructive suggestions for this issue.

7.5 Conclusion

The findings of the preceding chapters demonstrated that the concept of innovation should not be limited to the technical and mechanical aspects of goods and services. Instead, their biological, esthetic, qualitative, and suprafunctional aspects should also be considered. Development of ICT and business models has enabled the potential to harness such resources for innovation. The rules and regulations that coordinate producers and users change as they are transformed from a nondigital to digitalizing state (i.e., from physical to virtual space). The virtuous cycle that enables sustainable R&D growth and that avoids the dilemma of declining productivity can be constructed by a virtual cycle that bridges the nondigital and digitalizing states (i.e., bridging physical space and virtual space). Amazon's success in orchestrating the management of both technology and financing can be attributed to this virtual bridge.

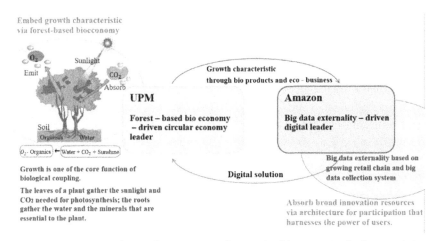

Figure 7.8 Concept of coevolutionary coupling embedding a growth characteristic.

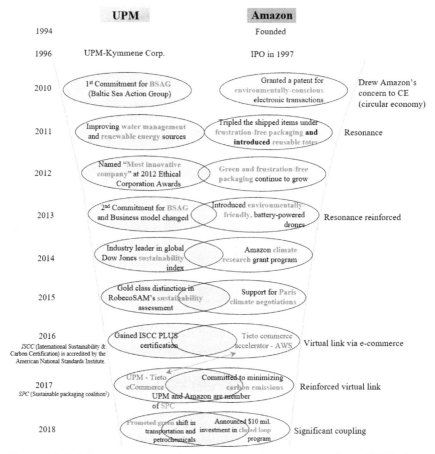

Figure 7.9 Reinforcing resonance leading to coevolutionary coupling of UPM- Kymmene Corporation and Amazon (1994–2018). *(Source: Naveed, N., Watanabe, C., Neittaanmäki, P., 2020. Co-evolutionary coupling leads a way to a novel concept of R&D: lessons from digitalized bioeconomy. Technology in Society 60, 101220.)*

These postulates highlight the significance of further innovative research on the following subjects:

(1) Conceptualizing and operationalizing the transformation process and identifying the rules and regulations that govern the post transformed world

(2) Tracking the return of the input journey as an outcome via digital transformation

(3) Embracing the novel concept of R&D that embeds a growth characteristic during an R&D process

It was realized in the preceding chapter that a pioneering endeavor at the forefront of global ICT leaders (such as Amazon) has demonstrated a remarkable virtuous cycle. It serves as a potential textbook for a solution to the R&D dilemma facing digital economies and corresponds to these insights concerning transformation of the traditional R&D model.

Inspired by these findings, this chapter attempted further conceptualization and operationalization of the above pioneering endeavor for a general solution to the current worldwide dilemma of R&D expansion coupled with declining productivity that most digital economies now confront. For this, further investigations were undertaken focusing on the following:

(1) A digital entrepreneurship ecosystem that integrates (a) digital ecosystems with a focus on digital infrastructure and users and (b) entrepreneurial ecosystems with a focus on agency and the role of institutions

(2) Return tracking of an journey inputs as an outcome via digital transformation inspired by the journey of salmon from the Sea of Okhotsk to the Bering Sea and back

(3) The novel concept of R&D that embeds a growth characteristic during an R&D process by reviewing reinforcing resonance, leading to the coevolutionary coupling of UPM and Amazon

Noteworthy suggestions obtained from these investigations include the following:

(1) Further empirical experimentation on Amazon's sophisticated virtuous cycle, which is based on the orchestration of its technofinancing system, from the viewpoint of integrating digital and entrepreneurial ecosystems, may provide significant insights into operationalization of the transformation process and identification of the rules and regulations that govern the post transformed world.

(2) In tracking Amazon's R&D journey via its virtuous cycle, trends in its assimilation capacity and self-propagating function represent evidence similar to that of the nitrogen content found in salmon bones. By comparing these trends with the elasticity of investor surplus to R&D, the prospect of tracking Amazon's R&D journey from a nondigital to digitalizing state may be obtained, because this elasticity represents an improvement in the performance of the economy toward stakeholder capitalization.

(3) It was identified that with a nature identical to a growth characteristic, biological organisms can achieve a variety of biological functions efficiently using the coupling effects of multiple factors. In this way, they can demonstrate optimal environmental adaptations. These notions support the significance of incorporating coevolutionary coupling with bioeconomy for embedding growth characteristics. Further investigation of the resonance between upstream and downstream leaders may provide constructive suggestions for conceptualization and operationalization of this notable characteristic.

These suggestions should aid in moving toward stable neo open innovation in the future, which could enable a general solution to operationalizing uncaptured GDP.

References

Ahmad, N., Schreyer, P., 2016. Are GDP and productivity measures up to the challenges of the digital economy? International Productivity Monitor 30, 4—27.

Brynjolfsson, E., McAfee, A., 2014. The Second Machine Age: Work, Progress, and Prosperity in a Time of Brilliant Technologies. W.W. Norton & Company, New York.

Berthene, A., 2019. How Amazon's whole foods acquisition changed the grocery industry. Digital Commerce 360. https://www.digitalcommerce360.com/2019/06/21/how-amazons-whole-foods-acquisition-changed-the-grocery-industry/ (retrieved 05.08.2019).

Evans, D.S., Schmalensce, R., 2016. Matchmakers: The New Economics of Multisided Platforms. Harvard Business Review Press, Boston.

Gestrin, M.V., Staudt, J., 2018. The Digital Economy, Multinational Enterprises and International Investment Policy. OECD, Paris.

Henfridsson, O., Bygstad, B., 2013. The generative mechanism of digital infrastructure evolution. MIS Quarterly 37 (3), 907—931.

Marshall, A., 1898. Mechanical and Biological Analogies in Economics. Reprinted in Pigou 1966.

Naveed, N., Watanabe, C., Neittaanmäki, P., 2020. Co-evolutionary coupling leads a way to a novel concept of R&D: lessons from digitalized bioeconomy. Technology in Society 60, 101220.

Nihon Keizai Shimbun (NKS), May 17, 2020. Tracing Salmon's Travel Record: Bones Analysis Approach. NKS: Japan's Financial Times. Nihon Keizai Shimbun, Tokyo.

Oracle, 2011. Oracle Directory Server Enterprise Edition Administration Guide. Oracle. https://docs.oracle.com/cd/E20295_01/pdf/821-1220.pdf (retrieved 20.08.2020).

Ren, L.Q., Liang, Y.H., 2010. Biological couplings: function, characteristics and implementation mode. Science China Technological Sciences 53 (2), 379—387.

Read, S., 2016. Organic or deliberate: a common on "applying the ecosystem metaphor to entrepreneurship — uses and abuses". Antitrust Bulletin 61 (4), 574—579.

Sussan, F., Acs, Z.J., 2017. The digital entrepreneurial ecosystem. Small Business Economics 49 (1), 55—73.

Stam, E., 2015. Entrepreneurial ecosystems and regional policy: a sympathetic critique. European Planning Studies 1—11.

Tilson, D., Lyytinen, K., Sorensen, C., 2010. Research commentary-digital infrastructures: the missing IS research agenda. Information Systems Research 21 (4), 748—759.

Tou, Y., Watanabe, C., Moriya, K., Naveed, N., Vurpillat, V., Neittaanmäki, P., 2019. The transformation of R&D into neo open innovation: a new concept of R&D endeavor triggered by Amazon. Technology in Society 58, 101141.

Tou, Y., Watanabe, C., Neittaanmäki, P., 2020. Fusion of technology management and financing management: Amazon's transformative endeavor by orchestrating techno-financing systems. Technology in Society 60, 101219.

University of Toronto, 2013. Amazon Business Model Case Study. APS1012 Management of Innovation — Final Team Projects, Spring 2013. University of Toronto, Faculty of Applied Science and Engineering, Toronto. http://www.amgimanagement.com/founder/ProjectSummaries/APS1012_2013_spring_03_Amazon%20business%20model%20case%20study.pdf (retrieved 10.01.2019).

Watanabe, C., Takayama, M., Nagamatsu, A., Tagami, T., Griffy-Brown, C., 2002. Technology spillover as a complement for high level R&D intensity in the pharmaceutical industry. Technovation 22 (4), 245—258.

Watanabe, C., Kondo, R., Ouchi, N., Wei, H., Griffy-Brown, C., 2004. Institutional elasticity as a significant driver of IT functionality development. Technological Forecasting and Social Change 71 (7), 723—750.

Watanabe, C., Hobo, M., 2004. Creating a firm self-propagating function for advanced innovation-oriented projects: lessons from ERP. Technovation 24 (6), 467—481.

Watanabe, C., 2009. Managing Innovation in Japan: The Role Institutions Play in Helping or Hindering How Companies Develop Technology. Springer Science & Business Media, Berlin.

Watanabe, C., Lei, S., Ouchi, N., 2009. Fusing indigenous technology development and market learning for greater functionality development: an empirical analysis of the growth trajectory of canon printers. Technovation 29 (2), 265—283.

Watanabe, C., Naveed, K., Zhao, W., 2015a. New paradigm of ICT productivity: increasing role of un-captured GDP and growing anger of consumers. Technology in Society 41, 21—44.

Watanabe, C., Naveed, K., Neittaanmäki, P., 2015b. Dependency on un-captured GDP as a source of resilience beyond economic value in countries with advanced ICT infrastructure: similarities and disparities between Finland and Singapore. Technology in Society 42, 104—122.

Watanabe, C., Naveed, K., Neittaanmäki, P., Tou, Y., 2016. Operationalization of un-captured GDP: the innovation stream under new global mega-trends. Technology in Society 45, 58—77.

Watanabe, C., Naveed, N., Neittaanmäki, P., 2018c. Digitalized bioeconomy: planned obsolescence-driven economy enabled by co-evolutionary coupling. Technology in Society 56, 8—30.

Watanabe, C., Tou, Y., Neittaanmäki, P., 2020. Institutional systems inducing R&D in Amazon: the role of an investor surplus toward stakeholder capitalization. Technology in Society 63, 101290.

Further reading

Amazon, 2019. Annual Report 2018. Amazon.Com, Inc., Seattle. http://www.annualreports.com/Company/amazoncom-inc (retrieved 22.03.2019).

Cowen, T., 2011. The Great Stagnation: How America Ate all the Low-Hanging Fruit of Modern History, Got Sick, and Will (Eventually) Feel Better. A Penguin Special from Dutton. Penguin, New York.

Watanabe, C., Tou, Y., Neittaanmäki, P., 2018a. A new paradox of the digital economy: structural sources of the limitation of GDP statistics. Technology in Society 55, 9—23.

Watanabe, C., Naveed, K., Tou, Y., Neittaanmäki, P., 2018b. Measuring GDP in the digital economy: increasing dependence on uncaptured GDP. Technological Forecasting and Social Change 137, 226–240.

CHAPTER 8

Conclusion

The dramatic advancement of the Internet has helped to create the digital economy. This economy has changed the way we conduct business as well as our daily lives. Continued progression of digitalized innovation over the last 3 decades, such as mobile services centered on smartphones, the cloud, and artificial intelligence, has further boosted this change and provided us with unprecedented services and levels of welfare.

However, contrary to such accomplishments, productivity in industrialized countries has been confronted with an apparent decline, and this has raised the question of a possible productivity paradox in the digital economy. The limitation of GDP statistics, the fundamental instrument for measuring and managing national economies across the globe, in measuring the advancement of the digital economy has become a critical subject. The trade-off between R&D expansion and productivity decline is a dilemma that has been heavily researched and discussed in advanced economies.

Key features of this economy can be highlighted as follows: (1) expansion occurs at a tremendous pace, (2) value can be provided free of charge, (3) information and communication technology (ICT) prices decrease while productivity declines, (4) digital goods are mobile and intangible, thus leading to substantially different business models, (5) the boundary between consumer and producer is thin and creates a "prosumer," (6) barriers to entry are low, which causes companies to innovate seamlessly, (7) companies can fully enjoy network externalities and subsequent self-propagation, (8) companies are bipolarized between those that enjoy network externalities and those that do not, (9) digital companies tend toward monopoly, and (10) contrary to traditional monopolies, this new monopoly can enhance convenience.

With these features of the digital economy in mind, this book has stressed the significance of the economy's increasing dependence on uncaptured GDP by revealing the two-faced nature of ICT. The Internet promotes a free culture, the consumption of which provides people with both utility and happiness, but its value cannot be captured through traditional GDP data, which measure revenue. This Internet-driven and uncaptured added value can be defined as uncaptured GDP.

Transforming the Socio Economy with Digital Innovation
ISBN 978-0-323-88465-5
https://doi.org/10.1016/B978-0-323-88465-5.00001-5

The shift in people's preferences from economic functionality to suprafunctionality beyond economic value, which encompasses social, cultural, and emotional values, induces further advancement of ICT initiated by the Internet, which intensifies the economy's dependence on uncaptured GDP. Therefore, the dramatic advancement of the Internet induces spin-off from the coevolution of traditional ICT, captured GDP, and economic functionality to a new form of coevolution. This new form encompasses Internet advancement, an increasing dependence on uncaptured GDP, and shifts in people's preferences.

A possible solution to the dilemma of productivity decline in the digital economy can be obtained by analyzing the dynamism of this coevolution.

In light of the increasing global significance of this dilemma, this book has presented a perspective on the solution to this critical issue by providing a transformative direction of innovation in the digital economy. This perspective was based on an intensive empirical analysis of national, industrial, and individual behaviors.

A five-dimensional empirical analysis was conducted to examine the following aspects: (1) the productivity paradox and limitations of GDP, (2) increasing dependence on uncaptured GDP, (3) soft innovation resources (SIRs) as the source of subsequent disruptive innovation, (4) neo open innovation that harnesses the vigor of this external innovation, and (5) the transformative direction of R&D into neo open innovation.

Based on the findings of these analyses, suggestions were made for further research on solid neo open innovation that enables a general solution to operationalizing uncaptured GDP.

Noteworthy findings and suggestions include the following:

ICT prices have continued to decline because of a trap in ICT advancement derived from the two-faced nature of ICT. That is, the advancement of ICT generally contributes to enhanced technology prices through new functionality development. However, the dramatic advancement of the Internet results in decreasing technology prices because of its characteristics of providing freebies, easy replication, and mass standardization. As a result, marginal productivity has declined in leading competitive economies.

To compensate for this price decrease, new unique services have been provided that are not necessarily captured by GDP, which measures only economic value, thus leading to increased dependence on uncaptured GDP.

These services correspond to the shift in people's preferences from economic functionality to suprafunctionality beyond economic value that encompasses social, cultural, and emotional values.

This shift induces the further advancement of the Internet, which intensifies the increasing dependence on uncaptured GDP. Therefore, a new spin-off coevolution has emerged among the combination of Internet advancement, the increasing contribution of uncaptured GDP, and shifts in people's preferences.

Due to the decline in both ICT prices and the marginal productivity of technology, the development trajectories of global ICT firms have been bipolarized. While firms with relatively low R&D intensity have maintained a virtuous cycle between R&D expenditures and marginal productivity relative to ICT increases, firms with high R&D intensity have fallen into a vicious cycle, as higher R&D investment results in declines in the marginal productivity of ICT. To deal with such circumstances, firms with high R&D intensity have endeavored to adopt digitalization with disruptive business models by harnessing the vigor of the untapped and noneconomic resources known as "soft innovation resources (SIRs)."

SIRs are latent innovation resources awoken and activated by the digital platform ecosystem. They are considered the condensates and crystals of the advancement of the Internet.

The identification of *SIRs* leads to envisioning a novel concept of neo open innovation that avoids the current dilemma over the decline in productivity and enables sustainable growth by increasing gross R&D to encompass assimilated *SIRs*. This innovation leads to operationalization of uncaptured GDP through effective utilization of *SIRs* and paves the way for the transformative direction of global ICT leaders.

It is widely agreed that technological change or innovation is the main source of economic growth and prosperity. However, the concept of innovation should not be limited to the technological aspects of goods and services. It should also include biological, esthetic, qualitative, and suprafunctional aspects.

Developments in ICT and digital technologies as well as in business models have enabled the potential to harness untapped and noneconomic resources for innovation. Assessment of innovation efforts that considers only hard R&D efforts without accounting for *SIRs* provides a limited and biased picture of total innovation activity. Another reason of the increasing significance of harnessing *SIRs* is the changing nature of research activities and research jobs in the digital era compared with those of traditional R&D.

Traditionally, firms and countries have focused on hard R&D investments for functional improvements in products and processes, but the dramatic advancement of ICT and digital technologies has enabled new ways of offering and consuming resources. New digital platforms are emerging. These platforms are effectively utilizing digital technologies, creating innovative business models, and harnessing a variety of untapped resources. In the process, they are disrupting traditional market players. Our research anticipates that the role of *SIRs* in innovation activity will be tremendously important in the future.

Pioneering endeavors at the forefront of global ICT leadership inspire a new and disruptive innovation model. These can serve as textbook examples of how to address the global productivity dilemma. In addition, they can represent a sophisticated digital machine that consolidates these insights to produce the following effects:

(1) a virtuous cycle among user-driven innovation, advancement of the Internet, and the coemergence of *SIRs* that leads to (2) a unique R&D model that transforms "routine or periodic alterations" into "significant improvements" during its R&D processes. This can exert the locomotive power of spin-off coevolution, which in turn creates (3) a "great coevolution" with digital innovation and shifts toward new trends that induce disruptive business models. These models then explore disruptive innovation by harnessing the vigor of activated *SIRs* that (4) orchestrate technofinancing systems that fuse technology management and financing management systems to enable (5) a high level of investor surplus that induces R&D bets from a broad array of stakeholders.

The unique contributions of this book include *uncaptured GDP, suprafunctionality beyond economic value, SIRs*, the *hybrid role of SIRs*, and *neo open innovation*.

Further insights include *transformation of the R&D concept, orchestration of the technofinancing system*, and *investor surplus that induces R&D bets from a broad array of stakeholders*.

Lastly, we suggest further research on stable neo open innovation in the future that enables a general solution for operationalizing uncaptured GDP:

(1) Conceptualize and operationalize the transformation process and identify the rules and regulations governing the post-transformed world.

(2) Track the inputted journey to outcomes via digital transformation.

(3) Use the novel concept of R&D embedding of growth characteristics during R&D processes.

Appendix I

Basic mathematics for technoeconomic analysis

AI-1. Development trajectories of global information communication and technology firms

A1.1 Innovation behavior in the digital economy

A1.1.1 The Internet's permeation of broad information communication and technology

The dramatic advancement of the Internet and further progression of digitized innovation over the last 2 decades have augmented the Internet's permeation of broad information communication and technology (ICT), as illustrated in Fig. A1-1 (Watanabe et al., 2018b). This permeation has

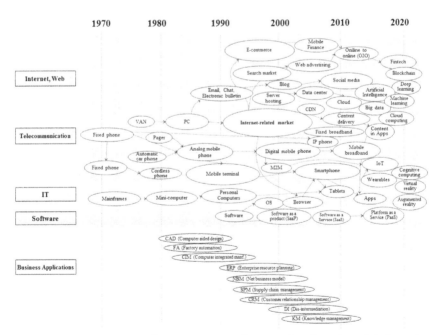

Figure A1-1 Permeation of Internet-oriented innovation into broad information communication and technology.

expanded to broad areas of technology as the IoT has progressed (McKinsey Global Institute, 2015).

A1.1.2 The conversion of R&D to Internet-relevant R&D

Such a permeation trend can be demonstrated by the convergence of R&D related to the Internet and to other ICT. Technology stock (technology knowledge stock) related to both the Internet and other ICT can be estimated by the ratio of respective R&D expenditures and the obsolescence factor. Here, the obsolescence factor can be estimated by the sum of the rate of technological obsolescence (ρ) and the increase in the rate of R&D at the initial period (g), in the long run (see Eq. A1-5 in A1.2).

With such understanding, Fig. A1-2 traces the trend in ICT's obsolescence factor related to 27 key areas scientific research consisting of (1) Internet R&D, (2) Internet-related peripheral R&D, and (3) other ICT R&D over the period 1980–2015.

Fig. A1-2 demonstrates that the values of obsolescence factors had diverged by 2005, they began to converge around 2010–15. This converging trend suggests that technology stock of both the Internet and other ICT can be treated as a sum of both types of R&D (Watanabe et al., 2018b).

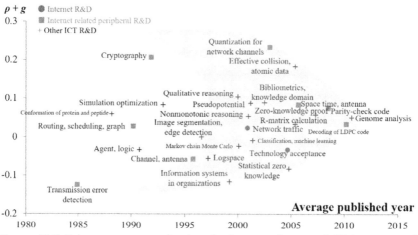

Figure A1-2 Value convergence in the obsolescence factors of 27 key areas of scientific research (1980–2015).

Given the increasing, seamless trend between Internet R&D and other-ICT R&D, this convergence supports the permeation trend of the Internet into broad areas of technology that are centered on ICT.

A1.1.3 Permeation of the Internet into production factors

Driven by the IoT, the physical world is becoming an ecosystem composed of physical objects embedded with sensors and actuators connected to applications and services through a wide range of networks. The Internet has permeated not only technology centered on ICT but also all production factors involved in moving toward an IoT society (McKinsey Global Institute, 2015; Kahre et al., 2017; EU, 2017a, 2017b).

Note 1: The analysis of Fig. A1-2 was based on the following bibliometrics approach (Watanabe et al., 2018a, 2018b):

The top 1% of scientific papers in *"Computer Science"* and *"Information Science & Library Science"* over the period 1960–2015 was traced (altogether 14,438 scientific papers retrieved from the Web of Science provided by Clarivate Analytics were examined).

First, by using the Academic Landscape System (Kajikawa et al., 2014; Innovation Policy Research Center, 2013), a citation network was constructed. Second, by means of the Newman method (Newman, 2004), the citation network was divided into 27 clusters. Each respective cluster contained more than 100 papers. Thus, the top 1% of scientific papers highlighted 27 scientific fields in broad ICT, as illustrated in Fig. A1-2 and which can be classified as (1) Internet R&D (2 clusters), (2) Internet-related peripheral R&D (8 clusters), and (3) other ICT R&D (17 clusters).

ρ can be estimated by calculating a reciprocal of the forward half-life after the peak with a negative value, whereas g can be estimated by calculating a reciprocal of the backward half-life before the peak with a positive value (see Note 2).

Note 2: Fig. A1-3 illustrates the method for calculating the obsolescence factor (ρ, g).

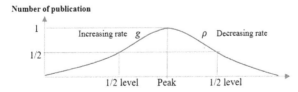

Figure A1-3 Method for calculating the obsolescence factor.

A1.2 Decisive factor of the development trajectories of global information communication and technology firms

A1.2.1 R&D-driven growth trajectories in global information communication and technology firms

The digital value, V, created by global ICT firms in an IoT society can be depicted as follows:

$$V = F(X, I_g) \qquad (A1\text{-}1)$$

where I_g is gross ICT stock $= I$ (ICT stock) $+ J$ (Internet dependence[1]) (see Fig. A1-1); and X is other production factors.

Translog (transcendental logarithmic) expansion on the first term is as follows:

$$\ln V = p + q \ln X + r \ln I_g \qquad (A1\text{-}2)$$

where p, q, and r are coefficients.

I_g is embodied in X in an IoT society as follows:

$$X = F(I_g) \quad \ln X = p_x + r_x \ln I_g \qquad (A1\text{-}3)$$

where p_x and r_x are coefficients.

Synchronizing Eq. (A1-2) and (A1-3):

$$\ln V = p + q(p_x + r_x \ln I_g) + r \ln I_g = (p + q \cdot p_x)$$

$$+ (q \cdot r_x + r)\ln I_q \equiv \alpha + \beta \ln I_g \qquad (A1\text{-}4)$$

where $\alpha = p + q \cdot p_x$, $\beta = q \cdot r_x + r$.

This demonstrates that V is governed by I_g under the above circumstances.

As the Internet permeates ICT in general (see Figs. A1-1 and A1-2), I_g increases proportionally to gross R&D, represented by gross R&D expenditures, R ($= R_i + R_j$), as follows[2]:

---

[1] See AI-5 for the definition, method, and original source of Internet dependence.

[2] ICT stock at time t can be measured by the following equation (Watanabe, 2009):

$$I_{g\,t} = R_{t-m} + (1 - \rho)I_{g\,t-1} \text{ and } I_{g\,0} = \frac{R_{t-m}}{\rho + g}, \text{ therefore, } I_{g\,t} = \frac{R_{t+1-m}}{\rho + g}, \text{ when } t \gg m - 1,$$

$$I_{g\,t} \approx \frac{R_t}{\rho + g}$$

where m : time $-$ lag between R&D and commericializtion.

$$I_g = I + J \approx \frac{R_i}{\rho_i + g_i} + \frac{R_j}{\rho_j + g_j} \approx \frac{R_i}{\rho + g} + \frac{R_j}{\rho + g} = \frac{R_i + R_j}{\rho + g} = \frac{R}{\rho + g}$$

(A1-5)

where R_j is R&D related to the Internet; R_i is R&D related to other ICT; ρ is the rate of obsolescence of ICT, and g is the R&D growth rate at the initial stage.

Substituting Eq. (A1-5) for I_g in Eq. (A1-4):

$$\ln V = \alpha + \beta \ln \frac{R}{\rho + g} = \alpha - \beta \ln(\rho + g) + \beta \ln R \equiv \alpha' + \beta \ln R \quad \text{(A1-6)}$$

where $\alpha' = \alpha - \beta \ln(\rho + g)$.

Thus, the digital value is governed by the gross R&D of global ICT firms in an IoT society, and global ICT firms demonstrate R&D-driven (R-driven) development trajectories.

A1.2.2 Digital value representing the behavior of global information communication and technology firms

It is generally understood that market capitalization, sales, and operating income represent the digital value created by global ICT firms in an IoT society (McKinsey Global Institute, 2015). While market value is greatly determined by external factors indigenous to respective firms, sales and operating income represent the due outcomes expected to be generated by R-driven growth endeavors common to global ICT firms.

Therefore, by taking the top 500 (by R&D level) global ICT firms[3] in 2016 and applying Eq. (A1-6), a comparative assessment of the correlation between R&D investment and the digital value arising from sales and operating income (OI) was conducted as summarized in Table A1-1.

Table A1-1 demonstrates that sales represent the R-driven digital value creation behavior of the 500 global ICT firms better than IO does. Also,

---

[3] Utilizing the EU Industrial R&D Investment Scoreboard 2016 (EC, 2017), the R&D of the top 500 global ICT firms were chosen. Using K-means cluster analysis, they are divided into the following three groups based on their R&D and sales level in 2016 as illustrated in Fig. 5.1: high-R&D-intensive firms D_1 (25 firms), R&D-intensive firms D_2 (140 firms), and low-R&D firms D_3 (335 firms).
ICT sectors are as follows: computer hardware, computer services, consumer electronics, electrical equipment and services, electronic and electrical equipment, Internet, IT hardware, leisure goods (partially), semiconductors, software and computer services, software, technology hardware and equipment, telecommunication equipment (fixed line telecommunication, mobile telecommunications, and telecommunication services were not included).

Table A1-1 Comparative assessment of the correlation between R&D and digital value in 500 global information communication and technology firms (2016).

$\ln S = 2.32 + 0.99 D_1 \ln R + 1.02 D_2 \ln R + 1.00 D_3 \ln R + 2.90 D$ $\quad\quad\;\; (4.43) \quad\; (15.18) \quad\quad\;\; (12.40) \quad\quad\;\; (9.65) \quad\quad\; (13.22)$	$adj.R^2 0.632$
$\ln OI = -1.28 + 1.01 D_1 \ln R + 1.05 D_2 \ln R + 1.03 D_3 \ln R + 2.33 D$ $\quad\quad\;\;\; (-0.18)^* \;\; (11.77) \quad\quad\; (9.39) \quad\quad\;\; (7.38) \quad\quad\; (8.33)$	$adj.R^2 0.525$

S: sales; OI: operating income; R: R&D investment; $D_1, D_2, D_3,$ and D: dummy variables. D_1: 25 high-R&D-intensive firms = 1, other firms = 0. Similarly, D_2: 140 R&D-intensive firms = 1, D_3: 335 low-R&D-intensive firms = 1, and D: outliers (5 in D_2 and 11 in D_3) = 1 (see classification of dummy variables in Fig. 5.1). The figures in parentheses indicate t-statistics: all are significant at the 1% level except *, which is not significant.

these results suggest that whereas elasticity increases as R-driven development proceeds (from D_3 to D_2), it reverses and begins to decrease as R-driven development exceeds a certain level (D_1), similar to a sigmoid curve in logistic growth (Watanabe et al., 2014, 2015).

A1.3 Bipolarization fatality and transformation of information communication and technology—driven growth

A1.3.1 Logistic growth trajectories of global information communication and technology firms

ICT in which network externalities function to alter the correlation between innovation and institutional systems creates new innovations that lead to exponential increases. Schelling (1998) portrayed an array of logistically developing and diffusing social mechanisms stimulated by these interactions. The advancement of the Internet further stimulates these interactions and accelerates the logistically developing and diffusing features of ICT that are typically traced by the sigmoid curve (Watanabe et al., 2004).

The digital value created by R-driven development in an IoT society can be depicted as follows:

$$V \approx F(R) \qquad (A1\text{-}7)$$

Given ICT's logistic growth nature, its R-driven growth, $\left(\frac{dV}{dR}\right)$, which can be approximated by the marginal productivity of R&D to digital value, $\left(\frac{\partial V}{\partial R}\right)$, in an IoT society, can be depicted by the following epidemic function:

$$\frac{dV}{dR} = aV\left(1 - \frac{V}{N}\right) \approx \frac{\partial V}{\partial R} \cdot \frac{dR}{dR} = \frac{\partial V}{\partial R} \qquad (A1\text{-}8)$$

This epidemic function leads to an R-driven simple logistic growth (SLG) function that depicts an R-driven digital value trajectory, $Vs(R)$, as a function of R&D investment as follows:

$$SLG = V_S(R) \frac{N}{1 + be^{-aR}} \qquad (A1\text{-}9)$$

where N is carrying capacity; a is velocity of diffusion; and b is a coefficient indicating the initial level of diffusion.

Table A1-2 R-driven sales growth trajectories of 500 global information communication and technology firms (2016).

$$S = \frac{N}{1+be^{-aR}} + cD$$

where N is carrying capacity, a, b, and c are coefficients, and D is a dummy variable ($D = 1$ for designated outlier firms, $D = 0$ for other firms)

N	a	b	c	$adj.\ R^2$	D (gigantic firms treated by dummy variable)
59.62 (17.39)	**1.32** (10.98)	**15.91** (21.87)	**99.09** (29.74)	*0.784*	**Apple, Samsung, Hon Hai**

Figures in parentheses indicate t-statistics; all are significant at the 1% level.

The development trajectories of global ICT firms follow this sigmoid trajectory, which continues to grow until it reaches carrying capacity (the upper limit of growth).

Because sales S represent the R-driven digital value creation behavior of the 500 global ICT firms, Table A1-2 analyzes the R-driven sales trajectories of the 500 global ICT firms in 2016 utilizing the SLG function,[4] which demonstrates statistical significance.

Table A1-3 compares the growth trajectories of R-driven sales growth, OI, and sales in 2005 and demonstrates that Table A1-2 is statistically most significant.

In this SLG trajectory, whereas the growth rate (marginal productivity of R&D to sales) continues to increase before reaching the inflection point corresponding to a level equal to half of carrying capacity, it decreases after exceeding the inflection point as follows:

$$be^{-aR} \equiv \frac{1}{x}\frac{\partial V}{\partial R} = aV\left(1 - \frac{V}{N}\right) = aN \cdot \frac{1}{1+1/x}\left(1 - \frac{1}{1+1/x}\right) = \frac{aN \cdot x}{(1+x)^2}$$
$$\text{(A1-10)}$$

$$\frac{d\frac{\partial V}{\partial R}}{dx} = \frac{d\frac{\partial V}{\partial R}}{dR} \cdot \frac{dR}{dx} = \frac{d\frac{\partial V}{\partial R}}{dR} \cdot \frac{1}{ax} = aN \cdot \frac{1-x}{(1+x)^3} \qquad \frac{1}{ax} = \frac{b}{a}e^{-aR} > 0 \quad \text{(A1-11)}$$

---

[4] Because the SLG function depends on a fixed carrying capacity (N) common to all 500 firms analyzed, in order to avoid a bias by particular gigantic "mutation" firms, based on comparative assessment of fitness to SLG, dummy variable treatment for these firms was attempted.

Table A1-3 Comparison of the R-driven growth trajectories of 500 global information communication and technology firms:

$$S = \frac{N}{1+be^{-aR}} + cD$$

where S is sales, R is R&D investment, N is carrying capacity, a, b, c are coefficients, and D is a dummy variable.

	N	a	b	c	adj. R^2	D	ln b/a
2005	**53.80**	**1.55**	**22.02**	**42.63**	**0.734**	Dell=1, others = 0	**2.0**
	(21.18)	(16.96)	(29.44)	(18.13)			
2016	**59.62**	**1.32**	**15.91**	**99.09**	**0.784**	Samsung, Apple, Hon Hai = 1, others = 0	**2.1**
	(17.39)	(10.98)	(21.87)	(29.74)			
OI in 2016	21.23	0.90	73.85	7.24	0.589	Apple = 1, others = 0	
	(18.44)	(10.74)	(13.82)	(11.37)			

Figures in parentheses indicate t-statistics; all are significant at the 1% level. N: carrying capacity; OI: operating income; R: R&D investment

Digitalization exceeding a certain level of R&D ($R > \ln b/a$) results in a decline in productivity:

$$d\frac{\partial V}{\partial R} = 0 \Leftrightarrow x = 1 \Leftrightarrow R = \frac{\ln b}{a} \rightarrow R > \frac{\ln b}{a} \Rightarrow \frac{d\frac{\partial V}{\partial R}}{dx} < 0 \qquad \text{(A1-12)}$$

Thus, ICT-driven logistic growth incorporates bipolarization fatality with an increase and decrease in marginal productivity, respectively, before and after the inflection point (Watanabe, 2009).

In the case of the 500 global ICT firms in 2016, an R&D level of € 2100 million identifies this inflection point, which demonstrates bipolarization between 25 high-R&D-intensive firms (HRIFs), represented by (D_1), and the remaining 475 firms (D_2 and D_3), as illustrated in Fig. 5.2.

A1.3.2 The dilemma of R&D expansion associated with declining productivity

This bipolarization causes the dilemma of R&D expansion coupled with declining productivity, as R&D expansion that exceeds the inflection point results in declining productivity and subsequent growth stagnation (Watanabe et al., 2015).

Confronting such a dilemma, global ICT leaders have endeavored to find an effective solution by transforming from traditional business models to new ones (Watanabe et al., 2018b).

Given that this dilemma stems from the unique feature of ICT, logistic growth, this feature should be transformed.

A1.4 Transformation to a virtuous cycle of neo open innovation

A1.4.1 Transformation of the unique feature of information communication and technology: *logistic growth within a dynamic carrying-capacity function*

As long as the development trajectory depends on the *SLG* trajectory, its digital value, $V_s(R)$, saturates with the fixed carrying capacity, N, inevitably resulting in the above dilemma. However, particular innovation can incorporate dynamic carrying capacity, $N_L(R)$, to create new carrying capacity during the diffusion process, and thus Eq. (A1-8), an epidemic function depicting digital value $V(R)$, can be developed as follows:

$$\frac{dV(R)}{dR} = a\, V(R)\left(1 - \frac{V(R)}{N_L(R)}\right) \tag{A1-13}$$

Eq. (A1-13) develops the following logistic growth within a dynamic carrying-capacity (*LGDCC*) function that incorporates a self-propagating function that enables its digital value, $V_L(R)$, to continue to increase as it creates a new carrying capacity successively during the process of development (Watanabe et al., 2004):

$$V_L(R) = \frac{N_k}{1 + be^{-aR} + \dfrac{b_k}{1 - a_k/a}e^{-a_kR}} \tag{A1-14}$$

where N_k is ultimate carrying capacity, and a, b, a_k, and b_k are coefficients.

Table A1-4 analyzes the development trajectories of 500 global information communication and technology firms in 2016 by comparing *SLG* and *LGDCC*.

Table A1-4 demonstrates that *LGDCC* is statistically more significant than *SLG*. This can be attributed to endeavors by *HRIFs* to overcome the dilemma by shifting from *SLG* to *LGDCC*. These endeavors correspond to their efforts to arouse and activate the latent self-propagating function indigenous to ICT.

Table A1-4 The development trajectories of 500 global information communication and technology firms (1996).

$V_S(R) = \frac{N_k}{1+be^{-aR}}$ $V_L(R) = \dfrac{N_k}{1+be^{-aR}+\dfrac{b_k}{1-a_k/a}e^{-a_kR}}$

	N	a	b	ak	bk	adj. R^2
Vs(R)	59.62	1.32	15.91			0.784
	(17.39)	(10.98)	(21.87)			
V_L(R)	102.23	0.77	15.84	0.43	1.32	0.999
	(178.83)	(26.13)	(9.72)	(7.06)	(2.53)	

$V_S(R)$, $V_L(R)$: digital values of *SLG* and *LGDCC*, respectively; *N*: carrying capacity; *a*, *b*, a_k, b_k: coefficients. Dummy variables are used for the $V_S(R)$ estimate (see Table A2). Figures in parentheses indicate t-statistics; all are significant at the 1% level.

A1.4.2 Activation of self-propagating function

The dynamic carrying capacity, $N_L(R)$, in $LGDCC$ that leads to the self-propagating function can be depicted as a function of digital value and its growth rate:

$$N_L(R) = V_L(R) \left(\frac{1}{1 - \frac{1}{a} \cdot \frac{\triangle V_L(R)}{V_L(R)}} \right) \quad \triangle V_L(R) = \frac{dV_L(R)}{dR} \quad \text{(A1-15)}$$

Once the development trajectory shifts from SLG to $LGDCC$, continued growth in digital value is enabled by incorporating a self-propagating function led by dynamic carrying capacity. An increase in digital value, $V_L(R)$, and its growth rate enhances dynamic carrying capacity as depicted in Eq. (A1-15), which enables sustainable growth in digital value.

Therefore, the key to sustainable growth in the ICT-driven development trajectories of global ICT leaders is to trigger increases in $V_L(R)$ without confronting the dilemma by constructing a virtuous cycle of increases in $V_L(R)$ that stimulate enhancements in $N_L(R)$ that in turn lead to growth in $V_L(R)$.

Because ICT incorporates an indigenous self-propagating function that utilizes network externalities (Watanabe and Hobo, 2004), the point for sustainable growth corresponds to activating this latent self-propagating function indigenous to ICT.

Induced by this self-propagating function, functionality (FD) increases in a spiral manner as $V(R)$ increases, as depicted in Eq. (A1-16):

$$FD = \frac{N_L(R)}{V_L(R)} = \frac{1}{1 - \frac{1}{a} \cdot \frac{\triangle V_L(R)}{V_L(R)}} \quad \text{(A1-16)}$$

As long as the development trajectory depends on the SLG trajectory, its digital value ($V_S(R)$) saturates with the upper limit depicted by fixed N without a self-propagating function. Once the trajectory shifts to $LGDCC$, digital value can continue to increase, supported by the self-propagating function and led by dynamically enhancing the upper limit $N_L(R)$. Therefore, the magnitude of the self-propagating function (*MSPF*) can be estimated by the ratio of $N_L(R)$ and $V_S(R)$ as follows:

$$MSPF = \frac{N_L(R)}{V_S(R)} = \frac{V_L(R)}{V_S(R)} \cdot \left(\frac{1}{1 - \frac{1}{a} \cdot \frac{\Delta V_L(R)}{V_L(R)}} \right) \qquad (A1\text{-}17)$$

A1.4.3 Assimilation of soft innovation resources

Efforts to create a new carrying capacity that leads to the self-propagating function and enables sustainable growth of the ICT-driven development trajectories of global ICT leaders reflect the repulsive power of price (marginal productivity) decreases consequent to bipolarization fatality arising from excessive R&D.

This repulsive power enforces the behavior of ICT leaders in absorbing resources for innovation, particularly soft innovation resources (*SIRs*), from the external market to advance innovation without confronting the dilemma by assimilating them into their businesses (Tou et al., 2019a). Here, *SIRs* are considered condensates and crystals of the advancement of the Internet (Tou et al., 2018b, 2019b) and consist of Internet-based resources that have been either sleeping or untapped or are results of multisided interactions in the markets where consumers are looking for functionality beyond economic value (Tou et al., 2018a).

A1.4.4 Suprafunctionality beyond economic value

Assimilated *SIRs* increase gross R&D, consisting of indigenous R&D (R_i) and assimilated external innovation resources centered on *SIRs*. This increase contributes to growth in digital value, $V_L(R)$, without confronting the dilemma. This growth induces increases in indigenous R&D, R_i, that contribute to increased assimilation capacity, z (Watanabe et al., 2002). Both are sources of R&D-driven growth that awakes and activates the latent self-propagating function indigenous to ICT (Tou et al., 2018b), as illustrated in Fig. A1-4.

The activated self-propagating function develops the *LGDCC* trajectory and induces functionality development that leads to the exploration of

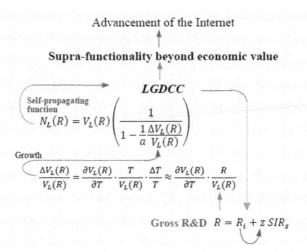

Figure A1-4 The dynamism of a core function of the disruptive business model.

suprafunctionality beyond economic value that encompasses social, cultural, and emotional values (Watanabe et al., 2015).

Since this functionality corresponds to a shift in people's preferences in the digital economy, this exploration further induces user-driven innovation and subsequent advancement of the Internet that accelerates the awakening and inducement of further *SIRs*.

Thus, a virtuous cycle in neo open innovation, effective utilization of *SIRs*, activation of a self-propagating function, sustainable growth, suprafunctionality creation, further advancement of the Internet, and coemergence of *SIRs* is constructed. *SIRs* play a core system role in inducing optimal coordination between innovation and growth by awakening and activating latent functions in the digital economy.

AI-2. Effects of information communication and technology advancement on price changes

A2.1 The two-sided nature of the development trajectory of information communication and technology prices

ICT's dual nature leads to price increases from new functionality developments that correspond to ICT advancement as a whole while prices decline in concert with increased Internet dependence, as illustrated in Fig. A2-1 (Watanabe et al., 2015).

While the former can be estimated by a logistic growth function initiated by ICT stock (*I*), the latter can be estimated by a reverse logistic

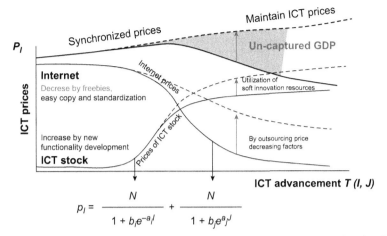

Figure A2-1 Development trajectory of information communication and technology prices.

growth initiated by Internet dependence (J) (Watanabe et al., 2001). Therefore, ICT prices, P_I, can be depicted by the following hybrid logistic growth function:

$$p_I = \frac{N}{1 + b_i e^{-a_i I}} + \frac{N}{1 + b_j e^{a_j J}} \tag{A2-1}$$

where I is ICT stock, J is dependence on the Internet, N is carrying capacity,[5] a_i, a_j and b_i, b_j are the diffusion velocity of I and J and the initial stage of diffusion of I and J, respectively.

Eq. (A2-1) can be developed as follows:

$$\frac{p_I}{N} = \frac{1 + b_j e^{a_j J} + 1 + b_i e^{-a_i I}}{\left(1 + b_i e^{-a_i I}\right)\left(1 + b_j e^{a_j J}\right)} = \frac{2 + b_j e^{a_j J} + b_i e^{-a_i I}}{1 + b_j e^{a_j J} + b_i e^{-a_i I} + b_i b_j e^{-a_i I} e^{a_j J}}$$

$$\approx \frac{2 + b_j e^{a_j J} + b_i e^{-a_i I}}{1 + b_i b_j + b_j e^{a_j J} + b_i e^{-a_i I}} = 1 + \frac{1 - b_i b_j}{1 + b_i b_j + b_j e^{a_j J} + b_i e^{-a_i I}} \quad (\because a_i I = a_j J)$$

$$\frac{p_I}{N} - 1 = \frac{1 - b_i b_j}{1 + b_i b_j + b_j e^{a_j J} + b_i e^{-a_i I}}$$

---

[5] Because the Internet has been playing a leading role in the whole ICT and providing significant impacts on the diffusion trajectory of ICT, carrying capacity of logistic growth in I and reverse logistic growth in J as well as their diffusion tempo ($a_i I$ and $a_j J$) were treated as behaved in the similar way $a_i I = a_j J$.

$$\frac{N}{N - p_I} = \frac{1}{1 - \dfrac{p_I}{N}} = -\frac{1 + b_i b_j}{1 - b_i b_j} - \frac{b_j e^{a_i J}}{1 - b_i b_j} - \frac{b_i e^{-a_i I}}{1 - b_i b_j}$$

$$\approx -\frac{1 + b_i b_j}{1 - b_i b_j} - \frac{b_j}{1 - b_i b_j}\left(1 + a_j J\right) - \frac{b_j}{1 - b_i b_j}\left(1 - a_i I\right)$$

$$= -\frac{1 + b_i b_j + b_i + b_j}{1 - b_i b_j} - \frac{a_j b_j}{1 - b_i b_j} J + \frac{a_i b_i}{1 - b_i b_j} I$$

$$\equiv \alpha + \beta J + \gamma I$$

where $\alpha = -\dfrac{1 + b_i b_j + b_i + b_j}{1 - b_i b_j} = -\dfrac{(1 + b_i)(1 + b_j)}{1 - b_i b_j}, \beta = -\dfrac{a_j b_j}{1 - b_i b_j},$

$$\gamma = \frac{a_i b_i}{1 - b_i b_j} \tag{A2-2}$$

$$\frac{\beta}{\gamma} = \frac{a_j b_j}{a_i b_i} = \frac{I}{J} \cdot \frac{b_j}{b_i} \quad (\because a_i I = a_j J)$$

$$b_j = \frac{\beta}{\gamma} \cdot \frac{J}{I} \cdot b_i \equiv \eta b_i \quad \left(\eta = \frac{\beta}{\gamma} \cdot \frac{J}{I}\right)$$

$$\alpha = -\frac{1 + \eta b_i^2 + (1 + \eta)b_i}{1 - \eta b_i^2}$$

$$\tag{A2-3}$$

$$(\alpha - 1)\eta b_i^2 - (1 + \eta)b_i - (\alpha + 1) = 0$$

$$b_i = \frac{(1 + \eta) - \sqrt{(1 + \eta)^2 + 4(\alpha - 1)(\alpha + 1)\eta}}{2(\alpha - 1)}, \quad b_j = \eta b_i$$

$$a_i = \gamma \cdot \frac{1 - b_i b_j}{b_i} = \gamma\left(\frac{1}{b_i} - b_j\right), \quad a_j = -\beta\left(\frac{1}{b_i} - b_i\right)$$

A2.2 Governing factors of information communication and technology prices

By means of Eq. (A2-2), the governing factors of ICT prices in Finland and Singapore over the period 1994—2011 were identified as Table A2-2 (Watanabe et al., 2015):

A2.3 Hybrid logistic growth function

Utilizing these results and applying Eq. (A2-3), the following hybrid logistic growth functions were identified in Finland and Singapore for 2011 as tabulated in Table A2-3 (Watanabe et al., 2018b):

AI-3. Elasticity of utility to consumption - Magnitude of consumption induced by uncaptured GDP

A3.1 Spin-off coevolution: Internet, uncaptured GDP, and shifts in preference

Fig. A3-1 illustrates spin-off coevolution among the Internet, uncaptured GDP, and shifts in people's preferences.

A3.2 Coevolution among the Internet, uncaptured GDP, and suprafunctionality

Table A3-1 demonstrates coevolution among the Internet, suprafunctionality, and uncaptured GDP in Japan over the period 1972—2012.

Because Internet dependence (J) and ICT stock (I) closely correspond to suprafunctionality beyond economic value (Q) and economic value (V) as demonstrated in (A3-1) and (A3-2), V and Q can be represented as a function of I and J.

Uncaptured GDP emerges according to the commercialization of the Internet (from D_3) and the induced preference shift to Q as demonstrated in (A3-3).

A3.3 Coevolution between consumption and increased GDP

Because consumption depends on GDP (income) as depicted in Eq. (A3-4), construction of a coevolution between consumption and increased GDP is the key to overcoming the economic stagnation derived from productivity declines due to a trap in ICT advancement:

$$C = a + b\,Y \tag{A3-4}$$

Table A2-2 Governing factors of information communication and technology prices in Finland and Singapore (1994–2011).

Finland

$$\frac{1}{1-\frac{p_t}{N}} = -1.605 + 0.052D_{F1}\cdot J - 0.052D_{F2}\cdot J - 0.030D_{F3}\cdot J + 0.005I + 0.268D_{Fa} - 0.568D_{Fb}$$
$$\;\;\;\;(-9.53)\quad(5.05)\quad\quad\quad(-3.87)\quad\quad\quad(-3.76)\quad\quad\quad(1.21)^{***}\;(1.94)^{*}\quad(-2.69)$$

$$adj.R^2\; 0.977\; DW\; 2.76$$
$$N=0.0170$$

Singapore

$$\frac{1}{1-\frac{p_t}{N}} = -1.869 - 0.180D_{S1}\cdot J - 0.112D_{S2}\cdot J + 0.03I$$
$$\;\;\;\;(-2.97)\quad(-4.83)\quad\quad\quad(-4.89)\quad\quad\quad(1.59)^{**}$$

$$adj.R^2\; 0.775\; DW\; 1.92$$
$$N=0.0570$$

pr: prices of ICT, N: carrying capacity, J: Internet dependency, I: ICT stock, D: dummy variables.
Finland: D_{F1}: 1994–99 = 1, others = 0; D_{F2}: 2000–08 = 1, others = 0; D_{F3}: 2009–11 = 1, others = 0; D_{Fa}: 1997, 1998, 2002 = 1, others = 0; D_{Fb}: 2001 = 1, others = 0.
Singapore: D_{S1}: 1994–2000 = 1, others = 0; D_{S2}: 2001–11 = 1, others = 0.
Figures in parentheses indicate t-statistics: all are significant at the 1% level except *10%, **15%, and ***20%.

Table A2-3 Two-sided information communication and technology price trajectories of Finland and Singapore *(2011)*—hybrid logistic growth function.

$$p_I = \frac{N}{1+b_i e^{-a_i I}} + \frac{N}{1+b_j e^{a_j I}}$$

	α	β			γ	a_i	b_i	a_j	b_j
Finland	−1.605	0.052 (1994—99)	−0.052 (2000—08)	−0.030 (2009—11)	0.005	0.005	0.191	0.102	0.278
Singapore	−1.869	−0.180 (1994—2010)	−0.112 (2001—11)		0.003	0.012	0.216	0.211	0.477

Status of both countries is as of 2011.

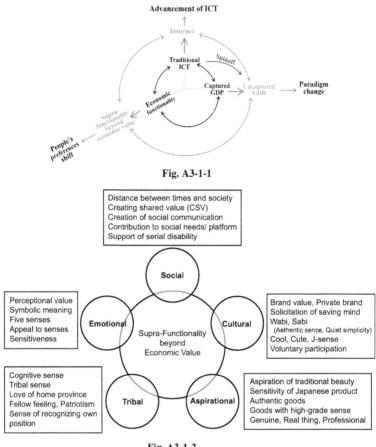

Fig. A3-1-1

Fig. A3-1-2

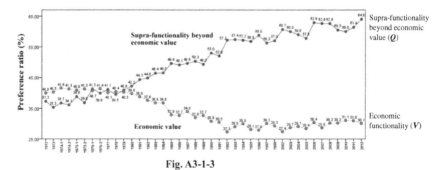

Fig. A3-1-3

Figure A3-1 Coevolution among the Internet, uncaptured GDP, and shifts in people's preferences. Figure A3-1-1. Coevolution of 3 Mega-trends. Figure A3-1-2. Concept of suprafunctionality. Figure A3-1-3. Trends in preference shifts in Japan (1972—2012). *Source: National Survey of Lifestyle Preferences (Japan Cabinet Office, annual issues).*

Table A3-1 Coevolution among the Internet, suprafunctionality, and uncaptured GDP in Japan (1972–2012).

Governing factors of the Internet

$$\ln J = -34.767 + 8.810 D_1 \ln Q + 9.495 D_3 \ln Q - 1.105 D \quad adj.R^2 0.937 \ DW \ 1.75 \quad (A3\text{-}1)$$
$$\underset{(-2.97^*)}{} \quad \underset{(3.05^*)}{} \quad \underset{(3.33^*)}{} \quad \underset{(-2.56^{**})}{}$$

with $+ 9.341 D_2 \ln Q$ $\underset{(3.24^*)}{}$

Governing factors of ICT stock

$$\ln I = -18.713 + 2.068 \ln V + (4.226 - 0.003 t^2 + 9.278 \times 10^{-5} t^3 + 2.153 \times 10^{-5} t^4) \ln Q + 0.305 D_2 \quad adj.R^2 0.909 \ DW \ 1.42 \quad (A3\text{-}2)$$
$$\underset{(-2.80^*)}{} \quad \underset{(2.04^{**})}{} \quad \underset{(3.70^*)}{} \quad \underset{(-3.25^*)}{} \quad \underset{(3.35^*)}{} \quad \underset{(2.92^{**})}{} \quad \underset{(3.28^*)}{}$$

J: Internet dependency, I: ICT stock, Q: suprafunctionality, V: economic functionality, t: time trend, D: dummy variables D_1: 1994–1996 = 1, D_2: 1997–2003 = 1, D_3: 2004–2012 = 1, D: 1994 = 1, *Other years* = 0, *respectively.*

Governing factors of the shift from economic functionality to supr-afunctionality

Captured GDP   Un-Captured GDP

$$\ln(Q/V) = -4.988 + 1.402 D_1 \ln Y + 1.043 D_2 \ln Y + 5.700 D_3 + 5.685 D_4 \quad adj.R^2 \ 0.964 \quad DW \ 1.52 \quad (A3\text{-}3)$$
$$\underset{(-9.63^*)}{} \quad \underset{(9.52^*)}{} \quad \underset{(10.33^*)}{} \quad \underset{(11.00^*)}{} \quad \underset{(10.96^*)}{}$$

Y: GDP, D_1–D_4: dummy variables correspond to four periods (D_i (i= 1–4) = 1, other years = 0). D_1: 1972–9 = 1, D_2: 1980–92 = 1, D_3: 1993–2008 = 1, D_4: 2009–12 = 1, other years = 0. The figures in parentheses indicate the t-statistics: *significant at the 1% level, **at the 5% level.

where C is consumption, Y is GDP (income), a is base consumption, and b is marginal propensity to consume.

Consumption is subject to utility (U), which represents satisfaction of consumption, and is depicted as follows:

$$C = C(U) \tag{A3-5}$$

Since U is governed by economic functionality (V) and suprafunctionality beyond economic value (Q) in the ICT-driven economy (Watanabe et al., 2015), and given that it is the total sum of utilities stemming from V and Q with constant returns to scale, it can be depicted as follows (Euler's theorem):

$$U = U(V, Q) = \frac{\partial U}{\partial V} \cdot V + \frac{\partial U}{\partial Q} \cdot Q \tag{A3-6}$$

The right-hand side of Eq. (A3-6) depicts utility stemming from economic functionality and suprafunctionality beyond economic value, respectively.

While Eq. (A3-6) can be further developed to determine Eq. (A3-7), the first three factors of the right-hand side of this equation demonstrate declines in the digital economy due to productivity declines stemming from the two-sided nature of ICT as declines in (1) marginal utility $\left(\frac{\partial U}{\partial C}\right)$ governed by the law of diminishing value, (2) marginal propensity to consume $\left(\frac{\partial C}{\partial Y}\right)$, and (3) marginal productivity of ICT $\left(\frac{\partial Y}{\partial I}\right)$:

$$U = U(V, Q) = \frac{\partial U}{\partial V} \cdot V + \frac{\partial U}{\partial Q} \cdot Q = \frac{\partial U}{\partial C} \cdot \frac{\partial C}{\partial Y} \cdot \frac{\partial Y}{\partial I} \cdot I \left(\frac{\partial I}{\partial V} \cdot \frac{V}{I} + \frac{\partial I}{\partial Q} \cdot \frac{Q}{I} \right) \tag{A3-7}$$

Under such circumstances, increased utility can be expected only through an engine function, χ, consisting of the product of I and sum of elasticity of V to I and Q to I as depicted in Eq. (A3-8) and suggesting that inducement of I by V and Q is one possible solution for enhancing utility under the current situation of declining productivity:

$$\chi = I \left(\frac{\partial I}{\partial V} \cdot \frac{V}{I} + \frac{\partial I}{\partial Q} \cdot \frac{Q}{I} \right) \tag{A3-8}$$

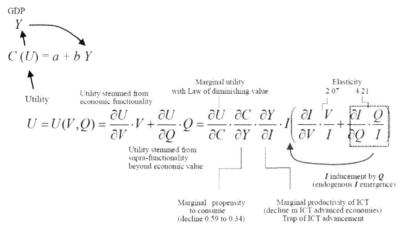

Figure A3.2 Structure of utility enhancement under a current decline in productivity. *V* is economic functionality, *Q* is suprafunctionality beyond economic value, *I* is information communication and technology stock, and *J* is Internet dependence. Figures demonstrate the case of Japan (1997−2007 and 2008−12 comparison) (Watanabe et al., 2015).

Based on the foregoing review, under a current decline in productivity caused by a trap in ICT advancement, a utility-enhancing mechanism without influences from declining factors can be illustrated as Fig. A3.2.

Fig. A3.2 demonstrates that the (1) marginal utility, (2) marginal propensity to consume, (3) marginal productivity of ICT, (4) ICT stock, and (5) elasticity of economic functionality as well as the suprafunctionality beyond economic value of ICT govern utility under the digital economy.

Because the (1) marginal utility, (2) marginal propensity to consume, and (3) marginal productivity of ICT decline due to the law of diminishing marginal utility, conflict between captured and uncaptured GDP, and a trap in ICT advancement, respectively, (4) ICT stock inducement by economic functionality and/or suprafunctionality can be one solution for enhancing utility to compensate for declines in consumption.

Given that suprafunctionality induces ICT with much higher economic functionality and a closer relationship to advancement of the Internet (Watanabe et al., 2015), enhancing utility through Internet inducement of ICT stock can be a possible solution for overcoming declines in productivity by reconstructing a virtuous cycle between consumption and increased GDP as follows:

$$J \rightarrow I \rightarrow U \rightarrow C \rightarrow GDP \rightarrow C$$

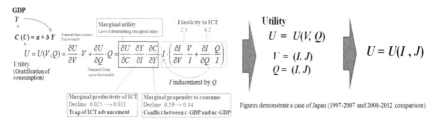

Figure A3.3 Dynamism highlighting the governing role played by information communication and technology stock and Internet dependence in enhancing utility. **Original source**: New Paradigm of ICT Productivity — Increasing Role of Uncaptured GDP and Growing Anger of Consumers (Watanabe et al., 2015).

Under the current productivity decline in the digital economy, as the marginal productivity of ICT and the marginal propensity to consume decline, the V and Q inducement of ICT stock is a possible solution for enhancing utility.

Provided that V and Q can be represented as a function of I and J, utility can be represented by a function of I and J under the productivity decline in the digital economy as illustrated in Fig. A3.3.

A3.4 Elasticity of utility to consumption

The foregoing review highlights the significance of the elasticity of utility to consumption in terms of the elasticities of I to C and J to C, which represent the magnitudes of consumption induced by uncaptured GDP, as depicted in (A3-9).

$$U = U(V, Q) \; V = V(I,J), \; Q = Q(I,J)$$

$$U = U(I,J) = \frac{\partial U}{\partial I}{\cdot}I + \frac{\partial U}{\partial J}{\cdot}J = \frac{\partial U}{\partial C}\left(\frac{\partial C}{\partial I}{\cdot}I + \frac{\partial C}{\partial J}{\cdot}J\right)$$

$$\underset{(\varepsilon_{cu})}{\frac{\partial C}{\partial U}{\cdot}\frac{U}{C}} = \underset{(\varepsilon_{ci})}{\frac{\partial C}{\partial I}{\cdot}\frac{I}{C}} + \underset{(\varepsilon_{cj})}{\frac{\partial C}{\partial J}{\cdot}\frac{J}{C}} \tag{A3-9}$$

U: Utility, C: Traditional consumption

V: Economic functionality, Q: Supra − functionality

J: Internet dependency, I: ICT stock

AI-4. Measurement of the magnitude of uncaptured GDP

A4.1 Analytical framework

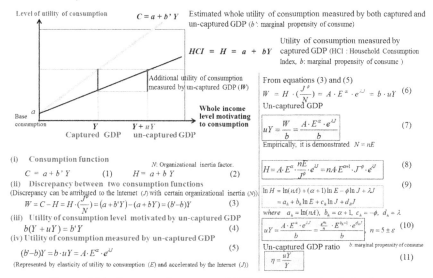

Figure A4-1 Concept of uncaptured GDP in consumption behavior.

A4.2 Empirical results

Uncaptured GDP can be attributed to the

Advancement of the **Internet** with **orgranizational intertia** →
Represented by **elasticity of utility to consumption** and **accelerated
by the Internet** → **Organizational intertia is propotional to the level
of this elasticity**

Table A4-1 Governing factors of household consumption in Finland and Singapore (1994−2013).

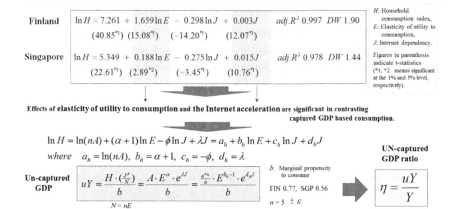

A4.3 Examination of results

Table A4-2 Correlation between Internet advancement and the uncaptured shift of GDP in Finland and Singapore (1996–2013).

		Before inflection	After inflection	Model 2 is most significant. Finland: shifted to new trajectory Singapore: clinging to same trajectory
Finland 1		$\ln \eta = 4.286 - 1.899 D_{9600} \ln I/J + 0.308 D_{0113} \ln I/J - 5.182 D_{0113}$		$adj.R^2$ 0.936 DW 2.35 $AIC - 83.43$
		$(3.93^{t})(-4.62^{t})$	(3.77^{t}) (-4.65^{t})	
	2	$\ln \eta = 4.817 - 2.093 D_{9601} \ln I/J + 0.259 D_{0213} \ln I/J - 5.560 D_{0213}$		$adj.R^2$ 0.982 DW 2.21 $AIC - 106.57$
		$(9.58^{t})(-10.96^{t})$	(5.93^{t}) (-10.74^{t})	
	3	$\ln \eta = 3.699 - 1.673 D_{9602} \ln I/J + 0.250 D_{0313} \ln I/J - 4.410 D_{0313}$		$adj.R^2$ 0.973 DW 2.05 $AIC - 99.04$
		$(10.28^{t})(-12.02^{t})$	(4.16^{t}) (-11.11^{t})	
Singapore 1		$\ln \eta = 0.980 - 0.817 D_{9698} \ln I/J - 0.861 D_{9913} \ln I/J$		$adj.R^2$ 0.766 DW 1.82 $AIC - 68.61$
		(3.02^{t}) (-7.21^{t})	(-6.65^{t})	
	2	$\ln \eta = 1.043 - 0.834 D_{9699} \ln I/J - 0.892 D_{0013} \ln I/J$		$adj.R^2$ 0.800 DW 1.90 $AIC - 71.27$
		(3.62^{t}) (-8.09^{t})	(-7.73^{t})	
	3	$\ln \eta = 0.869 - 0.787 D_{9600} \ln I/J - 0.819 D_{0113} \ln I/J$		$adj.R^2$ 0.761 DW 1.93 $AIC - 68.27$
		(2.96^{t}) (-7.27^{t})	(-7.02^{t})	

η : un-captured GDP ratio, I: ICT stock, J: Internet dependency, D_{mn}: dummy variable (period m-n =1, other period = 0) , mn reads as follows:9600 (1996-2000), 0113 (2001-2013), 9601 (1996-2001), 0213 (2002-2013), 9602 (1996-2002), 0313 (2003-2013), 9698 (1996-1998), 9913 (1999-2013), 9699 (11996-1999), 0013 (2000-2013), 9600 (1996-2000), 0113 (2001-2013). Figures in parenthesis indicate t-statistics (*t means significant at the 1% level).

Original source: Operationalization of Uncaptured GDP: Innovation Stream under New Global Mega-trends (Watanabe et al., 2016).

A4.4 Insight into integration of national accounts with microanalysis

The above analyses are based on the notion that stimulation by ICT advancement and inducement from shifts in people's preferences drive dependence on uncaptured GDP and that the equilibrium of the two inertias leads to the powerful emergence of uncaptured GDP, as illustrated in Fig. 3.9. This dynamism provides insight into the integration of national accounts with product/consumption-oriented microanalysis efforts.

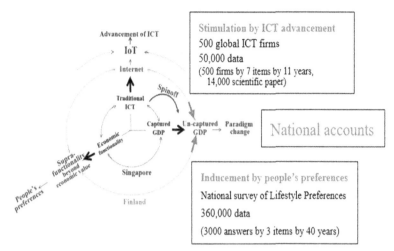

Figure A4-2 Coevolutionary dynamism: insight into the integration of national accounts with firm- and people-oriented microanalyses.

AI-5. Internet dependence

A5.1 Indicator percentage of individuals using the Internet

The proportion of individuals who have used the Internet from any location in the last 3 months (previously 12 months) reported in the HH7 (households and individuals) national survey conducted by the International Telecommunication Union (ITU) is summarized in Table A5-1.

A5.2 The International Telecommunication Union's World Telecommunication/ICT Indicators Database

ITU's World Telecommunication/ICT Indicators Database is the main source of global and internationally comparable telecommunication/ICT statistics.

A5.3 Definitions

Internet: The Internet is a worldwide public computer network. It provides access to a number of communication services including the World Wide Web, e-mail, news, entertainment, and data files irrespective of the device used.

Internet Access: Individuals may have accessed the Internet by any means including a computer, mobile phone, PDA, game machine, or digital TV. Access can be via a fixed or mobile network.

A5.4 Methods

The ITU conducted several surveys for the World Telecommunication/ ICT Indicators Database to measure ICT access and usage by households and individuals. The HH7 survey calculates the proportion of individuals who used the Internet from any location in the last 3 months.

A5.5 Survey Question: "Have you used the Internet from any location in the last 3 months?"

The proportion of individuals who have used the Internet is calculated by dividing the total number of individuals who used the Internet in the last 3 months by the total number of individuals surveyed.

A5.6 Source: International Telecommunication Union's World Telecommunication/ICT Indicators Database

ITU's World Telecommunication/ICT Indicators Database includes time series for more than 140 indicators and around 200 countries. The data are collected directly from telecommunication regulatory agencies and/or ministries and national statistical offices by means of an annual questionnaire and subsequently verified, harmonized, and complemented by ITU.

Table A5-1 The International Telecommunication Union's HH7 Survey for "Percentage of Individuals Using Internet"

	Indicators	Definitions and notes
HH7	**Proportion of individuals who have used the Internet (from any location) in the last 3 months**	The proportion of individuals who have used the Internet is calculated by dividing the total number of individuals who have used the Internet (from any location) in the last 3 months by the total number of individuals surveyed.
	Suggested model question: *"Have you used the Internet from any location in the last 3 months?"*	The Internet is a worldwide public computer network. It provides access to a number of communication services including the World Wide Web and carries e-mail, news, entertainment, and data files irrespective of the device used (not assumed to be only via a computer—access may also be provided by mobile phone, PDA, game machine, digital TV, and other means). Access can be via a fixed or mobile network.

Source: Manual for Measuring ICT Access and Use by Households and Individuals (International Telecommunication Union: ITU, 2009) (http://www.itu.int/dms_pub/itu-d/opb/ind/D-IND-ITC-MEAS-2009-PDF-E.pdf).

References

European Commission, Joint Research Center, 2017. The EU Industrial R&D Investment Scoreboard 2016. European Commission, Brussels.

EU, 2017a. Economics of Industrial Research and Innovation. EU, Brussels.

EU, 2017b. The Internet of Things: Digital Single Market. EU, Brussels.

Innovation Policy Research Center (IPRC), 2013. Academic Landscape System. http://academic-landscape.com/. (Accessed 9 April 2017).

International Telecommunication Union: ITU, 2009. Manual for Measuring ICT Access and Use by Households and Individuals. ITU, Geneva.

Japan Cabinet Office, 2019. National Survey of Lifestyle Preferences. Japan Cabinet Office, Tokyo.

Kahre, C., Hoffmann, D., Ahlemann, F., 2017. Beyond business-IT alignment-digital business strategies as a paradigmatic shift: a review and research agenda. Proceedings of the 50th Hawaii International Conference on System Sciences 4706—4715.

Kajikawa, Y., Tacoa, F., Yamaguchi, K., 2014. Sustainability science: the changing landscape of sustainability research. Sustainability Science 9 (4), 431—438.

McKinsey Global Institute, 2015. The Internet of Things: Mapping the Value beyond the Hype. McKinsey & Company, New York.

Newman, M.E.J., 2004. Algorithm for detecting community structure in networks. Physical Review E 69, 066133-1-5.

Schelling, T.C., 1998. Social mechanisms and social dynamics. In: Hedstrom, P., Swedberg, R. (Eds.), Social Mechanisms: An Analytical Approach to Social Theory. Cambridge Univ. Press, Cambridge, pp. 32—43.

Tou, Y., Moriya, K., Watanabe, C., Ilmola, L., Neittaanmäki, P., 2018a. Soft innovation resources: enabler for reversal in GDP growth in the digital economy. International Journal of Managing Information Technology 10 (3), 9—29.

Tou, Y., Watanabe, C., Ilmola, L., Moriya, K., Neittaanmäki, P., 2018b. Hybrid role of soft innovation resources: Finland's notable resurgence in the digital economy. International Journal of Managing Information Technology 10 (4), 1—22.

Tou, Y., Watanabe, C., Moriya, K., Neittaanmäki, P., 2019a. Harnessing soft innovation resources leads to neo open innovation. Technology in Society 58, 101114.

Tou, Y., Watanabe, C., Moriya, K., Naveed, N., Vurpillat, V., Neittaanmäki, P., 2019b. The transformation of R&D into neo open innovation: a new concept of R&D endeavor triggered by Amazon. Technology in Society 58, 101141.

Watanabe, C., Zhu, B., Miyazawa, T., 2001. Hierarchical impacts of the length of technology waves: an analysis of technolabor homeostasis. Technological Forecasting and Social Change 68 (1), 81—104.

Watanabe, C., Takayama, M., Nagamatsu, A., Tagami, T., Griffy-Brown, C., 2002. Technology spillover as a complement for high level R&D intensity in the pharmaceutical industry. Technovation 22 (4), 245—258.

Watanabe, C., Kondo, R., Ouchi, N., Wei, H., Griffy-Brown, C., 2004. Institutional elasticity as a significant driver of IT functionality development. Technological Forecasting and Social Change 71 (7), 723—750.

Watanabe, C., Hobo, M., 2004. Creating a firm self-propagating function for advanced innovation-oriented projects: lessons from ERP. Technovation 24 (6), 467—481.

Watanabe, C., 2009. Managing Innovation in Japan: The Role Institutions Play in Helping or Hindering How Companies Develop Technology. Springer Science & Business Media, Berlin.

Watanabe, C., Naveed, K., Zhao, W., 2014. Institutional sources of resilience in global ICT leaders — harness the vigor of emerging power. Journal of Technology Management in Growing Economies 5 (1), 7—34.

Watanabe, C., Naveed, K., Zhao, W., 2015. New paradigm of ICT productivity: increasing role of un-captured GDP and growing anger of consumers. Technology in Society 41, 21–44.

Watanabe, C., Naveed, K., Neittaanmäki, P., Tou, Y., 2016. Operationalization of un-captured GDP: the innovation stream under new global mega-trends. Technology in Society 45, 58–77.

Watanabe, C., Naveed, N., Neittaanmäki, P., 2018a. Digital solutions transform the forest-based bioeconomy into a digital platform industry: a suggestion for a disruptive business model in the digital economy. Technology in Society 54, 168–188.

Watanabe, C., Tou, Y., Neittaanmäki, P., 2018b. A new paradox of the digital economy: structural sources of the limitation of GDP statistics. Technology in Society 55, 9–23.

Appendix II

Database for technoeconomic analysis

AII-1. National development

The networked readiness index (NRI) measures the capacity of countries to leverage information communication and technologies (ICTs) for increased competitiveness and well-being. The NRI also provides a different lens through which to view recent years' innovation trends.

The networked readiness framework rests on six principles:

(1) A high-quality regulatory and business environment is critical in order to fully leverage ICTs and generate impact.
(2) ICT readiness—as measured by ICT affordability, skills, and infrastructure—is a precondition to generating impact.
(3) Fully leveraging ICTs requires a society-wide effort: the government, the business sector, and the population at large each have a critical role to play.
(4) The use of ICT should not be an end in itself. The impact that ICTs actually have on the economy and on society is what ultimately matters.
(5) The set of drivers— the environment, readiness, and usage—interact, coevolve, and reinforce each other to form a virtuous cycle.
(6) The networked readiness framework should provide clear policy guidance.

The networked readiness framework translates into the NRI, a composite indicator made up of four main categories (subindexes), 10 subcategories (pillars), and 53 individual indicators distributed across the different pillars:

A. Environment subindex: 1. Political and regulatory environment (nine indicators) 2. Business and innovation environment (nine indicators)
B. Readiness subindex: 3. Infrastructure (four indicators) 4. Affordability (three indicators) 5. Skills (four indicators)

Table AII-1 Level of information communication and technology advancement and GDP per capita in 139 countries (2016).

		Country	NRI	GDP/P			Country	NRI	GDP/P			Country	NRI	GDP/P
1	SGP	Singapore	6.0	56,722	51	MNE	Montenegro	4.3	7032	101	BWA	Botswana	3.5	6958
2	FIN	Finland	6.0	43,574	52	OMN	Oman	4.3	16,332	102	GHA	Ghana	3.5	1941
3	SWE	Sweden	5.8	51,599	53	AZE	Azerbaijan	4.3	3898	103	GTM	Guatemala	3.5	4141
4	NOR	Norway	5.8	70,224	54	HRV	Croatia	4.3	12,368	104	LAO	Lao	3.4	2325
5	USA	USA	5.8	57,901	55	PAN	Panama	4.3	14,356	105	PRY	Paraguay	3.4	5260
6	NLD	Netherlands	5.8	46,165	56	ARM	Armenia	4.3	3524	106	CIV	Côte d'Ivoire	3.4	1451
7	CHE	Switzerland	5.8	80,629	57	MNG	Mongolia	4.3	3577	107	SEN	Senegal	3.4	1235
8	GBR	UK	5.7	40,658	58	GEO	Georgia	4.3	3856	108	VEN	Venezuela	3.4	9092
9	LUX	Luxembourg	5.7	102,360	59	CHN	China	4.2	8116	109	KHM	Cambodia	3.4	1271
10	JPN	Japan	5.6	38,805	60	JOR	Jordan	4.2	4151	110	PAK	Pakistan	3.4	1440
11	DNK	Denmark	5.6	54,665	61	KWT	Kuwait	4.2	25,267	111	BOL	Bolivia	3.3	3095
12	HKG	Hong Kong	5.6	43,496	62	THA	Thailand	4.2	6113	112	BGD	Bangladesh	3.3	1459
13	KOR	Korea	5.6	29,296	63	LKA	Sri Lanka	4.2	3886	113	GMB	Gambia	3.3	684
14	CAN	Canada	5.6	42,440	64	UHR	Ukraine	4.2	2200	114	TJK	Tajikistan	3.3	796
15	DEU	Germany	5.6	42,116	65	ZAF	South Africa	4.2	5267	115	LSO	Lesotho	3.3	1207
16	ISL	Iceland	5.5	62,005	66	ROU	Romania	4.1	9539	116	ZMB	Zambia	3.2	1253
17	NZL	New Zealand	5.5	38,983	67	TTO	Trinidad and Tobago	4.1	15,938	117	DZA	Algeria	3.2	3919
18	AUS	Australia	5.5	51,979	68	COL	Colombia	4.1	5800	118	NPL	Nepal	3.2	777
19	TWN	Taiwan	5.5	22,573	69	BGR	Bulgaria	4.1	7496	119	NGA	Nigeria	3.2	2180
20	AUT	Austria	5.4	45,105	70	GRC	Greece	4.1	18,111	120	ETH	Ethiopia	3.1	777
21	ISR	Israel	5.4	37,333	71	MDA	Moldova	4.0	2273	121	UGA	Uganda	3.1	677
22	EST	Estonia	5.4	18,245	72	BRA	Brazil	4.0	8751	122	ZWE	Zimbabwe	3.0	1409
23	BEL	Belgium	5.4	41,540	73	IDN	Indonesia	4.0	3606	123	MOZ	Mozambique	3.0	379
24	FRA	France	5.3	38,349	74	SYC	Seychelles	4.0	15,219	124	CMR	Cameroon	3.0	1378
25	IRL	Ireland	5.3	62,938	75	SRB	Serbia	4.0	5756	125	GAB	Gabon	2.9	7082

	Code	Country	NR	Value		Code	Country	NR	Value		Code	Country	NR	Value
26	UAE	UAE	5.3	36,226	76	MEX	Mexico	4.0	8816	126	TZA	Tanzania	2.9	966
27	QAT	Qatar	5.2	57,965	77	PHL	Philippines	4.0	2953	127	MLI	Mali	2.9	802
28	BHR	Bahrain	5.1	22,652	78	MAR	Morocco	3.9	2997	128	BEN	Benin	2.9	1087
29	LTU	Lithuania	4.9	14,989	79	VNM	Vietnam	3.9	2172	129	SWZ	Swaziland	2.9	
30	PRT	Portugal	4.9	19,986	80	RWA	Rwanda	3.9	735	130	LBR	Liberia	2.8	772
31	MYS	Malaysia	4.9	9523	81	TUN	Tunisia	3.9	3666	131	NIC	Nicaragua	2.8	2100
32	LVA	Latvia	4.8	14,072	82	ECU	Ecuador	3.9	6046	132	MWI	Malawi	2.7	295
33	SAU	Saudi Arabia	4.8	20,289	83	JAM	Jamaica	3.9	4986	133	MMR	Myanmar	2.7	1157
34	MLT	Malta	4.8	25,420	84	ALB	Albania	3.9	4124	134	GIN	Guinea	2.7	680
35	ESP	Spain	4.8	26,682	85	CPV	Cape Verde	3.8	3084	135	MDG	Madagascar	2.6	406
36	CZE	Czech Republic	4.7	18,485	86	KEN	Kenya	3.8	1522	136	MRT	Mauritania	2.6	1235
37	SVN	Slovenia	4.7	21,640	87	BTN	Bhutan	3.8	2680	137	HTI	Haiti	2.5	735
38	CHL	Chile	4.6	13,776	88	LBN	Lebanon	3.8	8530	138	BDI	Burundi	2.4	298
39	KAZ	Kazakhstan	4.6	7662	89	ARG	Argentina	3.8	12,773	139	TCD	Chad	2.2	861
40	CYP	Cyprus	4.6	24,120	90	PER	Peru	3.8	6173					
41	RUS	Russia	4.5	8723	91	IND	India	3.8	1762					
42	POL	Poland	4.5	12,428	92	IRN	Iran	3.7	5027					
43	URY	Uruguay	4.5	15,139	93	SLV	El Salvador	3.7	3704					
44	CRI	Costa Rica	4.5	11,779	94	HND	Honduras	3.7	2383					
45	ITA	Italy	4.4	30,824	95	KGZ	Kyrgyz Republic	3.7	1132					
46	MKD	Macedonia	4.4	5153	96	EGY	Egypt	3.7	3686					
47	SVK	Slovakia	4.4	16,565	97	BIH	Herzegovina	3.6	4808					
48	TUR	Turkey	4.4	10,817	98	DOM	Dominican Republic	3.6	7521					
49	MUS	Mauritius	4.4	9681	99	NAM	Namibia	3.6	4854					
50	HUN	Hungary	4.4	12,823	100	GUY	Guyana	3.6	4531					

NR, networked readiness index.

Sources: World Economic Forum (WEF), 2016. The Global Information Technology Report 2016. WEF, Geneva; World Economic Outlook Database; International Monetary Fund (IMF), 2017. Measuring the Digital Economy: IMF Statistical Forum. IMF, Washington D.C.

C. Usage subindex: 6. Individual usage (seven indicators) 7. Business usage (six indicators) 8. Government usage (three indicators)
D. Impact subindex: 9. Economic impacts (four indicators) 10. Social impacts (four indicators)

The overall NRI is computed based on successive aggregations of scores—individual indicators are aggregated to obtain pillar scores, which are then combined to obtain subindex scores. Subindex scores are in turn combined to produce a country's overall NRI score.

Source: *The Global Information Technology Report 2016* (World Economic Forum, 2016).

AII-2. Company-level development

Table AII-2 2018 R&D investment for world's top 20 R&D leaders.[1]

R&D rank	Firms	Country	Sector	2018 R&D investment (USD mil. unless otherwise noted)	Investment execution timing (exchange rate)
1	Amazon	US	ICT	28,837 for technology and content	*FY* ended December 31
2	Google (Alphabet)	US	ICT	21,419 for research and development	*FY* ended December 31
3	Samsung Electronics	Korea	ICT	16,505 for research and development (18,650 bil. Korean won)	*FY* ended December 31 (1130 W/USD)
4	Huawei Investment	China	ICT	15,297 for research and development (CNY 101,509 mil.)	*FY* ended December 31 (6.636 CNY/ USD)
5	Microsoft	US	ICT	14,726 for research and development	*FY* ended June 30
6	Apple	US	ICT	14,236 for research and development	*FY* ended September 29
7	Intel	US	ICT	13,543 for research and development	*FY* ended December 29
8	Roche Holding	Switzerland	Pharma	12,260 for research and development (CHF 11,047 mil.)	*FY* ended December 31 (0.901 CHF/ USD)
9	Johnson & Johnson	US	Pharma	10,775 for research and development	*FY* ended December 30
10	Facebook	US	ICT	10,273 for research and development	*FY* ended December 31

Continued

Table AII-2 2018 R&D investment for world's top 20 R&D leaders.[1]—cont'd

R&D rank	Firms	Country	Sector	2018 R&D investment (USD mil. unless otherwise noted)	Investment execution timing (exchange rate)
11	Toyota Motor	Japan	Auto	10,039 for research and development (JPY 1,064.2 bil.)	*FY* ended March 31, 2019 (106 JPY/USD)
12	Volkswagen	Germany	Auto	9600 for research and development (EUR 13,640 mil.)* *double-counted between divisions.	*FY* ended December 31 *Eliminated double counting*
13	Novartis	Switzerland	Pharma	9100 for research and development (8489 mil. for continuing operations)	*FY* ended December 31 *Not include for regulatory process*
14	Robert Bosch	Germany	Auto	8700 for research and development (EUR 5.963 mil. by IFRS Foundation application)	*FY* ended December 31 *Same accounting as 2017 for consistency*
15	Ford Motor	US	Auto	8200 for engineering, research, and development	*FY* ended December 31
16	Pfizer	US	Pharma	8006 for research and development	*FY* ended December 31
17	General Motors	US	Auto	7800 for research and development	*FY* ended December 31

Table AII-2 2018 R&D investment for world's top 20 R&D leaders.[1]—cont'd

R&D rank	Firms	Country	Sector	2018 R&D investment (USD mil. unless otherwise noted)	Investment execution timing (exchange rate)
18	Daimler	Germany	Auto	7520 for research and development (EUR 6962 mil.) Mercedes-Benz Cars division	*FY* ended December 31 (1.08 USD/ EUR) covering other div. R&D
19	Honda Motor	Japan	Auto	7269 for research and development (JPY 806.9 bil.)	*FY* ended March 31, 2019 (111 JPY/USD)
20	Sanofi	France	Pharma	6719 for research and development (EUR 5894 mil.)	*FY* ended December 31 (1.14 USD/ EUR)

Sources: UNCTAD, World Investment Report 2019 based on statistical databases of Eikon and Orbis of Ghent University (2019) cross-evaluated by annual reports for *US firms* and *Sanofi*: US SEC, annual reports pursuant to the Securities Exchange Act for fiscal year 2019 for respective firms (2020); and Samsung Electronics, Consolidated Financial Statements (2019); Huawei Investment, 2019 Annual Report (2020); Roche, Finance Report 2019 (2020); Toyota, Annual Report 2019 (2020); Volkswagen, Annual Report 2019 (2020); Novartis, Annual Report 2019 (2020); Bosch, Annual Report 2019 (2020); Honda, Consolidated Financial Results 2018 (2019).

[1] A firm's annual R&D investment can be identified using data from its annual report (see the details in Table A1-1 in Appendix 1). In conducting an international and/or a time series comparison of firms' R&D investments, it should be noted that the fiscal year (*FY*) that applies to each firm's R&D investment timing differs by firm. Moreover, in response to the transforming trend in conducting R&D toward neo open innovation, Amazon, which has become the world's R&D leader since 2016, has insisted on describing traditional R&D investment as technology and content (see the details in Chapter 6). Similarly, Ford describes R&D as engineering, research, and development. In addition, due to difference in accounting standards, there is the possibility that actual R&D activities and the timing of their accounting may extend beyond the stated FY.

Table AII-3 Digital business structure of global information communication and technology (ICT) firms in 2016/2015 (top 50 R&D-intensive ICT firms by level of R&D).

R&D firm rank		R&D (R) EUR bil.	Net sales (S) EUR bil.	Operating income (OI) EUR bil.	R/S %	OI/S %	OI/R %
1	Amazon	12.9	109.5	2.9	11.8	2.6	22.4
2	Samsung	12.5	157.2	20.7	8.0	13.2	165.2
3	Intel	11.1	50.8	13.0	21.9	25.6	116.8
4	Google	11.0	68.8	17.7	16.0	25.8	160.9
5	Microsoft	11.0	78.3	18.6	14.1	23.8	169.7
6	Huawei	8.3	55.8	6.4	15.0	11.6	77.5
7	Apple	7.4	214.6	65.4	3.5	30.5	883.0
8	Cisco	5.7	45.2	11.8	12.6	26.3	208.3
9	Oracle	5.3	34.0	12.0	15.6	35.4	226.4
10	Qualcomm	5.0	23.2	5.4	21.7	23.5	108.1
11	Siemens	4.8	75.6	5.8	6.4	7.7	120.5
12	IBM	4.5	75.0	14.5	6.0	19.4	323.1
13	Facebook	4.4	16.4	5.7	26.9	34.7	129.3
14	Ericsson	3.8	26.8	2.3	14.2	8.8	61.9
15	Sony	3.5	61.7	2.2	5.8	3.6	62.8
16	Panasonic	3.4	57.5	2.7	6.0	4.9	81.6
17	HP	3.2	94.9	7.3	3.4	7.7	228.6
18	LG	2.7	44.2	0.9	6.1	2.1	34.4
19	SAP	2.6	20.7	4.2	12.9	20.4	158.1
20	Hitachi	2.5	76.4	4.5	3.3	0.1	180.7
21	Canon	2.5	28.9	2.7	8.6	9.3	108.1
22	Nokia	2.5	13.5	1.8	18.4	13.6	73.6
23	EMC	2.4	22.6	3.0	10.7	13.3	124.0
24	Alcatel	2.4	14.2	0.8	16.9	6.2	36.9
25	Toshiba	2.4	34.2	−1.8	7.0	−5.4	-77.0
26	Medtronic	2.0	26.4	4.8	7.7	18.4	237.9
27	ZTE	1.9	14.1	0.9	13.8	6.7	48.9
28	Taiwan SEM	1.8	23.5	9.1	7.8	38.7	498.4
29	SK Hynix	1.5	14.7	4.1	10.5	28.4	270.9
30	West Digital	1.4	11.9	0.7	12.5	6.3	50.5
31	Hon Hai	1.4	124.9	5.2	1.2	4.2	356.7
32	Baidu	1.4	9.3	1.6	15.4	17.6	114.3
33	Mitsubishi	1.4	33.4	2.2	4.3	6.9	161.0

Table AII-3 Digital business structure of global information communication and technology (ICT) firms in 2016/2015 (top 50 R&D-intensive ICT firms by level of R&D).—cont'd

R&D firm rank		R&D (R) EUR bil.	Net sales (S) EUR bil.	Operating income (OI) EUR bil.	R/S %	OI/S %	OI/R %
34	Micron Tec	1.4	14.8	2.7	9.5	18.5	194.9
35	MediaTek	1.3	5.9	0.7	23.2	12.2	52.6
36	Fujitsu	1.3	36.1	1.1	3.8	3.1	81.1
37	Applied Mat	1.3	8.8	1.3	15.0	15.6	104.1
38	Lenovo	1.2	41.2	3.1	0.0	−1.6	3.1
39	Fujifilm	1.2	18.9	6.5	7.7	117.3	6.5
40	NVidia	1.2	4.6	26.6	17.5	66.0	26.6
41	Tencent	1.1	14.5	8.1	39.3	485.5	8.1
42	Texas Inst	1.1	11.9	9.8	33.0	335.6	9.8
43	STM	1.1	6.3	18.1	1.9	10.6	18.1
44	Danaher	1.1	18.8	6.0	17.5	289.8	6.0
45	Seagate	1.1	10.2	11.1	4.0	36.0	11.1
46	Yahoo!	1.1	4.5	24.3	−93.5	−384.2	24.3
47	ASML	1.0	6.2	16.6	29.6	177.8	16.6
48	Elec Arts	1.0	4.0	25.2	20.4	81.0	25.2
49	Sharp	0.9	18.7	5.3	−7.6	−143.5	5.3
50	eBay	0.9	7.8	12.3	25.6	207.5	12.3

Original source: European Commission, Joint Research Center, 2017. The EU Industrial R&D Investment Scoreboard 2016. European Commission, Brussels.

Because Amazon's R&D investment, which it classifies as "technology and content," was not duly counted as R&D in the *Scoreboard*, its comparable R&D value and corresponding sales and operating income for 2015—2016 are based on its 2015 and 2016 annual reports.

Table AII-4 Trends in R&D investment and sales for Google, Apple, Facebook, and Amazon (1997–2018)—USD, millions.

R&D	Google	Apple	Facebook	Amazon	S	Google	Apple	Facebook	Amazon
1999		314		159	1999		6100		1640
2000		380		269	2000		7900		2762
2001		430		241	2001		5400		3122
2002	40	446		216	2002	400	5700		3933
2003	230	471		257	2003	1500	6200		5264
2004	395	489		283	2004	3200	8200		6920
2005	600	535		451	2005	6139	13,931		8490
2006	1229	712		662	2006	10,605	19,315		10,711
2007	2120	782	81	818	2007	16,594	24,578	153	14,835
2008	2793	1109	47	1033	2008	21,796	37,491	272	19,166
2009	2843	1333	87	1240	2009	23,651	42,905	777	24,509
2010	3762	1782	144	1734	2010	29,321	65,225	1974	34,204
2011	5162	2429	388	2909	2011	37,905	108,249	3711	48,077
2012	6083	3381	1399	4564	2012	46,039	156,508	5089	61,093
2013	7137	4475	1415	6565	2013	55,519	170,910	7872	74,452
2014	9832	6041	2666	9275	2014	66,001	182,795	12,466	88,988
2015	12,282	8067	4816	12,540	2015	74,989	233,715	17,928	107,006
2016	13,948	10,045	5919	16,085	2016	90,272	215,639	27,638	135,987
2017	16,625	11,581	7754	22,620	2017	110,855	229,234	40,653	177,866
2018	21,419	14,236	10,273	28,837	2018	136,819	265,595	55,838	232,887
2019	26,018	16,217	13,600	35,931	2019	161,857	260,174	70,697	280,522

(R&D investment on left, Sales on right.)

Sources: US Security and Exchange Commission (SEC), 2020a. Annual Report pursuant to Section 13 or 15(d) of the Security Exchange Act of 1934 for the Fiscal Year 2019, Alphabets Inc. SEC, Washington, D.C.; US Security and Exchange Commission (SEC), 2020b. Annual Report pursuant to Section 13 or 15(d) of the Security Exchange Act of 1934 for the Fiscal Year 2019, Amazon.com, Inc. SEC, Washington, D.C.; US Security and Exchange Commission (SEC), 2020c. Annual Report pursuant to Section 13 or 15(d) of the Security Exchange Act of 1934 for the Fiscal Year 2019, Apple Inc. SEC, Washington, D.C.; US Security and Exchange Commission (SEC), 2020d. Annual Report pursuant to Section 13 or 15(d) of the Security Exchange Act of 1934 for the Fiscal Year 2019, Facebook, Inc. SEC, Washington, D.C.; Macrotrends, 2020. The Premier Research Platform for GAFA Financial Statements 2005–2020. Zacks Investment Research Inc., Chicago. www.macrotrends.net/stocks/charts/GOOG/alphabet/financial-statements   https://www.macrotrends.net/stocks/charts/AMZN/amazon/financial-statements   https://www.macrotrends.net/stocks/charts/AAPL/apple/financial-statements   https://www.macrotrends.net/stocks/charts/FB/facebook/financial-statements   (Retrieved

Table AII-5 Trends in Amazon's key managerial factors (1997–2018)—USD million.

Year	Sales	Operating income	R&D	Net income	Operating CF	Free CF	Long-term debt
1997	148	−32	13	−30	1	−7	77
1998	609	−109	46	−125	31	3	348
1999	1640	−606	159	−720	−91	−378	1466
2000	2762	−864	269	−1411	−130	−265	2127
2001	3122	−412	241	−567	−120	−170	2156
2002	3933	64	216	−149	174	135	2277
2003	5264	270	257	35	392	346	1945
2004	6921	440	283	588	566	477	1855
2005	8490	432	451	359	733	529	1480
2006	10,711	389	662	190	702	486	1247
2007	14,835	655	818	476	1405	1181	1282
2008	19,166	842	1033	645	1697	1364	409
2009	24,509	1129	1240	902	3293	2920	0
2010	34,204	1406	1734	1152	3495	2516	1561
2011	48,077	862	2909	631	3903	2092	255
2012	61,093	676	4564	−39	4180	395	3084
2013	74,452	745	6565	274	5475	2031	3191
2014	88,988	178	9275	−241	6842	1949	8265
2015	107,006	2233	12,540	596	12,039	7450	8227
2016	135,987	4186	16,085	2,371	17,203	10,466	7694
2017	177,866	4106	22,620	3033	18,365	8307	24,743
2018	232,887	12,421	28,837	10,073	30,723	19,400	23,495

Sources: Amazon, 2019. Annual Report 2018. Amazon.com, Inc., Seattle. https://ir.aboutamazon.com/static-files/0f9e36b1-7e1e-4b52-be17-145dc9d8b5ec (Retrieved 02.07.2019).

Table AII-6 Amazon's consolidated income statement (2014–2018)—USD, millions.

	2014	2015	2016	2017	2018
Net product sales	70,080	79,268	94,665	118,573	141,915
Net services sales	18,908	27,738	41,322	59,293	90,972
Net sales	88,988	107,006	135,987	177,866	232,887
[Operating expenses]	[88,810]	[104,773]	[131,801]	[173,760]	[220,466]
(Cost of sales)	(62,752)	(71,651)	(88,265)	(111,934)	(139,156)
(Fulfillment)	(10,766)	(13,410)	(17,619)	(25,249)	(34,027)
(Marketing)	(4332)	(5254)	(7233)	(10,069)	(13,814)
(Technology and content)	(9275)	(12,540)	(16,085)	(22,620)	(28,837)
(General and administrative)	(1552)	(1747)	(2432)	(3674)	(4336)
(Other operating expense)	(133)	(171)	(167)	(214)	(296)
Operating income	178	2233	4186	4106	12,421
Interest income	39	50	100	202	440
(Interest expense)	(210)	(459)	(484)	(848)	(1417)
(Other balance)	(118)	(256)	90	346	(183)
(Provision for income taxes)	(167)	(950)	(1425)	(769)	(1197)
(Equity-method investment activity, net of tax)	37	(22)	(96)	(4)	9
Net income	(241)	596	2371	3033	10,073

Source: Amazon, 2019. Annual Report 2018. Amazon.com, Inc., Seattle. https://ir.aboutamazon.com/static-files/0f9e36b1-7e1e-4b52-be17-145dc9d8b5ec (Retrieved 02.07.2019).

Table AII-7 Amazon's cash flow trends (2012–2018)—USD, billions.

	2012	2013	2014	2015	2016	2017	2018
Net income before extraordinary	−0.04	0.27	−0.24	0.60	2.37	3.03	10.07
Depreciation, depletion, and amortization	2.16	3.25	4.19	5.65	7.48	11.48	15.34
Deferred taxes and investment tax credits	—	—	−0.32	0.08	−0.25	−0.03	0.44
Other funds	0.54	1.19	2.24	3.15	3.68	4.13	5.91
Changes in working capital	1.52	0.77	0.97	2.56	3.92	−0.24	−1.04
Net operating cash flow	4.18	5.48	6.84	12.04	17.20	18.37	30.72
Capital expenditures[a]	−3.79	−3.44	−4.89	−4.59	−6.74	−10.06	−11.32
Net assets from acquisitions	−0.75	−0.31	−0.98	−0.80	−0.12	−13.97	−2.19
Purchase/sale of investments	0.94	−0.52	0.81	−1.07	−3.02	−3.05	1.14
Net investment cash flow	−3.60	−4.28	−5.07	−6.45	−9.88	−27.08	−12.37
Issuance/reduction of debt. net	2.79	−0.62	4.42	−3.88	−3.74	9.93	−7.69
Other funds	−0.53	0.08	0.01	0.12	0.83	—	—
Net financing cash flow	2.26	−0.54	4.43	−3.76	−2.91	9.93	−7.69
Free cash flow (Net OCF less capital expenditures)	**0.40**	**2.03**	**1.95**	**7.45**	**10.47**	**8.31**	**19.40**

[a]Purchases of property and equipment, net of proceeds from property and equipment incentives. OCF: operating cash flow
Source: Amazon, 2019. Annual Report 2018. Amazon.com, Inc., Seattle. https://ir.aboutamazon.com/static-files/0f9c36b1-7e1e-4b52-be17-145dc9d8b5ec (Retrieved 02.07.2019).

Table AII-8 Trends in number of patent application by Google, Apple, Facebook, and Amazon (2004–2018).

Year	Google	Apple	Facebook	Amazon
2004	1783	534	186	24
2005	1587	565	188	55
2006	1813	645	209	46
2007	2202	925	221	60
2008	2003	1484	786	120
2009	1618	1685	236	143
2010	1791	2092	302	216
2011	1828	2451	333	306
2012	2980	3150	322	469
2013	4021	4368	749	806
2014	5338	4926	1055	1269
2015	6519	4429	933	1843
2016	5515	4935	1310	2249
2017	5237	4731	1780	2629
2018	4291	4407	1743	2732

Source: LexisNexis, 2019. Total Patent One. Ken Hattori of WHDA LLP, Washington, D.C.

AII-3. Trust and learning

AII-3.1 Information communication and technology advancement worldwide

Table AII-9 Information communication and technology advancement as measured by the networked readiness indices of 20 countries (2012–2015).

Country	2012–15 average	2012	2013	2014	2015
Finland	5.96	5.81	5.98	6.04	6.00
Singapore	5.95	5.86	5.96	5.97	6.00
Netherlands	5.75	5.60	5.81	5.79	5.80
Switzerland	5.65	5.61	5.66	5.62	5.70
USA	5.59	5.56	5.57	5.61	5.60
UK	5.57	5.50	5.64	5.54	5.60
Korea	5.49	5.47	5.46	5.54	5.50
Germany	5.44	5.32	5.43	5.50	5.50
Japan	5.38	5.25	5.24	5.41	5.60
Israel	5.36	5.24	5.39	5.42	5.40
New Zealand	5.35	5.36	5.25	5.27	5.50
France	5.12	5.12	5.06	5.09	5.20
Portugal	4.73	4.63	4.67	4.73	4.90
Spain	4.61	4.54	4.51	4.69	4.70
Czech Republic	4.43	4.33	4.38	4.49	4.50
Turkey	4.25	4.07	4.22	4.30	4.40
Italy	4.21	4.17	4.18	4.18	4.30
China	4.10	4.11	4.03	4.05	4.20
Greece	3.99	3.99	3.93	3.95	4.10
Brazil	3.94	3.92	3.97	3.98	3.90

Value measured by the networked readiness index.
Sources: World Economic Forum (WEF), 2012. The Global Competitiveness Report 2012–2013. WEF, Geneva; World Economic Forum (WEF), 2013b. The Global Information Technology Report 2013. WEF, Geneva; World Economic Forum (WEF), 2014. The Global Competitiveness Report 2014–2015. WEF, Geneva; World Economic Forum (WEF), 2015. The Global Competitiveness Report 2014–2015. WEF, Geneva.

AII-3.2 Coevolutionary structure in 20 countries

Table AII-10 Information communication and technology advancement measured by the networked readiness indices of 20 countries (2013).

	Country	Value		Country	Value		Country	Value		Country	Value
1	Finland	5.98	9	USA	5.57	21	Japan	5.24	45	Turkey	4.22
2	Singapore	5.96	11	Korea	5.46	26	France	5.06	50	Italy	4.18
4	Netherlands	5.81	13	Germany	5.43	33	Portugal	4.67	58	China	4.03
6	Switzerland	5.66	15	Israel	5.39	38	Spain	4.51	60	Brazil	3.97
7	UK	5.64	20	New Zealand	5.25	42	Czech Republic	4.38	64	Greece	3.93

The figures on the left-hand side indicate world rank out of 144 countries (see Table AII-9).
Source: World Economic Forum (WEF), 2013b. The Global Information Technology Report 2013. WEF, Geneva.

Table AII-11 Level of higher education in 20 countries (2013).

	Country	Value		Country	Value		Country	Value		Country	Value
1	Finland	6.27	7	USA	5.75	24	France	5.21	41	Greece	4.81
2	Singapore	5.91	9	New Zealand	5.68	26	Spain	5.19	42	Italy	4.75
3	Germany	5.90	17	UK	5.45	28	Portugal	5.15	65	Turkey	4.29
4	Switzerland	5.88	19	Korea	5.41	34	Israel	5.00	70	China	4.23
6	Netherlands	5.78	21	Japan	5.28	39	Czech Republic	4.85	72	Brazil	4.22

The figures on the left-hand side indicate the world rank out of 148 countries.
Source: World Economic Forum (WEF), 2013a. The Global Competitiveness Report 2013–2014. WEF, Geneva.

Table AII-12 Level of trust in teachers to deliver a good education in 20 countries (2013).

	Country	Value		Country	Value		Country	Value		Country	Value
1	Brazil	7.10	6	Portugal	6.62	11	Turkey	6.50	16	Germany	5.96
2	Finland	7.05	7	Singapore	6.60	12	UK	6.40	17	Czech Republic	5.94
3	Spain	6.86	8	Netherlands	6.56	13	France	6.15	19	Korea	5.40
4	China	6.74	9	New Zealand	6.54	14	Switzerland	6.10	20	Japan	5.35
5	USA	6.68	10	Italy	6.52	15	Greece	6.08	21	Israel	5.20

The figures on the left-hand side indicate world rank out of 21 countries (#18, Egypt, is excluded).
Source: Varkey Gems Foundation (VGF), 2014. 2013 Global Teacher Status Index, VGF, London.

Table AII-13 Composition of higher education level (2013).

Country	5th pillar: Higher education and training	5.01 Secondary education enrollment, gross %	5.02 Tertiary education enrollment, gross %	5.03 Quality of the education system	5.04 Quality of math and science education	5.05 Quality of management schools	5.06 Internet access in schools	5.07 Availability of research and training services	5.08 Extent of staff training
Finland	6.27	107.97	95.15	5.93	6.26	5.64	6.57	5.87	5.52
Singapore	5.91	107.00	72.00	5.77	6.29	5.75	6.30	5.44	5.23
Germany	5.90	103.32	–	5.14	5.05	5.10	5.03	6.10	5.12
Switzerland	5.88	95.46	56.75	5.98	5.80	6.09	6.11	6.47	5.57
Netherlands	5.78	121.46	65.41	5.17	5.31	5.66	6.25	6.09	5.14
USA	5.75	96.04	94.81	4.63	4.41	5.49	5.95	5.67	4.96
New Zealand	5.68	119.08	82.56	5.19	5.38	5.16	5.67	4.93	4.95
UK	5.45	105.34	59.75	4.62	4.37	5.89	6.16	5.61	4.73
Korea	5.41	97.08	103.11	3.82	5.10	4.45	6.11	4.81	4.21
Japan	5.28	102.20	59.74	4.10	4.66	4.04	5.16	5.52	5.35
France	5.21	113.59	57.67	4.21	5.19	5.80	4.41	5.42	4.33
Spain	5.19	128.52	82.63	3.60	3.86	5.83	4.92	4.82	3.72
Portugal	5.15	109.10	65.49	3.96	4.07	5.52	5.67	5.00	4.01
Israel	5.00	102.12	62.48	4.00	4.03	4.68	5.08	4.77	4.24
Czech Republic	4.85	90.78	64.85	3.69	3.96	3.95	5.79	5.00	4.03
Greece	4.81	109.46	89.38	3.10	4.28	3.85	3.91	3.83	3.47
Italy	4.75	100.40	64.98	3.64	4.26	4.98	3.67	4.79	3.21
Turkey	4.29	82.11	55.42	3.41	3.52	3.76	4.45	4.23	4.05
China	4.23	81.36	26.79	4.02	4.42	4.11	5.32	4.36	4.26
Brazil	4.22	105.83	25.63	2.98	2.56	4.54	3.60	4.71	4.30

AII-3.3 Higher education level

AII-3.3.1 Secondary education enrollment rate (International Standard Classification of Education levels 2 and 3)

Gross secondary education enrollment rate | 2011 or the most recent year available

Sources: UNESCO Institute for Statistics (accessed June 21, 2013, and April 21, 2013); ChildInfo.org Country Profiles; national sources

AII-3.3.2 Tertiary education enrollment rate (International Standard Classification of Education levels 5 and 6)

Gross tertiary education enrollment rate | 2011 or the most recent year available.

Sources: UNESCO Institute for Statistics (accessed June 21, 2013); national sources

AII-3.3.3 Quality of the educational system

How well does the educational system in your country meet the needs of a competitive economy? [1 = not well at all; 7 = extremely well] | 2012—3 weighted average

Source: World Economic Forum, Executive Opinion Survey

AII-3.3.4 Quality of math and science education

In your country, how would you assess the quality of math and science education in schools? [1 = extremely poor—among the worst in the world; 7 = excellent—among the best in the world] | 2012—13 weighted average

Source: World Economic Forum, Executive Opinion Survey

AII-3.3.5 Quality of management schools

In your country, how would you assess the quality of business schools? [1 = extremely poor—among the worst in the world; 7 = excellent—among the best in the world] | 2012—13 weighted average

Source: World Economic Forum, Executive Opinion Survey

AII-3.3.6 Internet access in schools

In your country, how widespread is Internet access in schools? [1 = nonexistent; 7 = extremely widespread] | 2012—13 weighted average

Source: World Economic Forum, Executive Opinion Survey

AII-3.3.7 Local availability of specialized research and training services

In your country, to what extent are high-quality, specialized training services available? [1 = not available at all; 7 = widely available] | 2012—13 weighted average

Source: World Economic Forum, Executive Opinion Survey

AII-3.3.8 Extent of staff training

In your country, to what extent do companies invest in training and employee development? [1 = not at all; 7 = to a great extent] | 2012—13 weighted average

Sources: *The Global Competitiveness Report 2013—*, Executive Opinion Survey (World Economic Forum, 2013a).

AII-4. Gender balance

Table AII-14 State of gender balance, cultural dimension, and Internet usage in 44 countries (2013).

Country	Country code	Gender Balance Index (GBI)	GDP per capita (current USD)	GBI intensity (GB I/GDP per capita X 1000)	Cultural dimension[a]			ICT advancement (NRI)	Women Internet usage (%)
					Ind	Mas	Mas/Ind ratio		
Norway	NOR	36.1	102,564	0.35	69	8	0.12	5.66	96.7
Sweden	SWE	27.0	60,005	0.45	71	5	0.07	5.91	91.1
Finland	FIN	26.8	49,766	0.54	63	26	0.41	5.98	93.2
France	FRA	18.3	44,105	0.41	71	43	0.61	5.06	83.7
South Africa	ZAF	17.9	6914	2.59	65	63	0.97	3.87	39.0
Denmark	DNK	17.2	60,494	0.28	74	16	0.22	5.58	96.4
Netherlands	NLD	17.0	51,595	0.33	80	14	0.18	5.81	93.5
Israel	ER	15.7	36,410	0.43	54	47	0.87	5.39	76.3
New Zealand	NZL	15.1	41,555	0.36	79	58	0.73	5.25	82.2
Germany	DEU	14.1	46,475	0.30	67	66	0.99	5.43	85.5
Australia	AUS	14.0	64,664	0.22	90	61	0.68	5.26	84.9
USA	USA	14.0	52,705	0.27	91	62	0.68	5.57	75.0
Poland	POL	13.6	13,773	0.99	60	64	1.07	4.19	66.9
Canada	CAN	13.1	52,345	0.25	80	52	0.65	5.44	79.2
Turkey	TUR	12.7	10,761	1.18	37	45	1.22	4.22	44.0
UK	GBR	12.6	42,453	0.30	89	66	0.74	5.64	90.4
Austria	AUT	11.3	50,585	0.22	55	79	1.44	5.25	79.7
Switzerland	CHE	10.0	85,237	0.12	68	70	1.03	5.66	84.3
Thailand	THA	9.7	6148	1.58	20	34	1.70	3.86	38.9
Hong Kong	HKG	9.5	38,170	0.25	25	57	2.28	5.40	83.3
Spain	ESP	9.5	29,397	0.32	51	42	0.82	4.51	77.1
Belgium	BEL	9.2	46,726	0.20	75	54	0.72	5.10	84.3
Ireland	IRL	8.7	52,094	0.17	70	68	0.97	5.05	81.2

Appendix II: Database for technoeconomic analysis 275

Czech Republic	CZE	8.6	19,913	0.43	58	57	0.98	4.38	80.1
China	CHN	8.4	7081	1.19	20	66	3.30	4.03	46.4
Italy	ITA	8.2	35,704	0.23	76	70	0.92	4.18	61.7
Philippines	PHL	7.9	2769	2.85	32	64	2.00	3.73	30.0
Greece	GRC	7.0	21,773	0.32	35	57	1.63	3.93	64.5
Singapore	SGP	6.9	55,617	0.12	20	48	2.40	5.96	77.3
Malaysia	MYS	6.6	10,700	0.62	26	50	1.92	4.82	69.0
India	IND	6.5	1480	4.39	48	56	1.17	3.88	17.0
Peru	PER	6.3	6626	0.95	16	42	2.63	3.39	38.5
Columbia	COL	6.0	8068	0.74	13	64	4.92	3.91	30.0
Indonesia	IDN	6.0	3676	1.63	14	46	3.29	3.84	20.3
Mexico	MEX	5.8	10,659	0.54	30	69	2.30	3.93	54.6
Brazil	BRA	5.1	12,260	0.42	38	49	1.29	3.97	54.2
Russia	RUS	4.8	15,559	0.31	39	36	0.92	4.13	73.0
Hungary	HUN	4.5	13,564	0.33	80	88	1.10	4.29	71.2
Taiwan	TWN	4.4	21,888	0.20	17	45	2.65	5.47	76.3
Egypt	EGY	4.4	3374	1.30	25	45	1.80	3.78	34.8
Portugal	PRT	3.7	21,626	0.17	27	31	1.15	4.67	65.7
Chile	CHL	2.8	15,714	0.18	23	28	1.22	4.59	60.0
Korea (Rep.)	KOR	1.9	25,998	0.07	18	39	2.17	5.46	87.1
Japan	JPN	1.1	38,552	0.03	46	95	2.07	5.24	89.3

[a]*Ind*: individualism, *Mas*: masculinity.

Original sources: GMI Ratings, 2013. 2013 Women on Boards Survey. GMI Ratings, New York; International Monetary Fund (IMF), 2014. World Economic Outlook Database, IMF, Washington, D.C; Hofstede, G., 1991. Cultures and Organizations. McGraw–Hill International, London; International Telecommunication Union (ITU), 2014. World Telecommunication Indicators Database. ITU, Geneva.

References

Amazon, 2019. Annual Report 2018. Amazon.com, Inc., Seattle. https://ir.aboutamazon. com/static-files/0f9e36b1-7e1e-4b52-be17-145dc9d8b5ec (Retrieved 02.07.2019).

Bosch, 2020. Annual Report 2019. Robert Bosch AG, Gerlinger. https://assets.bosch.com/ media/global/bosch_group/our_figures/pdf/bosch-annual-report-2019.pdf.

Daimler, 2019. Annual Report 2018. Daimler AG, Stuttgart. https://www.daimler.com/ documents/investors/reports/annual-report/daimler/daimler-ir-annual-report-2018.pdf.

European Commission, Joint Research Center, 2017. The EU Industrial R&D Investment Scoreboard 2016. European Commission, Brussels.

Ford, 2019. Annual Report 2018. Ford Motor Company, Dearborn. https://s23.q4cdn. com/799033206/files/doc_financials/annual/2018-Annual-Report.pdf.

Huawei Investment, 2020. 2019 Annual Report. Huawei Investment & Holding Co., Ltd., Shenzen. https://www-file.huawei.com/-/media/corporate/pdf/annual-report/annual_ report_2019_en.pdf?la=en.

General Motors, 2019. Annual Report 2018. General Motors Company, Detroit. https:// www.sec.gov/Archives/edgar/data/1467858/000146785820000028/gm201910k.htm.

GMI Ratings, 2013. 2013 Women on Boards Survey. GMI Ratings, New York.

Hofstede, G., 1991. Cultures and Organizations. McGraw-Hill International, London.

Honda, 2019. Consolidated Financial Results for FY 2018. Honda Motor Co., Ltd., Tokyo. https://global.honda/content/dam/site/global/investors/cq_img/library/ financialresult/FY201903_4Q_financial_ result_e.pdf.

International Monetary Fund (IMF), 2014. World Economic Outlook Database. IMF, Washington, D.C.

International Monetary Fund (IMF), 2017. Measuring the Digital Economy: IMF Statistical Forum. IMF, Washington D.C.

International Telecommunication Union (ITU), 2014. World Telecommunication Indicators Database. ITU, Geneva.

LexisNexis, 2019. Total Patent One. Ken Hattori of WHDA LLP, Washington, D.C.

Macrotrends, 2020. The Premier Research Platform for GAFA Financial Statements 2005–2020. Zacks Investment Research Inc., Chicago. www.macrotrends.net/stocks/charts/GOOG/ alphabet/financial-statements https://www.macrotrends.net/stocks/charts/AMZN/amazon/ financial-statements https://www.macrotrends.net/stocks/charts/AAPL/apple/financial-statements   https://www.macrotrends.net/stocks/charts/FB/facebook/financial-statements (Retrieved 30.01.2020).

Novartis, 2020. Annual Report 2019. Novartis AG, Basel. https://www.novartis.com/sites/ www.novartis.com/files/novartis-annual-report-2019.pdf.

Roche, 2020. Finance Report 2019. Roche Holding AG, Basel. https://www.roche.com/ dam/jcr:1e6cfce4-2333-4ed6-b98a-f6b62809221d/en/fb19e.pdf.

Samsung Electronics, 2019. Consolidated Financial Statements. Samsung Elecronics Co. Ltd., Seoul. https://images.samsung.com/is/content/samsung/p5/global/ir/docs/ 2018_con_quarter04_all.pdf.

Sanofi, 2020. Annual Report 2019. Sanofi, Paris. https://www.sanofi.com/-/media/ Project/One-Sanofi-Web/Websites/Global/Sanofi-COM/Home/common/docs/investors/2020_03_23_Sanofi-Report-2019-20F.

Toyota, 2020. Annual Report 2019. Toyota Motor Corporation, Tokyo. https://global. toyota/en/ir/library/annual/.

UNCTAD, 2019. World Investment Report 2019 based on Statistical Databases of Eikon and Orbis of Ghent University. UNCTAD, Geneva.

UNESCO, 2003. Towards Policies for Integrating Information and Communication Technologies into Education. UNESCO, Paris.

US Security and Exchange Commission (SEC), 2020a. Annual Report pursuant to Section 13 or 15(d) of the Security Exchange Act of 1934 for the Fiscal Year 2019. Alphabets Inc. SEC, Washington, D.C.

US Security and Exchange Commission (SEC), 2020b. Annual Report pursuant to Section 13 or 15(d) of the Security Exchange Act of 1934 for the Fiscal Year 2019. Amazon.com, Inc. SEC, Washington, D.C.

US Security and Exchange Commission (SEC), 2020c. Annual Report pursuant to Section 13 or 15(d) of the Security Exchange Act of 1934 for the Fiscal Year 2019. Apple Inc. SEC, Washington, D.C.

US Security and Exchange Commission (SEC), 2020d. Annual Report pursuant to Section 13 or 15(d) of the Security Exchange Act of 1934 for the Fiscal Year 2019. Facebook, Inc. SEC, Washington, D.C.

US Security and Exchange Commission (SEC), 2020e. Annual Report pursuant to Section 13 or 15(d) of the Security Exchange Act of 1934 for the Fiscal Year 2019. Intel Corporation. SEC, Washington, D.C.

US Security and Exchange Commission (SEC), 2020f. Annual Report pursuant to Section 13 or 15(d) of the Security Exchange Act of 1934 for the Fiscal Year 2019. Johnson & Johnson. SEC, Washington, D.C.

US Security and Exchange Commission (SEC), 2020g. Annual Report pursuant to Section 13 or 15(d) of the Security Exchange Act of 1934 for the Fiscal Year 2019. Microsoft Corporation. SEC, Washington, D.C.

US Security and Exchange Commission (SEC), 2020h. Annual Report pursuant to Section 13 or 15(d) of the Security Exchange Act of 1934 for the Fiscal Year 2019. Pfizer Inc. SEC, Washington, D.C.

US Security and Exchange Commission (SEC), 2020i. Annual Report pursuant to Section 13 or 15(d) of the Security Exchange Act of 1934 for the Fiscal Year 2019. Sanofi. SEC, Washington, D.C.

Varkey Gems Foundation (VGF), 2014. 2013 Global Teacher Status Index. VGF, London.

Volkswagen, 2020. Annual Report 2019. Volkswagen AG, Wolfsburg. https://www.volkswagenag.com/en/InvestorRelations/news-and-publications/Annual_Reports.html.

World Economic Forum (WEF), 2012. The Global Competitiveness Report 2012—2013. WEF, Geneva.

World Economic Forum (WEF), 2013a. The Global Competitiveness Report 2013—2014. WEF, Geneva.

World Economic Forum (WEF), 2013b. The Global Information Technology Report 2013. WEF, Geneva.

World Economic Forum (WEF), 2014. The Global Competitiveness Report 2014—2015. WEF, Geneva.

World Economic Forum (WEF), 2015. The Global Competitiveness Report 2014—2015. WEF, Geneva.

World Economic Forum (WEF), 2016. The Global Information Technology Report 2016. WEF, Geneva.

Appendix III
Remarkable disruptive business models and emerging new innovations

AIII-1. Suprafunctionality beyond economic value
Driving force in shifts in people's preferences

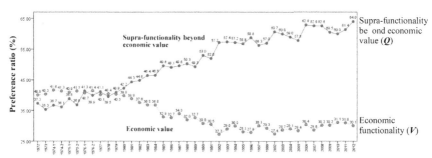

Figure AIII-1.1 Trend in the shift of people's preferences in Japan (1972–2012). *Source:* National Survey of Lifestyle Preferences *(Japan Cabinet Office, annual issues).*

Table AIII-1.1 Correlation between GDP and the shift in preferences in Japan (1972–2012).

$$lnV = 6.335 - 0.555D_1\ lnY - 0.549D_2\ lnY - 2.959D_3 \qquad \textbf{\textit{adj. R}}^2\ 0.913$$
$${\scriptstyle(17.36)}\quad {\scriptstyle(-7.21)}\qquad {\scriptstyle(-7.71)}\qquad {\scriptstyle(-8.11)}\qquad\qquad DW\ 1.09$$

$$lnQ = 1.283 + 0.500D_1\ lnY + 0.507D_2\ lnY + 0.515D_3\ lnY \qquad \textbf{\textit{adj. R}}^2\ 0.972$$
$${\scriptstyle(5.29)}\quad {\scriptstyle(9.76)}\qquad {\scriptstyle(10.73)}\qquad {\scriptstyle(11.55)}\qquad\qquad DW\ 1.66$$

Y: GDP Index (1972 = 100); V: economic functionality; Q: suprafunctionality beyond economic value; D: dummy variables—D_1: 1972–79 (Phase 1) = 1, D_2: 1980–92 (Phase 2) = 1, D_3: 1993–2012 (Phases 3 and 4) = 1, other years = 0. Figures in parentheses are t-statistics; all are significant at the 1% level.

Table AIII-1.2 Marginal propensity to consume of six selected countries.

	1990−2007[a]	2008−12[b]
Finland	0.42	0.23
Singapore	0.32	0.21
Japan	0.59	0.34
USA	0.74	0.64
Germany	0.55	0.44
UK	0.70	0.37

[a]1990−2006 for US and Germany.
[b]2007−12 for US and Germany.
Source: Watanabe et al. (2015).

AIII-2. Sleeping-capable resources
Uber's ridesharing revolution

Figure AIII-2.1 Uber's worldwide expansion to 479 cities (as of Jun. 2016).

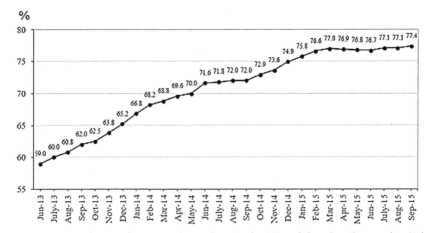

Figure AIII-2.2 The trend in smartphone share in the US mobile subscriber market (Jul. 2013−Sep. 2015). *Smartphone share of the US mobile subscriber market: percentage of mobile subscribers aged 13+ owning a smartphone.*

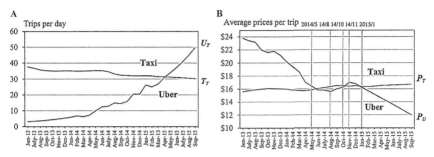

Figure AIII-2.3 Trends in trips and prices for Uber and taxis in New York City (Jun. 2013—Sep. 2015). *Sources: Taxi: Fig. 3-C. Uber—for Jun. 2013—Nov. 2014: Lunden (2014); for other periods: authors' estimates based on TLC, Uber, Stone (2015), and Silverstein (2014).*

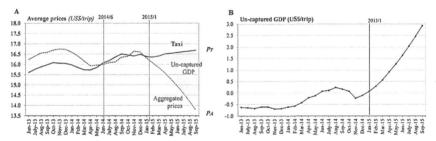

Figure AIII-2.4 Comparison between taxi prices and aggregate prices, and the emergence of uncaptured GDP due to Uber, in New York City (Jun. 2013—Sep. 2015).

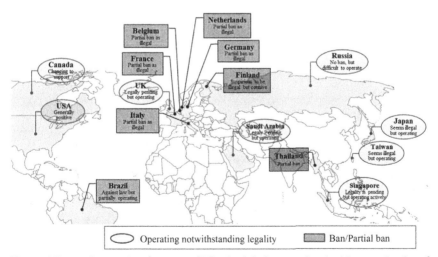

Figure AIII-2.5 Contrasting features of Uber's global expansion in 16 countries (as of Jun. 2016).

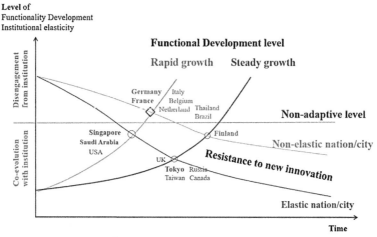

Figure AIII-2.6 Adaption of Uber in institutional systems. *Source: Watanabe et al. (2017).*

Countries without legal battle

Uber induced CCSD leading to a co-evolution between ride-sharing revolution and advancement of the institutional systems.
Singapore: Induced incorporating user's requirements into the tripartism framework (company, employee, government) by stimulating social demand (transport, job, productivity).
Saudi Arabia: Enabled women's social participation by providing the reliable transportation leading to co-evolution.
Tokyo: Stimulated better service seeking competitive market broader stakeholder's involvement for social demand solution.

Countries with legal battle

Traditional quasi-monopolistic market protected by non-innovative government impeded Uber's revolution resulting in disengagement from the institutional systems.
Germany: Government non-innovative policy urging traditional legal requirements in response to traditional taxi companies' requirement to preserve existing profit securing system based on quasi-monopolistic market impeded Uber's disruptive innovation resulting in failing CCSD construction.

France, Italy follows the similar results.

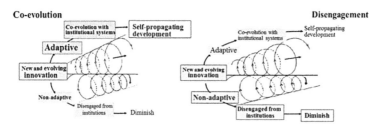

Figure AIII-2.7 Uber's coevolution and disengagement with host institutions. *Source: Watanabe et al. (2017).*

AIII-3. Trust derived from overdrawing past information
Trust-based digitally rich learning environments

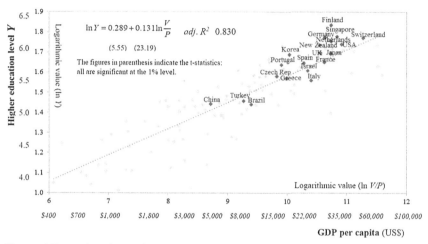

Figure AIII-3.1 Correlation between economic development and higher education level in 112 countries (2013). *Sources: IMF (2013); WEF (2013a).*

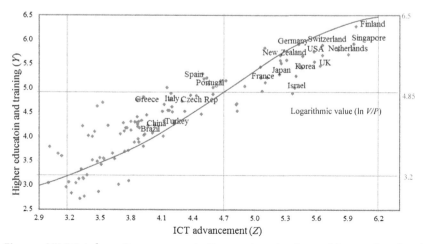

Figure AIII-3.2 Information communication and technology—driven educational development in 120 countries (2013). *Sources: WEF (2013a,b).*

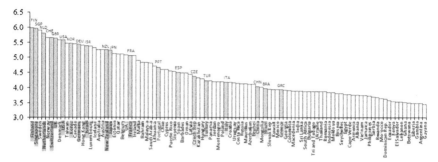

Figure AIII-3.3 Level of information communication and technology (ICT) advancement by networked readiness index (NRI) in 100 countries (2013). *Source: WEF (2013b).*

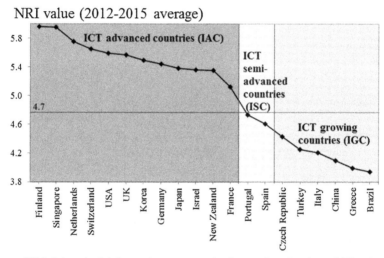

Figure AIII-3.4 Level of information communication and technology (ICT) advancement by networked readiness index (NRI) in 20 countries (2012–15 average). *Sources: WEF (2012, 2013, 2014, 2015).*

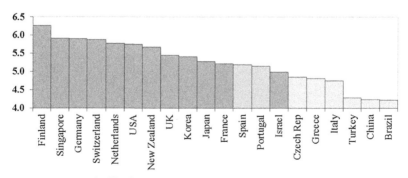

Figure AIII-3.5 Level of higher education in 20 countries (2013). *Source: WEF (2013a).*

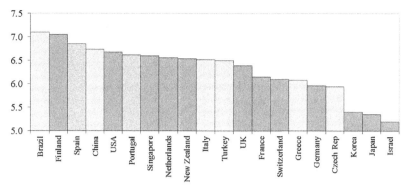

Figure AIII-3.6 Level of trust in teachers to deliver a good education in 20 countries (2013). *Source: VGF (2014).*

	State of digitally-rich learning environments and subsequent co-evolution		Priority countermeasures
ICT advanced countries (IAC)		**Shifted to DILE** Constructed co-evolutionary dynamism between Z, Y and X.	1. Continued transcending innovation to transform learning environments into DILE 2. Transfer transforming experiences to ISC and IGC. 3. Harnessing the vigor of growth potential from IGC.
ICT semi-advanced countries (ISC)		**Transition from TTLE to DILE** Unsuccessful co-evolution due to a vicious cycle between Z and Y.	1. Transforming Y-Z disengagement into co-evolution by making full utilization of X-Y co-evolution 2. Learning the DILE shift experiences from IAC 3. Accelerating the shift to DILE.
ICT growing countries (IGC)		**Remain TTLE** Disengagement due to a mismatch between Z and X.	1. Enhancing Y by making full utilization of external resources on Z based on Z-Y co-evolution 2. Transforming X-Y disengagement into co-evolution by learning experiences from ISC and IAC 3. Stepwise introduction, absorption, application, diffusion and transformation of Z by collaborating with ISC and IAC

Figure AIII-3.7 State of digitally rich learning environments, subsequent coevolution, and priority countermeasures.

DILE: Digitally-rich Innovative Learning Environments

TTLE: Traditional Teaching and Learning Environments

    X: Trust in teachers   *Y*: Higher education level   *Z*: ICT advancement

+ ⟵⟶ Co-evolution (virtuous cycle),   ⁻ ⟵----⟶ Disengagement (vicious cycle).

AIII-4. Utmost gratification ever experienced
The commodification of past experiences

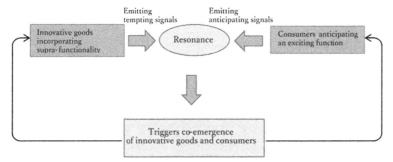

Figure AIII-4.1 Resonance of signals emitted by innovative goods and consumers.

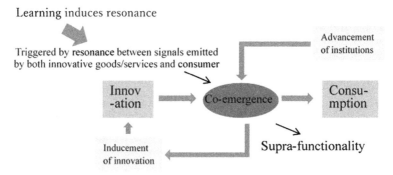

Figure AIII-4.2 Dynamism in coemerging innovation and consumption.

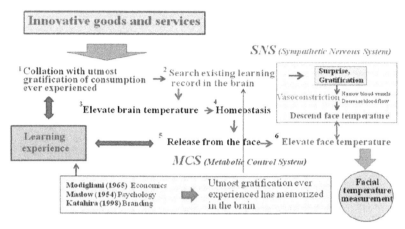

Figure AIII-4.3 Scheme of facial temperature feedback hypothesis.

33.4

Record in a PC

Analyze the recorded data by the exclusive software

"FLIR Research IR" (able to identify a pin-point temperature)

Figure AIII-4.4 Thermography for monitoring facial temperatures. *Source: Watanabe (2013).*

Event wagon on which sweetened ban is displayed (15 February)

Installation of PC for data recording (15 February)

Hanging situation of the thermography (15 February)

Shelf on which PC is stalled (15 February)

Positions of event wagon and the thermography (15 February)

Angle of the thermography and target of monitoring (21 February)

Figure AIII-4.5 Pilot experiment at leading Japanese supermarket in Tokyo (Feb. 2011). *Source: Watanabe (2013).*

Cosmetics corner

Thermography connected to PC

Shoppers accessing to cosmetics corner

Examining anticipating cosmetics

Inducement by sales promoter

Trial makeup

Figure AIII-4.6 Pilot experiment at leading Finnish supermarket in Jyväskylä (Mar. 2012). *Source: Watanabe (2013).*

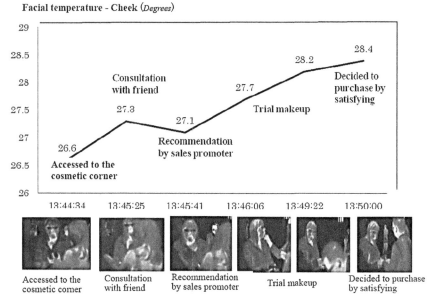

Figure AIII-4.7 Standardized pattern of facial temperature change in purchasing (Jyväskylä). *Source: Watanabe (2013).*

AIII-5. Memories and future dreams
Coevolution of streaming and live music

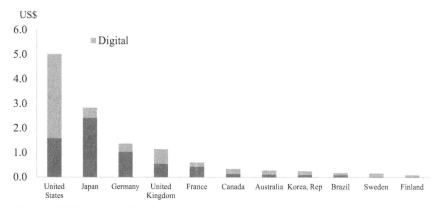

Figure AIII-5.1 International comparison of music industry by country revenues (2014). *Source: Music Ally (Music Ally data map, global music industry data on Sales.).*

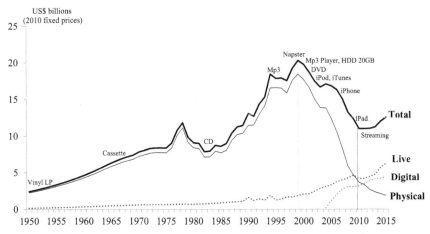

Figure AIII-5.2 Development trajectory of the US music industry by revenues (1950–2015). *Sources: RIAA (Recording Industry Association of America), Pollstar (trade publication for the concert tour industry).*

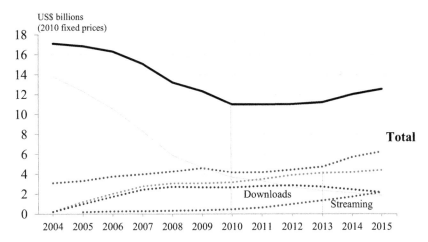

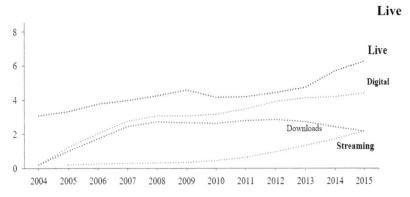

Figure AIII-5.3 Development trajectory of the US music industry by revenues (2004–15). *Sources: RIAA and Pollstar.*

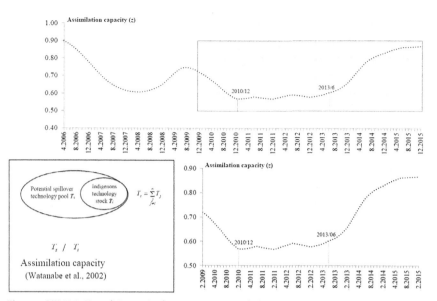

Figure AIII-5.4 Trend in assimilation capacity of the live music industry in the US (2006–15), 6-month moving average.

Table AIII-5.1 Hybrid logistic growth for three product segments of the music industry in the US (Jan. 1985–Dec. 2015).

$$Y = \frac{N_X}{1 + b_{X1}D_1e^{-a_{X1}D_1t} + b_{X2}D_2e^{-a_{X2}D_2t}}$$

	N_X	D_1		D_2		adj. R^2
		a_1	b_1	a_2	b_2	
Physical		*1985/1–1999/12*		*2000/1–2015/12*		
	1.705	0.015	1.980	−0.026	0.001	0.983
	(60.89)	(15.00)	(28.46)	(−26.00)	(−36.76)	
Digital		*1985/1–2007/12*		*2008/1–2015/12*		
	0.443	0.066	42.08×10^6	0.016	84.775	0.981
	(14.29)	(22.00)	(21.51)	(5.33)	(6.97)	
Live		*1985/1–2013/3*		*2013/4–2015/12*		
	0.868	0.007	14.145	0.024	41.123×10^2	0.966
	(7.54)	(19.75)	(23.32)	(5.48)	(6.41)	

Y: music input into the market/its assets; N_x: upper limit of diffusion (carrying capacity); X: P (physical music), D (digital music), L (live music); D_i: dummy variables corresponding to the change in external circumstances; t: time trend; and a_{Xi}, b_{Xi} ($i = 1, 2$): coefficients.

AIII-6. Untapped resources and vision

Harnessing the vigor of women's untapped resource potential

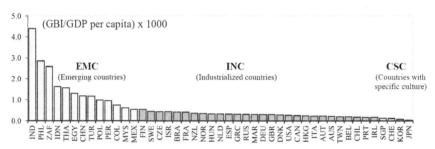

Figure AIII-6.1 Gender balance intensity in 44 countries by three clusters (2013).

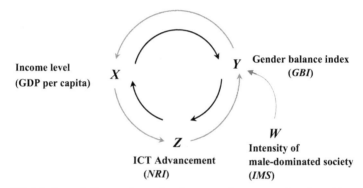

Figure AIII-6.2 Coevolutionary dynamism between the econocultural position, gender balance index, and information communication and technology (ICT) advancement. *GBI*: gender balance index as a proxy of gender balance improvement, *NRI*: networked readiness index, *IMS*: intensity of male-dominated society (*M/I*).

Based on this dynamism, the following six coevolutions were first analyzed:

1. $Y \rightarrow X$ Contribution of gender balance improvement to economic growth
2. $X \rightarrow Z$ Contribution of economic growth to information communication and technology (ICT) advancement
3. $Z, W \rightarrow Y$ Gender balance improvement induced by ICT and impeded by male-dominated society
4. $X, W \rightarrow Y$ Gender balance improvement supported by income growth and impeded by male-dominated society
5. $Z \rightarrow X$ ICT Contribution to income growth
6. $Y \rightarrow Z$ ICT advancement stimulated by gender balance improvement

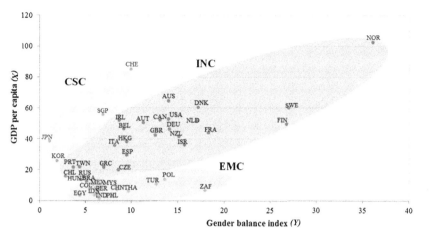

Figure AIII-6.3 Correlation between Gender Balance Index and GDP per capita in 44 countries (2013).

$$lnX = \underset{(34.81)}{8.41} + \underset{(1.73)^*}{0.21D_1} \, lnY + \underset{(8.44)}{0.86D_2} \, lnY + \underset{(7.60)}{1.26D_3} \, lnY + \underset{(4.48)}{1.49D_a}$$

$$- \underset{(-4.25)}{1.21D_b} \quad \textbf{adj. } \textbf{\textit{R}}^2 \; 0.866$$

X: GDP per capita (x 10^3 US$); Y: Gender Balance Index; D_1, D_2, and D_3: coefficient dummy variables corresponding to emerging countries (EMCs), industrialized countries (INCs), and countries with specific cultures (CSCs), respectively; D_a, D_b: dummy variable (D_a: JPN, KOR = 1, others = 0. D_b: IND, PHL = 1, others = 0). Figures in parentheses are t-statistics; all are significant at the 1% level except*10%.

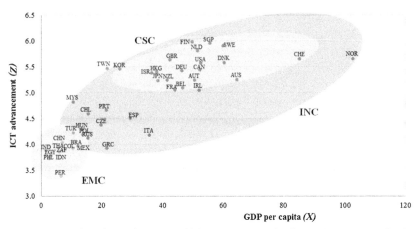

Figure AIII-6.4 Correlation between GDP per capita and information communication and technology (ICT) advancement in 44 countries (2013).

$$lnZ = 0.33 \underset{(1.58)^*}{} + 0.12D_1 \; lnX \underset{(4.87)}{} + 0.12D_2 \; lnX \underset{(6.10)}{} + 0.13D_3 \; lnX \underset{(6.50)}{} \quad \textbf{\textit{adj. R}}^2 0.739$$

Z: ICT advancement (NRI); X: GDP per capita (x 10^3 US\$); D_1, D_2, and D_3: coefficient dummy variables corresponding to EMCs, INCs, and CSCs, respectively. Figures in parentheses are t-statistics; all are significant at the 1% level except *10%.

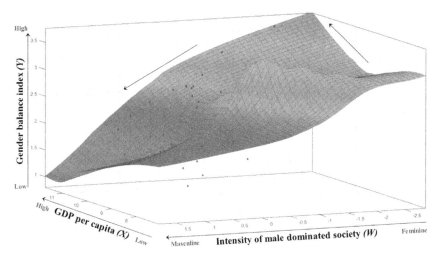

Figure AIII-6.5 Correlation between GDP per capita, intensity of male-dominated society, and Gender Balance Index in 44 countries (2013).

$$lnY = -2.35 \underset{(-2.53)}{} + 0.56D_1 \underset{(5.13)}{} lnX + 0.44D_2 \underset{(4.91)}{} lnX + 0.41D_3 \underset{(4.92)}{} lnX \quad \textbf{\textit{adj. R}}^2 \, 0.794$$

$$- 0.48D_1 \underset{(-2.60)}{} lnW - 0.32D_2 \underset{(-3.87)}{} lnW - 0.87D_3 \underset{(-1.92)**}{} lnW - 1.04D_3 \underset{(-4.28)}{}$$

Y: Gender Balance Index; W: intensity of male-dominated society (M/I); and X: GDP per capita, all of which are represented with logarithmic values; D_1, D_2, and D_3: coefficient dummy variables corresponding to EMCs, INCs, and CSCs, respectively; D: dummy variable (JPN, CHL = 1, others=0). Figures in parentheses are t-statistics; all are significant at the 1% level except *5% and **15%.

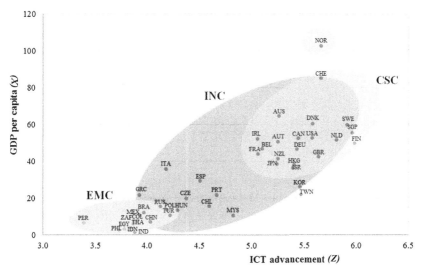

Figure AIII-6.6 Correlation between information communication and technology (ICT) advancement and GDP per capita in 44 countries (2013).

$$lnX = 4.631 \underset{(5.30)}{} + 3.028D_1 \underset{(4.66)}{} lnZ + 3.579D_2 \underset{(6.84)}{} lnZ$$

$$+ 3.564D_3 lnZ \quad \textbf{\textit{adj.R}}^2 \quad 0.815$$

X: GDP per capita (x 10^3 US\$); Z: ICT advancement (NRI); D_1, D_2, and D_3: coefficient dummy variables corresponding to EMCs, INCs, and CSCs, respectively. Figures in parentheses are t-statistics; all are significant at the 1% level.

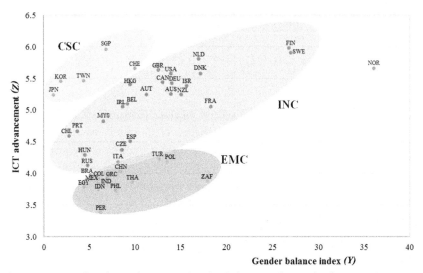

Figure AIII-6.7 Correlation between Gender Balance Index and information communication and technology (ICT) advancement in 44 countries (2013).

$$lnZ = 1.227 + 0.061D_1 \; lnY + 0.162D_2 \; lnY + 0.089D_3 \; lnY$$
$$\underset{(23.16)}{} \quad \underset{(2.30^*)}{} \quad \underset{(7.19)}{} \quad \underset{(2.39^*)}{}$$

$$+ 0.351D \quad adj.R^2 \quad 0.771$$
$$\underset{(5.47)}{}$$

Y: Gender Balance Index; Z: ICT advancement (NRI); D_1, D_2, and D_3: coefficient dummy variables corresponding to EMCs, INCs, and CSCs, respectively; D: dummy variable (CHE, JPN, KOR, SGP, $TWN = 1$, others $= 0$). Figures in parentheses are t-statistics; all are significant at the 1% level except *2%.

Table AIII-6.1 Elasticities of coevolution in 44 countries (2013).

		Emerging countries	Industrialized countries	Countries with specific cultures
1	$Y{\rightarrow}X$	0.21	0.86	1.26
2	$X{\rightarrow}Z$	0.12	0.12	0.13
3	$Z{\rightarrow}Y$	2.63	2.12	2.05
	$W{\rightarrow}Y$	−0.41	−0.37	−2.49
4	$X{\rightarrow}Y$	0.56	0.44	0.41
	$W{\rightarrow}Y$	−0.48	−0.32	−0.89
5	$Z{\rightarrow}X$	3.03	3.58	3.56
6	$Y{\rightarrow}Z$	0.06	0.16	0.09

X: income level (GDP per capita); Y: Gender Balance Index; Z: ICT advancement (NRI); W: intensity of male-dominated society (IMS).

Glossary

Coevolution Coevolution is a mutually inspiring virtuous cycle.

Digital economy The digital economy is an *economy* based on Internet-driven advancements in information and communication technology (ICT), which have dramatically changed aspects of business and daily life. The *digital economy* is also referred to as the Internet *economy*, new *economy*, or web *economy*. The OECD (2020) defines the digital economy as follows: The digital economy incorporates all economic activity reliant on, or significantly enhanced using digital inputs, including digital technologies, digital infrastructure, digital services, and data. It refers to all producers and consumers, including government, that utilize these digital inputs in their economic activities.

Dilemma between R&D expansion and productivity decline Contrary to the decisive role of R&D centered on ICT in the digital economy, excessive expansion in R&D has resulted in declining productivity due to the two-sided nature of ICT.

Great coevolution This process is coevolution among the new streams of the digital economy under the spin-off dynamism, digital innovations with unique natures, and shifts to new socioeconomic trends.

Internet of Things (IoT) Contrary to the traditional computer-initiated ICT innovation of the Product of Things (PoT) era, an IoT network's connectivity and computing capability extend to objects, sensors, and everyday items not normally considered by computers, thus allowing these devices to generate exchanges and consume data with minimal human intervention.

Neo open innovation This innovation is the novel concept of innovation emergence that maintains sustainable growth by avoiding the dilemma of productivity decline through increases in gross R&D, including soft innovation resources (*SIRs*) assimilated through the harnessing of their vigor.

Shift to new socioeconomic trends This shift is a move toward an ecoconscious smart consumer society, a sharing economy, a circular economy, and a noncontact socioeconomy.

Soft innovation resources (*SIRs*) SIRs are latent innovation resources in the digital economy that can be awoken and activated by deploying an ICT-driven disruptive business model with the consolidated challenge for social demand. The activation possibility of *SIRs* can be attributed to ICT's indigenous self-propagating nature.

Spin-off dynamism This dynamism is a spin-off from traditional coevolution among traditional computer-initiated ICT innovation, captured GDP, and economic functionality to new coevolution occurring among Internet advancement, uncaptured GDP, and suprafunctionality beyond economic value.

Suprafunctionality beyond economic value This term represents sophisticated functionality that satisfies shifts in people's preferences and encompasses social (e.g., creation of and contribution to social communication), cultural (e.g., brand value, cool, and cute), aspirational (e.g., aspirations to traditional beauty), tribal (e.g., cognitive sense, fellow feeling), and emotional (e.g., perceptional, five senses) values.

Trap in ICT advancement Contrary to expectation, the excessive advancement of ICT results in declining marginal productivity due to price decreases derived from its two-sided nature.

Two-sided nature of ICT While the advancement of ICT has generally contributed to enhanced technology prices via the development of new functionalities, dramatic advancement of the Internet has resulted in decreased technology prices due to its characteristics of freebies, easy replication, and mass standardization.

Uncaptured GDP The Internet promotes free culture, the consumption of which provides people with utility (satisfaction of consumption) and happiness. Uncaptured GDP is the value of this utility, happiness, and their related cultural elements that cannot be captured though GDP data, which measure revenue.

Index

Printed in the United States
by Baker & Taylor Publisher Services